enough candy

enough candy
ALAN JACKSON

BANTAM PRESS

LONDON · NEW YORK · TORONTO · SYDNEY · AUCKLAND

TRANSWORLD PUBLISHERS LTD
61–63 Uxbridge Road, London W5 5SA

TRANSWORLD PUBLISHERS
c/o Random House Australia Pty Ltd
20 Alfred Street, Milsons Point, NSW 2061, Australia

TRANSWORLD PUBLISHERS
c/o Random House New Zealand
18 Poland Road, Glenfield, Auckland, New Zealand

TRANSWORLD PUBLISHERS
c/o Random House Pty Ltd
Endulini, 5a Jubilee Road, Parktown 2193, South Africa

Published 1999 by Bantam Press
a division of Transworld Publishers Ltd
Copyright © Alan Jackson 1999

A catalogue record for this book is available from the British Library.

ISBN 0593 045041

Typeset in 11/14pt Bembo by
Phoenix Typesetting, Ilkley, West Yorkshire.

Printed in Great Britain by

Mackays of Chatham plc, Chatham, Kent.

1 3 5 7 9 10 8 6 4 2

for my father

acknowledgements

My sincere thanks go to the many artists, management and record-company personnel, present and former colleagues and friends who have each contributed so much to my experiences as a journalist and, as a result, to this book, whether or – as in many cases – not they appear in it. You'll know who you are and, I hope, also just how appreciative I am. For especial support and encouragement, meanwhile, I would like to record my gratitude and thanks to Dawn Bartlett, Nicola Bathurst, Robert Bell, Deborah Bodenham, Martin Brammer, Len Brown, Paul Buchanan, Mary Costello, Sheena Easton, Rebecca Gooch, Kathleen Jackson, Heather Jones, Ben Laurance, the late Mabel Lyon, Gill Morgan, Paul Joseph Moore, Trish and Ann-Marie Ostojitsch, Ian Pye, Steve Reagan, David Sinclair, Anne and Max Smith, and Howard Warren. I thank also my agent, Barbara Levy, not least for your patience, and, among all those at Transworld, Shauna Newman, Bill Scott-Kerr, Henry Steadman, Claire Ward, Sally Wray and the sales and marketing staff for your hard work on my behalf. Above and beyond that, I am deeply grateful to Clive King for proving to be a much-valued (though unofficial) editor, as well as a true friend, and, in particular, to Broo Doherty, for proving to be a much-valued friend as well as (very officially) a true editor. Thank you both, and thank you again. Finally, my ultimate debt is to Christine, for always, always making everything seem possible.

a prologue

As a child I knew Epiphany to be a holy day of obligation, observed on Twelfth Night, the sixth of January. So early into the new year, it was more than usually cold in the vast, modern church adjoining my school. Class by class, we had been led across the white-frosted playground to worship there, all of us shivering in our uniforms. Accordingly, the fingers with which we turned the pages of our mass books were raw and clumsy. When we made our responses to the priest, or lent thin voice to his chosen hymns, our breath curled in the air like smoke from those rows of sputtering candles banked before the side altar, each lit for a special intention.

It was the occasion of Christ's manifestation to the Magi that we honoured, and I did so in the very same way I recited my Catechism answers: unquestioningly, by rote. With toes frozen and mouth on automatic pilot, I was able to join in with the Our Father while at the same time effortlessly re-running 'Downtown' or 'I Feel Fine' or 'Baby Love' in my head. All the while, the hands of the clock above the

ere edging towards 10 a.m., break time. Soon
receiving the Eucharist, the Body of Christ. Then
be back across the thawing tarmac for a bottle of milk
a chocolate bar. It was 1965. I was eight years old.

My own epiphany took place much later, one foggy
midweek evening in early autumn, 1988. Nearly a quarter of
a century had passed and despite all I'd seen and learned, I was
still a believer. I believed in pop music and its ability to transport me beyond my physical surroundings into a whole other
world. I believed in all the joy, pain and sheer, unadulterated
nonsense that could be contained within the grooves of a
black vinyl record. Most of all, however, I believed in the
people who sang the songs and made the records that I loved.
And I wanted to get close to them.

It was my dad who first taught me to love music and to
respect the individuals responsible for it. But I wanted to be
more than just a grateful consumer. I wanted to be part of
what Joni Mitchell, in her song 'Free Man In Paris', called the
star-maker machinery behind the popular song. Which is
why, on the day life slapped me in the face with a reminder
that I was expected to pay my way in the world, not just graze
endlessly through its record stores, I was able to make an
instant career choice. As a journalist, you might expect to do
more than just gaze, wide-eyed and from a distance, at your
heroes and heroines. As a journalist, you might actually get to
meet them.

But not immediately. First, there was a host of council
officials, golden-wedding celebrants, crime victims and other
small-town characters to encounter in the altogether more
prosaic world of provincial news-gathering. So when, finally,
I got close to where I'd always wanted to be, it was as if I
were approaching the new Jerusalem, some magical kingdom

wherein everyone was talented, larger than life and d̶
with stardust. All in all, it was just as I had hoped – had know̶
– it would be. Which brings me to that foggy autumn evening
in 1988.

The woman I was due to meet remains one of the most
enduringly successful figures in American rock music. I had
loved the records she'd sung on, and had played them repeatedly in the bed-sits and tiny flats of my early independence.
Her looks and idiosyncratic style had fascinated me too. She
had always been beautiful, and I had no doubt that she would
still be so now. In my hand was a selection of newly commissioned publicity photographs, each of them showing her
pale, thin and lovely, magically untouched by time. How
calm, how fulfilled, she must feel, I reflected, with so many
gifts at her disposal, the object of so much collective love.
Except, of course, that she turned out not to be. Anything
but.

Quite why it had taken me so long to realize I'd been
worshipping a false god, I can't explain. The packaging had
been so pretty, the myth it promoted so seductive, that I
had suspended all disbelief. Here, at last, was the reality. The
rich and famous are human beings, like any other, despite
the talents they were born with and the wealth they have
amassed. And when our paths crossed, this particular rich and
famous human being was tired and unhappy – with herself,
with others, with life.

It was only afterwards that I was able to see how these very
facts made our interview so much more honest and revealing
than any I'd done before. This time, there was no possibility
of falling back on the breathlessly enthusiastic, upbeat tone of
writing I had relied upon to date. But, at the time, all I could
register was the fact that she didn't look as she was supposed

...ographs I'd been given only a day earlier
...e still would. And so the scales fell from my eyes.
...sn't the heavenly kingdom I'd imagined it to be. Nor
...opulated only by perfect angels.

This latter point was driven home to me as I made hesitant progress up a spiral staircase, *en route* to the bedroom where our interview was to take place. I'm not proud of myself for having retained my observational skills in such a situation, but the fact is that you don't follow in the wake of someone world-famous without taking the opportunity to register, even subconsciously, the size of their arse.

I

Religious instruction of any kind will probably do, but it was junior-style Catholicism that gave me the basic training needed to develop a fan's mentality. Humility, constancy, devotion – submissive qualities like these don't grow on trees, not without careful husbandry. Luckily, I was raised in a world of plaster saints and sweets given up for Lent, of Stations of the Cross and being seen but not heard. Only transference from a junior school staffed by nuns to that chilly and forbidding place, the seminary, could have prepared me better for a lifetime's enslavement to beings and ideals infinitely greater than myself. But I had my wits about me the day I was summoned by the headmistress, Sister Paul, to meet an emissary from the diocesan bishop's office. After he had spoken with gloomy import to my seven-year-old self about the honour and responsibility of vocations, I surprised myself by asking him, 'But you don't have to be a priest to do God's work, do you?' I didn't see how he could say you did, and I was right. He couldn't and didn't. I had escaped.

Yet I still suspected I was born to serve some form of

...ing around me for guidance, I made an exciting
...here were false gods, too, in addition to the bona-
...sanctioned by Rome. Some kids find their lives given
...ture and meaning by the tribalism of sport; I became a
convert to pop music. There was a lot of catching up to be
done, however. That the Devil has all the best tunes had been
kept from me by the wimple-wearing staff of St Mary's
Roman Catholic Primary, and I had been steered instead
towards happy-clappiness. Other men my age will boast
that the first record they owned was 'A Hard Day's Night' or
'Nineteenth Nervous Breakdown'. I confess that mine was
'Dominique' by The Singing Nun (Santa planted it on
me, honest), and duly ask forgiveness. Hopefully, an offering
of ten Hail Marys, three Our Fathers and a verse or two of
'Michael, Row The Boat Ashore' will be enough to clear up
this unfortunate little matter. OK, the whole of it, if you really
think I sinned so badly.

Briefly a worldwide phenomenon, thanks to that one-off
hit single, Belgium's inappropriately named Sister Sourire
later left her convent, was hounded by the tax authorities and
eventually committed suicide: God must really have hated
that song. Today, it's almost impossible to conceive of a
woman of the cloth appearing on *Top Of The Pops* – unless it
were Madonna, perhaps, in costume to explore some aspect
of her own Catholic past. But back then it didn't seem at all
strange to me. From the day I first started school, nuns were
a significant part of my early life. They conducted morning
assembly, stood before the blackboard in lesson after lesson
and waved us off at the end of the afternoon. Not even in the
outside world was there any escape from them. In our road
stood the Cross and Passion Convent, a handsome, modern
building that has since been replaced by an old people's home

of mock-Georgian design. I had to pass by its gates on m[...]
to and from home, and was frequently intercepted there b[...]
Sister Alphonsus, the most senior inmate.

To a small boy, she seemed older than time, her body
humped within its floor-length black robes, her face crumpled
and pleated by the years. 'Would you go to the post box for
me, young Alan?' she would call, holding in a shaking hand
an envelope bearing an Irish address, adding, 'And for your
trouble . . .' Then she would rummage deep within the folds
of her habit for the handkerchief she kept in some hidden
pocket, and from it she would prise a sweet. I knew that
accepting gifts from strangers was a mortal sin, but nuns
weren't strangers; it would be an insult to refuse. But did I
actually want to eat the unwrapped toffee or fluff-covered
piece of fudge she proffered? Only when out of her sight
would I throw it away. I always mailed the letters, though,
each bound for the same recipient. 'Don't tell,' she would say,
waving me on my way. 'It's our little secret.' And it was years
before it dawned on me why. Did she ever win the
Sweepstake back in her native Ireland? It's just possible that
she did. Certainly, one day my father, whilst mowing the
front lawn, was stunned to see a lime-green Opel fastback
lurch past, a white-faced Sister Paul gripping its wheel, Sister
Alphonsus, tiny but smiling beatifically in the passenger seat.
'A bequest from a grateful parishioner,' we were told at mass,
but I just wonder . . .

Confectionery was a strong currency in those far-off days,
a fact brought home to us each spring during the six long,
self-denying weeks of Lent. Each child was urged – all but
forced, in truth – to make some form of extended sacrifice
at this time, and to divert the money they saved by doing so
towards the Black Baby Fund. Giving up sweets and ice cream

..most popular option. Each sixpence saved and ... in this way allowed your individual cut-out-and-...-in black baby to move one rung higher on a chart ...d to the classroom wall by the fund's administrator, ...ster Eugenie. The intended result was a boost in funds for Catholic missionary work overseas, particularly in Africa, and as a cunning incentive she had legislated that a name could be bestowed on each paper baby launched onto that ladder. If you were sufficiently self-denying to be able to donate a full ten shillings, the baby would climb to the top. Then, we were told, a child in Africa would be christened with the very same name.

Naturally, this brought an element of grand-prix-like excitement to the otherwise joyless process of abstention. There would be personal variations on a theme of, 'Look, my Cilla's overtaken your Elvis, so nur-nur-nur-nur-nur!', or more Murray Walkerish overviews, along the lines of, 'Sandie and Dusty are neck and neck, but it's Engelbert who's come through on the outside – that's 'cos Lesley Lampwick said no to her mum's offer of a packet of Fruit Pastilles and a Strawberry Mivvi and took the money instead!' Meanwhile, thanks to my own efforts, there was already a young Petula and a young Cher somewhere on that far-off, dark continent. Allegedly, that is. I realize now that I was never offered any conclusive proof.

The Catholic primary schools of the 1960s were hardly hotbeds of progressive social thinking – or certainly not those sited in north-east England – so Sister Eugenie can be forgiven for not having anticipated the eventual advent of political correctness. But perhaps she could have been a little more sensitive. The school's only non-white pupil was in our class, a beautiful, serious-natured boy called Aubrey. Only recently his mother had given birth to twins – real black babies, not the brightly crayoned variety pinned to our noticeboard like so many butterflies. And rather than being sensitive to Aubrey's subsequent feelings of exclusion, Sister Eugenie chose him as the object of her irritation at our on-going fixation with the world of entertainment.

'Now, you can't be having a Lulu,' she told him, her big face wearing its vexed expression, as he attached a new cut-out to the wall. 'For sure, we've got three on the ladder as it is, and there's one that's already gone over the top. If it's a girl baby your heart's set on, then why don't we make her a nice Bridie or Maureen or Maeve? Now, which is it to be?'

'Lulu,' repeated Aubrey gravely, eyes unblinking.

'Well, you're a very stubborn, foolish boy, then. Haven't I just told you there's to be no more Lulus? Are you looking to populate the whole of Africa with silly pop stars? Is that the idea?'

As a slow, sad tear rolled down Aubrey's left cheek, Carol Harkin stepped in to save the day. 'I've got five sixpences here and I'd like to start off five new black babies all at the same time,' she said, wriggling with superiority. 'I'm going to call them Dave Dee, Dozy, Beaky, Mick and Tich. I've got them all coloured in ready. Here's my two-and-six!'

What's black and white and red all over? Sister Eugenie exploding in apoplexy. However, while the memory of her sudden eruption of anger has all but faded, I can vividly recall my feeling of being cheated at the final assembly that Easter term. It was the Friday before Palm Sunday and a special mass had been celebrated. By the rules existent in our house, there were just another eight days of Lent to endure; it would end at 12 noon precisely on Easter Saturday. Only then, after all those weeks of prohibition and piety, would sweets become permissible again. In a cupboard at home, a small but exciting array of chocolate eggs had been inadequately hidden. And, as every year, there was one absolute corker – a huge, glittering, beribboned beauty, sent to me and my sister, Trish, three years older and my only sibling, by our elderly Great Aunt Jennie. Although I didn't have a particularly sweet tooth, six weeks of privation and my frequent sneaked peeks at this treasure trove were more than enough to have me aching with anticipation. But first there was an end-of-term address from Sister Paul.

It would culminate, as it did every year, with an announcement about the Black Baby Fund – the amount that had been raised, and a reminder of the sterling work done by Catholic missionaries overseas on our behalf. Beside our thin, sallow-skinned headmistress was an Easter egg bigger and grander even than the one from Auntie Jennie. A prize for the child, or related children, who had made the greatest donation to the fund, it was like a giant chocolate rugby ball decorated with coloured icing, and it was more luxurious than anything I'd ever seen before. If only it were destined for our house . . .

'And now, in recognition of their excellent contribution, I'd like to call forward Patricia Jackson from Junior Four and her little brother, Alan, from Junior One,' said Sister Paul, in a tone several degrees warmer than the one she normally used.

I waited enviously to see who these two might be, the lucky pair. 'It's you, stupid,' said an aggrieved Lesley Lampwick, poking me hard in the ribs at exactly the same moment as Trish took my hand and yanked me towards the stage. As we walked towards an Easter egg almost half as tall as I was, my upturned hands levitated, as if by magic, until they were ready to take possession of it. Quite how it came to be ours, I couldn't imagine. Yes, we had handed over all our pocket

money each week, but I knew we weren't rich and I'd auto-
matically assumed that others would give more than us.
Whatever the explanation, it was a wonderful stroke of luck.
I couldn't wait to carry it home to show my mum and dad.

'It's very kind of you, Sister, and we'd truly love for it to
be ours. But Alan and I think it should go to children more
deserving than us. We'd like it to be given to a hospital or an
orphanage, if that's all right.'

It was my sister who had spoken. The same sister who was
now leading me back from the stage amid a frenzy of applause.
The one who was smiling graciously to left and right in
acknowledgement of it all. The one who had given away not
only her share of the most marvellous Easter egg in the world,
but my share, too. These days, I like to think I'd have done
exactly the same thing. But back then, I didn't understand
altruism or know that giving could be better than receiving.
I'd just wanted that egg, and now my bottom lip was
twitching in a way I knew to be dangerous. If I wasn't careful,
any minute now I'd start crying.

'A most noble gesture, school, I'm sure you'll all agree. If
only more of you children could be so generous,' said Sister
Paul, beaming her approbation. 'Now, to our final hymns.
Piano please, Sister Ignatius. And let's start with a nice, rousing
rendition of "Soul Of My Saviour!" Come on, boys and girls!
Let's really make those rafters ring!'

Religion and music, music and religion – the two main
external forces to impact on my childhood world. Superficially, at least, and despite the best efforts of Sister Eugenie
and all the others, I would say that music had the greater influence on me. Certainly, whenever I rerun even the earliest
memory, I am aware of a radio playing the hits of the day softly

in the background – the theme from 'A Summer Place' by Percy Faith and his orchestra, perhaps, or 'Can't Get Used To Losing You' by Andy Williams. And in between there would be the mellifluous tones of a BBC presenter. In particular, I remember Brian Matthew, who hosted mid-morning studio sessions by the emergent beat groups of the early 1960s on *Saturday Club*. Then later, during the lunch hour, there would be Jack Jackson, his urbane Transatlantic voice as exotic to me then as the tail fins and chrome of the occasional American dream car brought home by our next-door neighbour Mr Grayson, who worked for a second-hand car dealership.

Because, at that time, we didn't yet have a car of our own, I was thrilled and fascinated – I'd been conditioned not to be envious – by the weekly, even daily, appearance of different models outside his house. Sometimes I was even allowed to sit on a cushion in the driver's seat of one or other of them and grip the wheel. My main recreation, though, was listening to my mother's radio and, later, the records she and my father played on the gramophone he'd built from a kit, its speakers vast and plywood-fronted, their insides lined with egg boxes. I didn't really care what the source was, as long as there was music. I was even enthralled by the record collection of another neighbour, Mrs Lapworth, a swimming instructress given to wearing pedal-pushers and jaunty tops, who, it seems to me now, identified closely with put-upon screen heroines.

Her back-garden gate was opposite ours, with just a cinder track running in between, and on warmer Sunday mornings the air between our respective houses would vibrate to the yearning voice of Doris Day singing 'Secret Love' or 'Whatever Will Be Will Be'. Were she in a brisker mood, however – a bout of rug-beating, possibly in the aftermath of a dispute with her husband, the little seen Mr L. – we might hear selections from the *Calamity Jane* or *South Pacific* sound-tracks. Only recently have I seen the latter film and thus appreciated the circumstances in which Mitzi Gaynor sings 'I'm Gonna Wash That Man Right Out Of My Hair'. How that song puzzled me, though, as a literal-minded child. Figures of speech were, as yet, an unknown conceit – for years I believed the wronged lover singing 'I Heard It Through The Grapevine' was eavesdropping from behind a bush – so just how a man could have become entangled in Mitzi's tresses was a mystery. Whatever the explanation, the song was frequently played on those long-gone Sunday mornings. Perhaps it was Mr Lapworth who was put-upon.

It was after breakfast one Saturday in January 1963 that the first Britpop explosion struck our house. Soon after the shops had opened, it became clear that the thirteen-year-old son of our other neighbours, the Woodfields, had discovered the Beatles. Newly resplendent in my dad's cast-off Fleet Air Arm leather flying jacket, and with his parents safely out for the morning, he had been to spend an accumulation of pocket money on a copy of their first British Top-10 single, 'Please Please Me'. In order that we might discover them, too, he proceeded to play it over and over again. Stuart Woodfield both intrigued and frightened me, with his downy upper lip, twitching permanently in a hopeful imitation of an Elvis sneer, and with bubble gum forever threatening to blossom from his sullen, open mouth. He even had a catapult. But though the record sounded great, I sensed the tension caused by its repeated, thudding intrusion through the party wall of our dining room during *The Jack Jackson Show*. There was already unease, caused by the soft-hearted Mrs Woodfield's habit of rewarding our cat, Tuppence, with tinned tuna whenever – naturally, it was ever more frequently – he ventured over the dividing fence into her garden. Now came the additional provocation of the Fab Four.

Any fear that I might be turned into a pre-school delinquent by passive exposure to their revolutionary sound was groundless. I was too easily seduced by a pretty female voice to be corruptible by four male mop-tops. Six years younger than the swaggering Stuart, but equally obsessed with pop music, I had identified a favourite of my own. I hadn't seen her, because we had yet to acquire our own television set. Only my Auntie Carol had one, and if we were visiting her on a Sunday teatime it would be switched on for me to watch the antics of the two puppet pigs, Pinky and Perky. Hit records were often featured on their show. But frustratingly, they were performed by facsimiles of other farmyard animals, and on the one occasion I recognized her voice, it was coming from the mouth of a Friesian cow wearing a red necklace and earrings. No matter, because I'd heard her songs many, many times on the radio. And so, on the first occasion that I entered a record shop, I bought not 'She Loves You' or some other Beatles release, but a single by a woman I would end up loving myself.

Hearing of my preoccupation with music, Great Aunt Jennie, a spinster, retired headmistress and a stalwart of her church parish in rural Buckinghamshire, had sent me a record token as a birthday present. She probably imagined I would spend it on something as cosy and church-youth-club-friendly as a version of 'Kumbaya'. In fact, I didn't know what to buy with it and, having never possessed such a token before, spent many hours listening to the radio and trying to make up my mind. Then some DJ played 'Baby It's Me' by Petula Clark and the issue was settled. Recently, having not heard the track in years, I sought out the old Pye 45, its pink and white sleeve tattered by time. Why had it so appealed to me? I wondered, playing it once again. Perhaps because it had the kind of silly but insistent chorus that a seven-year-old could grasp and commit to memory. For whatever reason, and despite its chirpy mediocrity, my primary-school-aged self knew he loved it. For this reason, and because it was the very first of the many thousands of records, tapes and CDs I have subsequently bought, it has import for me still.

Back in 1963, I didn't really know who Petula was – the child stardom and unhappy adolescence, her eventual metamorphosis into a world-conquering pop star. But her profile would soar when the altogether superior 'Downtown' was released the following year, followed by 'I Know A Place' and all the various others, and as a result I became increasingly aware of the person behind the voice. AT 32, LIFE IS TENSE is a headline I recall from the *Sunday Express* of the time, accompanying a profile of her. Still my interest in her was largely academic; schoolboys were meant to collect something, be it cigarette cards, marbles or model planes, and so I began to collect her records. Before I knew it, I was a ten-year-old vinyl junkie, stuck with an expensive habit and in danger of losing his heart.

In retrospect, I suppose my romantic awakening occurred because, finally, we got our own telly. And in May 1967, on a Thursday evening so sunny that I had to draw the curtains in order to see the screen, I switched it on in anticipation of *Top Of the Pops*. I was hoping Petula might feature – she had a new hit, 'Don't Sleep In The Subway' – but the presenter said she was working in America and couldn't be in the studio. In compensation, he introduced footage of her strolling pensively along a deserted beach in Brazil – an early forerunner of the pop video, this – with the occasional close-up revealing her preoccupied, almost troubled expression. That pop singers could look anything but cheerful or wildly dramatic was a revelation to me, and this sad and lovely Petula, familiar yet remote, was exactly the icon I had been waiting for.

Eagerly following the path mapped out by the clip's director, I hurried to the conclusion that here was someone trying to tell us that she was something more than the jolly, wholesome figure of her cherished public image. And therein lay our common bond. Just as the world at large stereotyped Petula as the bright, Mary Poppins-ish singer of bright, Mary Poppins-ish songs, so I felt it persisted in seeing me only as cheery, well-mannered and good in class, not the anxious-to-be-accepted, slightly melancholic kid I knew myself to be underneath. I wanted the world to recognize that I had feelings, too, but the world wasn't looking hard enough. It thought it knew who I was without asking.

Thus misunderstood and aged eleven, I won a place at Carmel Grammar School in Darlington, the nearest town of any size. Only a handful of other boys from my primary class would be going there, none of whom lived near by. That meant my making the half-hour bus journey alone, then walking for some twenty minutes to the school itself. For an unwilling pupil like myself, a door-to-door, unsupervised journey time of around an hour represented a prolonged exercise in resisting temptation. And I wasn't good at it. The opportunity to just turn around and go home presented itself again and again, and in that first autumn term of 1969 I seized it many times. It was a poor course of action. I quickly became known as the scaredy-cat, the kid who kept running away. Only towards Christmas, when faced with the ultimatum of either knuckling down or being removed from the school altogether, forced to start all over again somewhere else, did I finally resign myself to my fate. If this was where I absolutely had to be for the next seven years, then I might as well make the most of it.

In tandem with this outbreak of common sense my musical tastes broadened. Carmel Grammar may have been dedicated to the manufacture of reasonably educated, God-fearing heavy-rock fans, but I saw that as no reason why I should toe the line. For a couple of years the words Black Sabbath, Deep Purple or Genesis seemed to be Humbrol-painted on every haversack but mine, which remained advert-free, and that of Sean O'Brien, a walking billboard for the late John Denver – when it was his turn to choose an inspirational reading at morning assembly, he bravely but misguidedly recited the lyrics of 'Annie's Song'. During that time I was, for a while, the school's lone soul boy, then its one disciple of the sublime singer-songwriter Joni Mitchell. But throughout these various changes, my affection for Petula was unwavering. The LPs that the rest of her public overlooked were the ones that spoke most persuasively to me. In particular, I remember *Memphis*, recorded at the legendary Muscle Shoals studios in 1970 and, from the following year, *Warm and Tender*, made with Aretha Franklin's producer Arif Mardin and his coterie of musicians.

I would look for these and other of her releases each Friday lunchtime when, on sorties into Darlington town centre's various record departments, I made it my mission to put Petula to the fore in every available rack – not just Female Vocal but Male, too, plus Light Orchestral, Brass Band and Spoken Word, and even, as I recall, Railway Engine Noises. The best friend I eventually found, Andy, an avid supporter of Marc Bolan, would compete for space with T. Rex releases. In companionable silence, we would go about our work in up to six different locations, depending on how much time we had. And it was a strangely satisfying feeling to head back towards double French or triple Latin in the knowledge that, even as we did so, vexed assistants and afternoon shoppers in Boots, W.H. Smith and Woolworth were being spooked by multiple brooding images of our respective favourites.

Who knows what impact that may have had, subliminally? Though musically disparate, the two performers were united at this point in time in their loyalty to that most singular of hairstyles, the poodle perm. It's possible that every salon and barber's shop in walking distance of the market square felt the knock-on effect of our endeavours during the final hours of the working week. Scores of puzzled housewives might have found themselves sinking into the stylist's chair and sighing, 'A Petula, please,' without ever understanding why. And who knows how many brainwashed office workers surprised themselves by saying, 'Give us a Bolan, will you, mate?' when all they'd envisaged going home with was a short back and sides. Indeed, had we been operational across all five weekday lunchtimes, Andy and I might have succeeded in making Darlington a centre of special anthropological interest: the only town in Britain peopled entirely by Afro-haired Anglo-Saxons. One can only begin to imagine the cultural implications.

Earth, Wind and Fire might have been formed not by the cream of Chicago's black session musicians, but by a collection of skinny white blokes from up the North Road. The late, lamented soul singer Minnie Riperton would have hailed from the Mowden Estate and have gone to the same school as my sister. Starsky and Hutch's streetwise pal Huggy Bear would have had freckles, a ginger moustache and a season ticket to Darlington F.C. It was not to be. I suspect however that we were influential somewhat closer to home, specifically in the matter of Kevin Keegan, The Dodgy Barnet Years.

Clearly, the then young and impressionable footballing hero had one day got off at the wrong railway station, wandered into town and found himself assailed by countless seductive, curly-haired pictures of Petula and Marc. And, equally clearly, he really had been bonkers enough to enter A Cut Above or Curl Up And Dye and ask for something along the same lines. What other explanation can there be for the hairstyle-made-in-hell he sported in the mid to late Seventies? My abiding fear is that, should I ever meet him, he will identify me as the man responsible and swiftly break my nose. Either that or he'll extract his revenge by shoving my finger into an electrical socket, so turning what's left of my hair into some absurdly retro Clarkian or Bolanesque frizz.

Needless to say, this campaign of retail terrorism was covert; we had no wish to trigger the scorn of our classmates, and its likely manifestation in hearty physical abuse. Hence it took all my powers of self-containment not to fall to my knees and kiss the sixth-form common room's grubby concrete floor one day when, flicking through the pages of the *Northern Echo* and tapping my Tuf Pathfinder lace-up in pretend appreciation of a Jethro Tull album, I happened upon an advert for the ABC Theatre, Stockton-on-Tees. There, making a one-night, two-show appearance, was to be Petula herself. The very same woman who had walked along that Brazilian beach in such splendid isolation was coming to a high street not twenty miles away. For a brief while, the world of a sad and lovely famous person was to collide with my own.

19 October 1974: it would be the eve of my eighteenth birthday – a sign in itself, I decided, while queuing for tickets

for the second performance. There was no question in my mind but that Andy would come with me: 'I'd do the same for you if Marc were playing,' I repeated, mantra-like, until he agreed. What to wear on such an important occasion then became my preoccupation. Eventually, I decided upon a three-piece suit in a bold brown check, which had recently caught my eye – how could it have failed to? – from the window of Mr Harry's Boutique for Men, and I wore it on the night with misplaced pride. Andy, a snappy dresser, turned up with a new trenchcoat draped nonchalantly over the shoulders of his best velvet jacket, so protecting it from the evening's drizzle. Thus brutalized by low-budget, mid-Seventies male fashion, we joined the queue outside the ABC as the first of the evening's two shows drew to a close.

From within, we could hear the final bars of a brassy, up-tempo version of 'You've Got A Friend' and the audience's subsequent, extended applause. This hint of what was in store should only have increased my anticipation but, instead, I found myself tormented by a secret, one so immense that possession of it was starting to make me feel sick. Earlier in the week, I had sent Petula an earnest letter via the theatre, explaining that I would come of age the day after I saw her second set, and asking if she might dedicate a song to me – any song, and not verbally, but in her own head. This very strange idea had been prompted by a revelation in the *New Musical Express* that she silently offered up each of her concerts to the goal of world peace, and the presumption of my resultant request had yet to strike me. Global unity is a glorious ideal, of course, but quite why I imagined that the small matter of my own birthday deserved parallel inclusion on Petula's spiritual agenda, let alone God's, is beyond me now. And not only that.

My main aim throughout adolescence had been to avoid drawing attention to myself. Now, unwittingly, I had created a situation where Petula, misreading my letter in superstar haste, might believe that what I actually wanted was to be publicly identified as the birthday boy, made to stand up in a spotlight and be rewarded with a round of applause. What if she went so far as to call me up on stage and present me with a cake? There might even be community singing and a picture in the paper. Suddenly I wanted to die – then I realized that, by doing so outside a packed theatre, I would only increase my chances of making Monday's papers. Regrets, however, were futile, because the doors had opened, the matinee audience had spilled out and we were on our way to our seats. The ensuing hundred minutes were wonderful, of course, though time has erased most details other than that no ritual humiliation of me, however benignly intended, was involved. Then it was all over and we were back outside in the rain.

Enervated, but also massively relieved, I forgot my habitual shyness when Andy said, 'Why don't we ask to say hello?' And so we did, although a curmudgeonly stage doorman was having nothing of our hopeful, starstruck presence. 'Get your-selves off home, lads,' he advised, kettle in hand, as we attempted to shelter in the doorway outside his cabin. 'She won't want to be talking to the likes of you.' But just before he could eject us into the night, Petula emerged, newly changed into flared jeans and a fluffy crew neck that had a Scottie-dog motif on the front. 'Please! Please! These young gentlemen are my friends,' she remonstrated, causing my heart to swell. Suddenly paralysed with self-consciousness, I struggled to speak.

Finally, the words 'I wrote to you' emerged, but in a tone

that, through nervousness, sounded accusatory, if not down-right rude. As patient and kind as a special-needs teacher, Petula explained that she received quite a lot of mail, and coaxed from me my letter's specific details. Then puzzlement clouded her face. 'But did I make a mistake? I'd thought you were going to be at the first show. I dedicated "You've Got A Friend" especially to you. Right out loud!'

'That's right!' exclaimed one of the other polyester-clad admirers who had somehow materialized behind us. 'I'm sooo jealous! Everybody heard it.' Everybody except me, of course, a fact which, later, I would view as a double triumph: somehow, I had realized every fan's dream of impinging on their idol's consciousness, yet had also avoided my ultimate fear, that of being stared at by other people. 'Well,' concluded Petula, discreetly noting the arrival of the limousine due to return her to whatever constituted Stockton's best hotel, 'at least you know I was thinking of you. Happy birthday for tomorrow!'

Awash with gratitude, I crunched her hand in mine and grinned stupidly. Then Andy curtailed what could have been an awkward moment by edging past me, raincoat still draped elegantly about his shoulders – had he sewn it to his jacket? – and kissing her on either cheek with a confidence of which I hadn't suspected him capable. 'A great evening,' he assured her as she and a small entourage stepped out into the night. Feeling slightly as if I'd been mugged by a guest at my own party, I joined him in waving until the long black car had turned a corner and disappeared from sight.

Old loyalties die hard, as was proved when I arrived in New York on another Saturday evening twenty years later, an interview with Carly Simon for *Harpers & Queen* scheduled for the Monday, but no plans whatsoever for the hours in between. My hotel was in the heart of the theatre district and, after registering and tidying myself up, I went back outside and began to walk. Turning a corner on to West 45th Street, I saw the neon lights of the Music Box Theatre, home to a production of Willy Russell's musical *Blood Brothers*, which featured David and Shaun Cassidy and starred – yes, thank you – Petula Clark.

'Only one ticket left, sir. Sixty-five dollars,' I was told at the box office. I bought it gratefully and slipped into my seat, for the show was about to begin.

The plot scarcely matters; if you haven't seen the play already, suffice it to say that it's set in breadline Liverpool and boasts a couple of stirring musical numbers, delivered in bravura fashion on this occasion by my boyhood heroine. In fact, all the performances had a genuine charm, and the audience cheered long and raucously at its conclusion. Petula had sung beautifully and, though it was strange to see her moving about within stage-set Toxteths and Skelmersdales in such a venue, she had authenticated what was necessarily a melodramatic depiction of working-class northern Britain. Also, despite the odd combination of high heels and frilly ankle socks, she still looked impossibly young and glamorous.

One scene in particular stays with me, when David Cassidy, suddenly retreating into a recreation of his childhood self, runs frightened towards his stage mother and throws himself into her arms. Fondly and gently, she cradles his head, protecting him from the world. It's a poignant and affecting moment, and brought a lump to the theatre's collective throat. Then, 'Lucky Puh-tew-la!' came the sudden, involuntary and very loud exclamation of the woman sitting next to me, obviously a diehard fan of the former teen star. All around us, people turned to stare, causing my neighbour to look mortified at her outburst and the partner on her other side to sink his face into his hands. Personally, I thought she'd got it back to front. 'No,' I said to myself, thinking of 19 October 1974, 'Lucky David!'

Early on in my school career, I realized that my reputation as a bit of a delicate flower, combined with a certain look of butter-wouldn't-melt studiousness, could be exploited for comic effect. I could never hope to be the toughest kid in the class, nor the star of the football or cricket teams, but sometimes I could make people laugh. I could ask cheekier questions of the teachers than anyone else, disguising my intentions with a saintly expression, or whip the bearded, drooling English master of our first year into a salivating frenzy of gratitude by mimicking his overly theatrical delivery of a poem like 'MacCavity The Mystery Cat' while everyone around me monotonously droned. In this way, if not actually making myself universally popular, I won acceptance. In so far as it qualifies as a talent, it was one I was grateful to have.

Carmel Grammar was an all-male preserve, in terms of pupils at least, its female equivalent being the Immaculate Conception School for Girls, which my sister Trish had already gone on to attend. Though directly related, the two buildings were a mile or so apart, and had no formal programme to integrate the two sets of students; if anything, boys meeting girls was actively discouraged. On becoming old enough and hormonal enough to sense it properly, I realized that this lent a particular charge to the atmosphere we worked in. The subject of sex bubbled below the surface constantly, erupting with even the most feeble provocation. A geography master had only to make reference to the peaks of a mountain range or the particular curves of a river valley and the class would collapse into giggles and wisecracks. Even aspects of history or geometry could cast a thrall across the form room, while biology was, of course, all but a non-stop mental orgy. When tall, toothy John Forward claimed to have seen head boy, Keith Hadleigh, kissing French teacher, Miss Howell – one of two female members of staff, and the only one under fifty-five – we debated the subject for weeks, despite none of us believing it to be true. When the two left at the end of term, allegedly to set up home together, we were stunned into an awed and appalled silence.

My own education in worldly matters began officially when my mum presented me with a booklet published by some Catholic propaganda outfit, 'Answering Boys' Questions About Sex'. It didn't answer any of the ones I wanted to ask, but concentrated instead on two things: the sinfulness of spilling one's own seed – the writers couldn't even bring themselves to use the word masturbation – and the fact that sexual relations were a gift from God that could only be enjoyed between a man and a woman who together had entered the state of holy matrimony. It illustrated these points with line drawings of the reproductive organs of the male and female bunny. They mucked you up, those authors. They may not have meant to, but they did. After all, rabbits are famed for one thing and one thing only: the energy and frequency of their reproductive congress. An entire generation of Catholic boys must have gone out into the adult world in the belief that they must shag like crazy and then feel horribly guilty afterwards. I know I did.

What 'Answering Boys' Questions About Sex' didn't tell me, I could pick up by eavesdropping on the conversations of John Forward and his mates. The knowledge, and, of course, misinformation, I gathered in this way only confirmed what

I was already beginning to suspect: that not everyone believed in, or lived by, the same restrictive religious and moral codes I had been brought up with. I had been told these codes were universal, not to be doubted or argued with, and that failure to comply with them would mean eventual condemnation to the cleansing flames of purgatory, if not to hell itself. The evidence I was gathering from all around me suggested the world was an altogether more complex, potentially wicked place than I could possibly have imagined. The thought both disquieted and excited me.

I remember being truly shocked when, while visiting my grandfather and finding myself alone in his kitchen for a minute or two, I picked up his copy of the *News of the World*, a paper I'd never seen before. Its lead story detailed the goings-on at parties organized by the vice queen-cum-recording star Janie Jones, and featured a wonderfully prurient report of orgies watched through two-way mirrors by disc jockeys and pop stars of the day. I hadn't known, or even imagined, that such things could go on, let alone that people in the public eye might be participants. And, in a decade when getting your kit off was not the familiar career move it is today, I was almost equally shocked that teen idol David Cassidy should lose all his clothes before the lens of *Rolling Stone* photographer Annie Liebovitz. It seemed everyone, not just Darlington schoolboys, was obsessed with sex. Lulu, the epitome of Saturday-night light entertainment at the time, had been to a performance of Kenneth Tynan's controversial, nudity-filled revue *Oh Calcutta!*, and had reportedly told the tabloids that she would like to have been offered a part in it. Even the divine Petula, discussing her possible casting in a proposed film adaptation of the John Updike novel *Couples*, told interviewers that she would be prepared to strip if it were essential to the role.

Thus, by the time I read in my parents' *Sunday Express* that the actress and singer Jane Birkin had completed a steamy photo shoot for the French men's magazine *Lui*, my imagination had reached something close to fever pitch. She was in her underwear, or less, throughout, I read, and in one instance was shown handcuffed to the radiator of a Parisian hotel bedroom. Why didn't matter. I just had to see those pictures, and there was only one place in Darlington where I could hope to do so: at the news stand in the town's indoor market. So clandestine did the mission seem to me that I didn't even tell partner-in-crime Andy of my intentions on the afternoon I left school intent on buying a copy. I already knew it was stocked there, because I'd identified it among a top shelf of foreign titles while walking casually back and forth the previous day. Now all I had to do was ask the stallholder for it.

Rehearsal one: 'The *Darlington & Stockton Times*, please. Oh, and I'll take that copy of *Lui* while I'm at it, too. That one up there, tucked behind *Paris-Match*.' No. A little too contrived. If he doesn't already know what sort of magazine it is, that'll only draw his attention to it.

Rehearsal two: 'I'm studying French at school and have been told I should read as many native publications as I can lay my hands on. Could I take a copy of every French magazine in the rack, please. Yes, including that copy of – what is it? *Lui*? Oh, whatever. Chuck it in the bag. The more the merrier.' No again. Far too expensive. There's easily twenty quids' worth of stuff up there and I've only got £5.

The actuality: it was raining and getting dark. Within the market, there was a constant traffic of damp commuters looking for something to read on the journey home and – a nightmare I hadn't anticipated – the proprietor had abandoned his post to chat with the owner of the adjoining vegetable counter, leaving a woman of my mum's age to operate the till. Mortified and unsure of what to do, I lingered by a nearby butcher's concession for so long that its female assistant was moved to ask if I was feeling all right. 'Fine, thank you,' I told her. 'Well, bugger off then,' she replied. 'You're giving me the willies, hanging about like this.'

There were only five minutes left before my own once-every-half-hour bus was due. Miraculously, the queue at the news-stand suddenly evaporated. Despite my misgivings about approaching someone else's mother with such a delicate request, I knew it was now or never. So, 'Hello there!' I began brightly. 'I'd like to buy a copy of that French magazine up there. *Lui*, it's called. Directly above *Caravaning Today*, and a little to the right. D'you see it?'

'Louis?' repeated the assistant doubtfully.

'No, *Lui*,' I corrected, pointlessly, as she finally identified the object of my desire and pulled it from the tightly racked display. 'Thank you. How much is that?'

'Hold your horses, bonny lad,' she replied, scrutinizing the publication. 'I'm not sure I should be selling you this. Boss! Young man I've got here wants to buy this. It looks a bit grown-up to me. Is it OK to let him have it?'

Already, the length of this exchange had been sufficient for a small line of customers to gather behind me. And when the proprietor strolled over, curious, it was with his grinning friend from the vegetable stall in tow. 'So why d'you want a magazine like this, eh, son?' he asked, playing to the gallery. '*Health & Efficiency* not good enough for you, is it?'

There was a small ripple of laughter from around me, but I was in too deep to think of bailing out. 'I'm doing French A level,' I told him, 'and we've been told to read as much in the actual language as we can. And so' – here, I made a desperate appeal to him, boy to man – 'I thought that, if I'm going to look at a magazine like this, it might as well be a French one.'

'I can't believe you'll be spending much time reading the text,' he said, nudging his mate and flashing him the centre-fold. 'Looks like some things are the same, no matter which country they come from. But if you're so keen to have this, and you really want it for your studies, let's hear you ask for it in French.'

This was awful. Too awful. Especially with an audience. But there was no going back. '*Je voudrais . . . Non! Je veux acheter ce journal, s'il vous plaît. C'est pour mes études.*'

'Let the lad have it, for God's sake,' came a woman's voice from behind me. 'Some of us have buses to catch. If I was wanting to learn French, I'd be taking evening classes.'

Seconds later I fled the scene, managing to climb aboard my homeward-bound bus with just seconds to spare, a copy of *Lui* secreted within my haversack, and a crimson flush of embarrassment still on my face. Not until we'd passed through the outlying housing estates and were into open countryside did the number of fellow passengers diminish enough for me to be able to sneak the magazine out and, under cover of the *NME*, examine its contents. I flicked through page after page after page in an increasing panic. Then, unable to believe my eyes, I went back to the beginning and started flicking through again. A glance at the cover confirmed the awful truth: I'd been sold a back copy. There was no Jane Birkin, clothed, unclothed, handcuffed or otherwise. It was the wrong bloody issue.

Two years ago, I met the woman in question for the first time. By then she was forty-nine years old, a respected actress, and in London from her Paris home to launch a retrospective collection of her past recordings, among them the notorious 'Je T'Aime . . . Moi Non Plus', that kitsch, cod-orgasmic duet with her former partner, the late French troubadour Serge Gainsbourg. She and I arrived at the concierge's desk of the appointed hotel at exactly the same moment, I full of anticipation, she in the throws of a coughing fit. 'What a beastly state in which to present oneself,' she apologized while all but doubled over. There then followed a volley of sniffs and the search for a tissue with which to make a robust blowing of the nose.

The real Jane Birkin was not a schoolboy's erotic dream, being dressed in grubby plimsolls, faded jeans, a sweater and an outsize mac. But she had a beauty beyond anything that my younger, hormonal self could have imagined, standing awkwardly and full of anticipation at the news stand that day. And when we talked, she seemed so gentle, warm and wise that I felt impelled to confess my little secret to her. She listened solemnly as I spoke, then, when I'd finished, clapped her hands together with delight. 'Perfect!' she exclaimed. 'To be displayed among the cutlets and sprouts of a northern English market! Imagine! Or, rather, how could one? Imagine, that is, when one does these things, that one will end up being presented in that way.' And so saying, she subsided apologetically into yet another volley of coughs.

Thanks or no thanks to *Lui*, I passed my French A level. I got passes in English and art too, sufficiently good ones to qualify for a place at university. Initially, I'd imagined that I wanted to go as far away as possible, in order to reinvent myself and start my adult life as a degree student of English. Accordingly, I had put relatively remote destinations, such as Lancaster and

Lampeter, towards the top of my UCCA form, with nearby Newcastle in fifth and final place, just in case I lost my nerve. My mum bought me a new sports jacket and trousers, in case I was called to interview – at all of those I attended, I was far more smartly, and awkwardly, dressed than the members of department assessing me – and the University of Kent at Canterbury provided me with a first opportunity to wear them. Nervously, I stepped onto the London-bound train at Darlington station. Settling into a vacant seat, I noticed that the rather glamorous girl sitting opposite me was, by chance, reading a University of Kent prospectus. This piece of serendipity empowered me to speak to her. Yes, she was going to Canterbury. Yes, she had an interview tomorrow, just like me.

Cheerfully ditching the arrangements made for me by my mother, I readily fell in with the suggestion that I should stay at the same place she was booked into and not somewhere else in town. The landlady, exotic in a handkerchief skirt and low-necked blouse, and with dyed black hair piled artfully upon her head, was so eagerly complicit in the plan that she volunteered to call and cancel the existing reservation on my behalf. 'Mr Jackson has been unavoidably detained,' I heard her say, in strangulated, pseudo-upper-class tones, 'and will be unable to fulfil the booking he made with you earlier. He asks me to convey to you his sincere apologies, and 'opes he has not inconvenienced you too greatly.' Then, replacing the receiver, she came in search of us. 'The deed is done,' she said with a conspiratorial wink. 'And it serves her right. Thinks she's a cut above, does that particular party. Cups of tea all round, I think. I'll go and warm the pot.'

And so it was that I came to have dinner that night in a wine bar with someone who, though of a similar age, was infinitely more sophisticated and poised than I was. For starters, a wine bar? I don't think I'd ever tasted wine before, let alone eaten mushrooms à la Grecque, lasagna and tiramisu. All of which went to explain why, when Emma tapped on my bedroom door later that night and made a surreptitious entrance, she found me being copiously and noisily sick into the hand basin. Needless to say, she didn't linger.

I would like to be able to report that I felt better by the following morning. But, within seconds of joining a decidedly frosty Emma in a taxi to the university campus, I knew that I didn't. The dean reportedly made a jolly speech to welcome all potential students, but I missed most of it through being violently ill in a bathroom near by. Some kind first years gave us a guided tour of the living accommodation and communal facilities afterwards, but I missed most of that, too, through being opportunistically sick in toilets, sports changing rooms and a corridor waste basket – I successfully sluiced the afflicted item under someone's shower, but was rewarded with rising damp to the legs of my nasty brown flares. Somehow, subsequent to this, I managed to discuss the dinner-party scene in Virginia Woolf's *To The Lighthouse* with a professor from the English faculty – and all without throwing up across his desk at the mention of beef en daube. To my astonishment and relief, I was offered a place on his course. The trouble was, whenever I thought of Canterbury afterwards, it was in terms of me on my knees, making intimate acquaintance with a toilet bowl.

'I'm due to meet some friends, actually, and probably won't head north until tomorrow,' said Emma that afternoon. 'I'll leave you here, if that's OK.' And with that, she feinted an escape from my attempted embrace and disappeared towards the underground at Waterloo station. When I saw her less than an hour later, at King's Cross and boarding the same Newcastle-bound train that I was already sitting on, I had sufficient respect for her and myself to hide behind my copy of the *NME*. Did she ever take up a place at the University of Kent? I doubt it. She probably feared I'd be there, too, looking permanently queasy while trailing doggedly hither and thither across the campus in pursuit of her.

When my mum handed over my sports jacket at the dry cleaners the following weekend, the assistant wondered about the precise nature of the stain on its very large lapel. 'He was sick,' she said confidentially, with a you-know-how-it-is-with-teenage-boys type of glance in my direction. 'It was a stomach bug that flared up quickly. He's over it now.' They weren't interested in the details. 'Vomit mark, upper left front,' read the ticket I was obliged to surrender a few days later.

My jacket may have been returned to me in pristine condition, but I was left feeling strangely careworn. The humiliating circumstances of my first venture into the world of academe had dented my confidence badly, and I was no longer certain that I could meet the challenge of far-away places with strange-sounding menus. Safer altogether, I decided, to head up the road to Newcastle. It still represented pastures new. Though it was little more than half an hour away by train, I'd only been there twice. Perhaps I would fit in on Tyneside. Maybe that was where I could best reinvent myself as Mr Confident, Mr Successful, even Mr Stable-Stomached. Determinedly putting hope into my heart and a predictable assortment of dodgy, late-Seventies fashion into the trunk my father had bought me, I prepared to leave home for the first time.

2

For reasons that are now lost to me, I believed my university education would never end. It did. Yet right up until the end of my third year, even beyond the final exams themselves, I maintained my ostrich pose. Perhaps it was because I'd seen the newly released film *Grease*, in which every high-school student appears to be at least thirty years old. Perhaps I thought that I too could just resit and resit, year after year, finally ending up as handsome as John Travolta. Whatever my reasoning, I felt I needn't trouble my head with the business of selecting a career, let alone of getting a job. And as a result, I was able to smile blithely as my friends and flatmates obsessed about the yearly milk round, or debated the relative merits of dedicating their futures to P&O or ICI. Leaving them to fill in endless application forms, I would walk through the sunshine to Newcastle's Northumberland Street and my favourite record store, Callers, to sift through the latest releases on A&M or RCA, and to daydream about the hazily unspecific but star-filled future that doubtless lay ahead.

In retrospect, I think this attitude of denial stemmed from

the fact that I had never been so happy before. At university I had found friends, had enjoyed my course, liked the city I was living in and, through arriving late at a French conversation class two years earlier, had identified the love of my life – true, there was the small matter of her not being in agreement about this – Christine Costello. The future of the family unit had been under discussion at the moment I burst through the door, apology rehearsed. But it was the wrong door, and Joelle Dupont, a notoriously tetchy *lectrice* with a Mireille Mathieu bob and a serious jewellery habit, was not pleased to see me.

'But no!' she snapped when, having had my mistake pointed out to me, I began to retreat into the corridor. 'You have already disrupted one group with your comings-late and your oh-so-very-sorrys. Don't now disrupt another. Sit. In silence. And learn.'

I sat. And minutes later, when I dared to raise my eyes to a horizontal position, I found myself looking at the loveliest face I'd ever seen. Not that it was merely lovely. It could talk, too. In French. 'Oh, at least six. I think,' it was saying – like many language students, I was far more successful at translating other people's sentences than I was at formulating any of my own. 'But then, I'm the youngest of seven. And I think there's much to be gained from being part of a large family. It makes you less selfish, less inward-looking. It gives you a better sense of your own role within the greater scheme of things.' Hallelujah! Not only was she clearly a Catholic, like myself, but also she was super-intelligent, socially aware, kind and generous. And, er, beautiful, too. Anyone else might have thought, Bingo! She's the one for me. With my religious training, however, I preferred to believe I had died and gone to heaven.

'*Très bien*, Christine!' purred Joelle, pausing for a moment to admire her own outstretched and beringed fingers before turning to me. '*Et vous, Alain? Combien des enfants voudriez-vous avoir, nous nous demandons?*'

It was my big chance to impress and I was paralysed – by surprise, fear and, most effectively of all, by a woefully inadequate command of the French language. 'Er, *deux, peut-être?*' I said uncertainly, and smiled, also uncertainly. Joelle was decidedly unimpressed. '*Une fille et un fils, sans doute*,' she replied with disdain. 'Ladies and gentlemen, the crasher of our gate is clearly one of life's great original thinkers.'

I could never have anticipated that my going to university – for years, it had been the combined ambition of me, my mother and father – would result in my being made to feel so stupid so regularly. No doubt many students are similarly disabused of a belief in their own potential brilliance as they make the transition from the smallish ponds of secondary school to the more competitive waters of university. My mistaken notion that I was some kind of linguist was making things considerably worse for me. That I had sat through five whole years of Latin instruction – much of it with a folded-up copy of the *NME* hidden beneath my text books – and still achieved the worst possible O level grade should have alerted me to my limitations in this field. It hadn't.

Because I'd passed French A level and, in my final year of sixth form, had scraped through German O level after just two terms, I'd indulged the idea that various glittering, multi-lingual careers were open to me, should I choose to select them: as a fast-track junior diplomat-cum-secret agent, for example, or as a male Katie Boyle, smoothly intoning, '*La Norvège, nul points*; Norway, no points,' as the international juries cast their votes in the Eurovision Song Contest – this latter scenario had the stronger appeal, because pop music of a kind was involved. Thus, when its prospectus revealed to me that Newcastle University had one of the country's few departments of Scandinavian studies, I abandoned my plans to apply for Single Honours English and opted instead for a general arts degree. In the interests of the entente cordiale, I would do English and French, while also learning a new language, Swedish.

This latter decision had proved a terrible mistake. The other eleven students in my group had one, if not two, Swedish parents, or had been brought up there because their fathers were in the employ of Volvo or Saab. I'd never had so much as a lift in either; my dad drove a Vauxhall Viva. So, effectively, my classmates were fluent speakers already and I was the dunce, barely able to pronounce the names of Abba's four members, let alone read aloud an untranslated Strindberg text. This, combined with my pedestrian abilities at French, meant I had spent much of my first year at university cramming to pass two subjects I should never have selected, simply in order to drop them and do the course I should have chosen in the first place.

No degree of fluency would have been enough to win Christine's heart that day in Mlle Dupont's conversation class, however. Over the two and a half years that followed, she variously tolerated, took pity on and seemed genuinely amused by my attempts to woo her, but gave little encouragement and yielded no ground. I was persistent, obsessive even. When, at the end of the first summer term in Newcastle, she issued a general invitation to anyone travelling through Europe that summer to look her up in Bonn, where she would be working as a hotel chambermaid, I brooded for a few days, withdrew what money I had in a building-society account and flew out to meet her. It was the first time I'd ever been on a plane.

I arrived late on the night that Elvis Presley died, and we sat up until the early hours, listening to tearful presenters pay tribute to him on Radio Luxemburg. She had found me a room in a male students' house close to her workplace, and I drifted through the city by day, or spent hours reading in the American Library, getting by on my minimal German and waiting for the hour when she finished work and I could meet her. I don't think it occurred to me that she might need time to herself after working hard all day, or that a spaniel-like devotion might actually not help my cause. Every day I would be there when she came off shift – smiling, ever-hopeful, looking forward to an evening that would end with Christine getting on the tram that took her back to the fearsome land-lady of her all-female rooming house.

One particular evening, I remember, we fell out, and it felt like the end of the world. My parents had never exchanged cross words in front of my sister and me, so I had no idea that you could argue and make up, that it was what people did. So there was no question of me sleeping that night. Before first light, I was standing outside the Hotel Bristol, where Christine worked. I knew the name of the road she lodged on, but not where it was; all I knew was that she caught a tram home from outside the hotel. So, with dawn breaking, I walked through the empty streets towards suburbia, the tram line always beneath my feet, checking the street signs to the left and right at each intersection I passed. In this way, finally, I found my way to her door. I was there, waiting to apologize, when she emerged at six thirty to leave for work.

Was I Romeo or just a sad limpet? Probably the latter, for all my good intentions. Certainly when, around the time of my finals, I announced that I wouldn't actually be leaving Newcastle to begin a career, but intended to hang around until Christine's four-year course finished the following summer, her reaction was unequivocal: on your bike and get a job. Finally, I understood that she could only be attracted to someone who had their own life and their own ideas, and who wasn't seeking to be a passenger in hers. Despite my immediate disappointment, I was energized by this revelation and hurried off towards the university careers office.

'What's the best way of becoming a journalist?' I asked the counsellor to whom I was assigned. She invited me to draw up a chair, withdrew some files from a rank of grey steel cabinets and then proceeded to tell me.

A human dynamo in a blue nylon overall, Mrs Mullet seized possession of my suitcase as I hovered awkwardly on her doorstep, and then, at a speed I wouldn't have thought her capable of, lurched with it up a set of thickly Axminstered stairs. She looked like an elderly luggage thief in flight. I'd got as far as, 'Hello, I'm Alan, your lodger,' when she interrupted me with a brusque, 'I know. Now, give me that,' and took off. As a result, I missed out on whatever conversational niceties might have eased me into the household – the 'Welcome to Cardiff!' or the 'How was your journey?' No matter. The new, purposeful, knows-where-he's-going me I had so carefully constructed wasn't about to be unravelled by a hyperactive pensioner with a home perm and carpet slippers. I crossed the threshold of the dark, three-storey house uninvited, closed the front door behind me and followed upwards in her wake.

'Here! Your new home!' she called back to me, defiant, tumbling into a rear bedroom, situated, I would soon discover, precisely where the Welsh sun never shone. Ever. I entered the room to find her patting the thin, gold-quilted counterpane upon a large divan. 'I know you'll sleep well in this bed,' she said in a softer tone. 'It's the one my late husband died in. Just six weeks ago, it was.' An ominous hollow in the centre of the double mattress made it all too easy to imagine the spectral presence of Mr Mullet still lingering between a set of brown nylon sheets.

As she spoke, she paused briefly before the mirrored dressing table, then turned away again, as if unable to recognize her own reflection. Had I not been so young, so callow and self-absorbed, I might have registered and been humbled by the mini-revelation I was offered of a tiny, tight-skinned woman in her early seventies, brittle and busy and too much in denial of her new lone status to dare to stand still. Indeed, I might even have succeeded in offering more than just a mumbled, 'I'm very sorry to hear that,' shuffling uncomfortably as I did so. As it was, I effortlessly read the situation only in relation to myself. Fantastic! I thought to myself bitterly. A seven-hour journey to start a new life, only to find I'm lodging with the un-merry widow!

After ringing my way unsuccessfully down the list of possible accommodation addresses sent to me by the local Institute of Technology, where the NCTJ or National Council for the Training of Journalists was to run its pioneer four-month post-graduate course, I had finally struck lucky with Mrs Mullet. Or I'd believed I had. 'Tell Mum not to worry,' she urged me, after confirming she had a vacancy. 'I've always had a lodger or two on the go since my Graham flew the nest; he's big in the biscuit world, you know. I take good care of my young men. You'll be snug as a bug in a rug down in this cozy corner.'

Great. Only, now that I was here, there was no hint of the kindly surrogate granny I'd spoken to on the phone. At twenty-two, I wasn't yet smart enough to read her unexpected frostiness as a bad disguise, to sense that beneath it hid someone desperate to give love, but made afraid of doing so by her recent loss. Instead, I had to get to know her from scratch. This was no easy thing, especially given her confusing habit of stating one thing, quite vehemently, then demonstrating that actually she meant the exact opposite.

'Let's get one thing established right away,' she said, all the while flying about the gloomy room, adjusting already-straight pictures and snatching imaginary specks of lint from the floor. 'Don't think I've got time to be running here and there after you, picking up your shopping and rinsing your smalls. It's a very busy schedule I have, what with poor Phyllis next door and all her troubles, and another boy from your course already moved into my de luxe *en-suite*. Steve, his name is. From Lancashire. Is that the time?'

'I'll be no trouble at all,' I promised, and believed it. 'I can pick up whatever I need locally and I'm fine with a launderette. Everything seems to be on hand. I saw the parade of shops as I arrived in the taxi.'

'Hand over your money to those robbers down the road when I could get your tinned stuff at near half price from Leo's, where I do my big Friday shop? You'd have to be mad,' snapped Mrs Mullet, as if personally insulted. 'And as for that launder-so-called-ette? A filthy, dirty place. Your things'll come out worse than when you put them in. No, you don't want to go there. Anyway, take a moment or two to get your things unpacked, why don't you? Then get yourself downstairs to the front parlour, pronto. I'm making tea and you can introduce yourself to Steve. A nice boy, and cheeky with it – a real rip! You'll like him. He's got dark hair, too.'

When the hurricane had passed out on to the landing, I went to the window and pulled aside the starched nets. Late on the first Saturday afternoon of January, I could see more of my own reflection than I could of the immediate vista of dark brick walls, dustbins and a thin-looking square of grass. Potentially, a strange new world lay beyond the glass, but what I could see of it was somehow only too familiar. Before I had time to feel properly melancholy, though, a shrill voice reached up from below and boxed me round the ears. 'Alan? Downstairs, now! I've a Battenburg here cut up and ready! We're waiting for you.'

Entering the room, I expected to find Steve flagging beneath the onslaught of Mrs Mullet's ministrations and desperate for whatever solidarity I could offer. But no. Cheerful and bespectacled, he sat upright amid the mass of cushions camouflaging the sofa and waved a half-eaten slice of pink and yellow chequered cake at me in greeting. Pushed into place alongside him, I listened to his brief biographical self-portrait and responded with one of my own. A china cup and saucer and plate were placed in my hands as I did so.

'Working class, like us, but with lower-middle-class aspirations,' said Steve in David Attenboroughish tones, during the brief moment in which Mrs Mullet was out of the room, refilling a teapot covered with a knitted version of a crinolined lady.

'What makes you say that?' I asked, looking for the definitive social signifier in a room stuffed with items of fatly upholstered furniture, and in which every available surface was covered with a doily boasting an item of glassware or a figurine.

'That,' he said, gesturing at a teak bowl on the glass-topped coffee table standing between us and the hearth of a vast electric fire. 'Fruit on the table when no-one's sick. It's a dead give-away.'

Mrs Mullet was right when she said that I'd like Steve. He was smart, funny and, to my great deference, had spent the six months since his graduation working not in a factory, as I had, but on an actual newspaper, a Lancashire weekly called the *Darwen Advertiser*. I couldn't have been more impressed if I'd been told he'd won the Pulitzer Prize. Our landlady smiled benignly to see us getting on so well, but that didn't stop her insinuating a slight sense of betrayal when I announced, post-tea, that we intended going out for a drink together later. 'You feel free to come and go as you please,' she said, thrusting a front door key into my hand in a way that suggested I'd wrenched it directly from her heart. 'I don't drink myself. Never have, never will. It's the Lord I turn to when I need comfort and strength. But you two go and enjoy yourselves. I'm no killjoy. I like to see young people happy.' And it was with the merest hint of a self-righteous sniff that she vanished, leaving me alone in the overheated hall.

Later, waiting hopefully at the bar of our nearest pub, we watched customer after customer give their order and then walk away, drink in hand. But not us. First I tried to catch the barmaid's eye, then Steve did. Then we both tried, but from different ends of the same counter. When, finally, there was no-one else left to serve, the barmaid at whom we'd been staring beseechingly for all of ten minutes – in a year when most women wanted to look like Debbie Harry, she was Dusty Springfield with a bad attitude – approached Steve and snapped, 'What would you be wanting then, eh?'

'Two pints of Brains bitter, please,' said Steve. Brains was the local brewery, and selecting one of its beers was bound to establish us as discerning drinkers, keen to integrate.

'Brains bitter, is it?' she replied, her crimson lips curling energetically this way and that, in a manner recently popularized by Sue-Ellen, a character in the new American TV import *Dallas*. 'That's B B; or Boys' Beer, as I call it. I should've known. You sure you wouldn't rather have halves?'

On the day that we began our journalism course, we walked in early through tree-lined streets of bay-fronted semis towards the institute, Steve jocular and bright, me with the kind of dull foreboding I remembered from the first days of term in my adolescence. My sense of regression was intensified by the familiar dreariness of the building that confronted us. Low-rise, economy-sized post-modern, it could have been any one of a thousand secondary schools in cities the length and breadth of Britain; there was even a playground in which other reluctant students dawdled, smoking cigarettes.

My face fell, confronted with this unlikely first rung on my ladder towards a glittering, celebrity-filled future. Bike sheds, litter bins and 'No Running In The Corridors' signs hadn't featured in my dreams of writing glory. But, 'Hold the front page!' said Steve confidently to no-one in particular, leading the way towards our designated classroom. 'Woodward and Bernstein have arrived!' His enthusiasm was contagious, and I felt pleased to be given sidekick status with someone of his experience. Perhaps we really were a journalistic Batman and Robin. Perhaps the world had better watch out.

Thus it was with relative confidence that I joined the five other male and three female trainees who, with Steve and myself, comprised course tutor Peter's inaugural post-grad class. Seats had already been allocated to us in the small room and, in the U-shaped arrangement of desks facing a black-board, I was placed between tall, drawling David, born to wear a blazer and with the innate self-confidence of the upper middle classes, and Carol. How to describe her? For a tabloid photo-caption writer in the pre-political-correctness era in which I first met her, it would have been easy: blonde bomb-shell, college cutie. It was if the Rank Charm School of the 1950s had suddenly been recreated in south Wales, and I had been positioned between Dirk Bogarde and Barbara Windsor.

Yet Carol was much more than just an amalgam of peroxide hair, Essex vowels and frequently applied lip-gloss. Ruthless in her determination to get first look at our class copy of the *Guardian*, and completely devoted to her dreamboat boy-friend, Jack, she was perhaps brighter and more ambitious than anyone in the room; when I last heard of her, she was lecturing in media studies at an American university. For now, she was giving a first airing to what we would soon discover was her catchphrase. 'Blimey! Leave it out!' she exclaimed, and giggled, after being told by Peter, a man with bone structure straight out of Mount Rushmore, that it was his intention to make men of us, journalistically at least.

The first step in this process involved an introduction to shorthand and typing from the delightful, twittering Mrs B – so committed was she to brevity, that this was how she preferred to be known. And through her we were also intro-duced to the many pressing social, financial and planning issues facing the administrators of our new patch, that teeming metropolis of Anytown. 'Come on, my dearie-dears, you know what the short form for multi-storey carpark is,' she would urge. 'Remember? Of course you do! We only learned it yesterday. It's those four horizontal lines, one on top of the other, and with just enough room between them for a little bitty car to scoot along. Now, let's get back inside that town hall and continue taking down our report of those speeches.'

And with an encouraging smile and a deep breath, she would resume her address, 'Mr Mayor, Fellow Councillors, Ladies and Gentlemen, I must protest in the strongest possible terms about the proposal to build a multi-storey carpark within this densely populated residential area. While I appreciate that drivers must have somewhere close to the central business and shopping area to leave their vehicles, I would suggest that a site external to the ring road – remember that short form! – perhaps one adjoining the existing industrial and retail estate, would make a far more cost-effective, less environmentally damaging alternative. Also, we have yet to fully discuss the implementation of a park–and–ride scheme – short form, Alan! short form! – as detailed within sub-section fourteen of the report prepared for us by . . .'

As my notepad filled up with the hieroglyphics of the Teeline system, I would sometimes allow myself to reflect that local-government reportage was not what I'd had in mind when I made my choice of profession. A more thrusting and confident cub reporter than myself would have just tipped up in London and talked themselves into a job on some paper or magazine, learning his or her profession from the shop floor up. Instead, I had taken to heart all my careers counsellor had told me: the need to serve indentures on a provincial title, to sit and pass the proficiency exams of the NCTJ, to gradually work up the news-desk hierarchy. As a result, multi-storey car parks, ring roads and industrial estates were to be my bread and butter, my stock-in-trade. It was like being an architect or town planner, but without the job satisfaction.

What, I wondered idly, were the Teeline short forms for film première, champagne reception and London's glittering

West End? And when was I to be told how best to tease information from the lips of 007 starlets and pop idols? In the face of Mrs B's relentless oration, such questioning was fatal. 'Our previously agreed policy for regeneration within the inner-city boundaries clearly states that . . .' she was now dictating, leaving me trailing two half-remembered sentences behind, with no chance remaining of typing up an accurate transcript.

'Shit!' I said to myself. 'Blimey!' said Carol out loud, her pencil point having snapped under the strain.

During those first dark weeks of January, the streets of Anytown became as real to me as those I trod to and from Mrs Mullet's. It was there that I and the others – young, enthusiastic and eager to succeed – were required to prove ourselves. Steve, having already had journalistic experience in the real world, had a head start, of course. 'Anytown Council last night gave the green light to a controversial new traffic system which . . .' he would type instinctively, while I struggled to arrange a jumble of local-government jargon and subordinate clauses into an opening sentence longer than one of his paragraphs. Conversely, if the facts we were given made it appropriate, he would rattle off stories in which brakes were applied or U-turns made. Where the wielding of local-newspaper clichés was concerned, Steve was in a class of his own, and I hero-worshipped him for it. Because he had honed this talent there, the *Darwen Advertiser* acquired a status in my mind to rival that of the *Guardian* or the *Financial Times*. I watched and learned from him, and gradually my own intros got shorter – 125 words, 100 words, a finely wrought and breathtakingly pacy 75 words.

And all the while I was becoming accustomed to the idiosyncratic domestic routine of my temporary home. Steve's accommodation allowed him a measure of independence which, increasingly, I came to envy. My bedroom adjoined Mrs Mullet's and the fact that she slept with her door ajar made me even more aware of her hovering presence. Privacy was an alien concept to her, and I quickly became used to her bursting in each morning without a preliminary knock. Thus, my first sight on being woken was of her rushing to my window, flinging apart the long, lank curtains and barking out some variation on what soon became a familiar theme. 'It's raining again. Pouring. The postman was dripping, poor love. No mail for you, by the way. Not a sausage. Now chop-chop, shake a leg, I can't be doing with stay-a-beds.'

Then there was the matter of my smalls, as she termed them. The combination of my mother's training and three years at university meant that I was self-sufficient in the laundry department. And anyway, Mrs Mullet had made it very clear that she was far too busy to think of taking on such a chore. But within days there had been a change of position, and she had started to demonstrate a near-obsession with my supply of clean underwear. As I left the breakfast table on the Friday of my first week with her, things reached a head. 'Oh, and I'll have a few minutes spare when I get back from the supermarket with Phyllis, so you might as well give me your smalls to wash through,' she said.

'It's very good of you to offer, but really, there's no need,' I told her. 'It's Saturday tomorrow and I'll have plenty of time to go to the launderette.'

'I've told you what I think of that place,' she countered darkly. 'Now, no arguing; I've neither the time nor the inclination. Just give me your smalls!'

Then, when I showed no sign of complying, she hardened

her tone, 'Come on! I haven't got all day,' she said. 'Hand over your smalls.'

Determined to maintain autonomy in at least one area of my new life, I left the house with Steve, whose underwear she seemed less concerned about, without having caved in to the demand. But that afternoon, when the two of us returned from college with fellow classmates Heather and Anne, the first visitors we had dared bring back for a friendly cup of tea, an unanticipated sight greeted me in the hall. There, ranged along a pair of electric storage heaters for all to see, were six steaming pairs of pre-Calvin-Klein-era pants. Thus displayed, the accumulation of damp unnatural fibres in such high-fashion colours as black, purple and red was enough to make me feel dizzy with shame and anger. This was a step too far. 'These yours? I'm a Y-front man myself,' said Steve. Heather and Anne merely smirked.

'Ah, now what have we here? It's Alan and The Rip!' exclaimed Mrs Mullet, her extra-sensitive ears causing her to spring from the kitchen before we could take a further step. 'And you've brought some nice friends home with you, too. Well now, let's get you all straight into the front parlour and I'll bring in some tea and biscuits. Better move Alan's socks from on top if you turn up the fire now, Steve. We don't want them catching alight.'

Then she confided to the girls, 'Alan's bits and bobs – every-where, they are! I've been rinsing things through, though heaven knows I haven't the time. Had them hidden away in a hold-all at the bottom of the wardrobe, he did. Men! The trouble they cause us, eh? Now, in you go, girls, and I'll pop that kettle on. Back in a mo and you can tell me all about yourselves.'

* ★ ★

As the winter weeks sped by, I became ever better versed in the principles of fair and accurate reporting. With this accumulation of knowledge there came a certain growth in confidence. I began to feel that, when eventually launched into the world of magistrates' court hearings, inquests and council sub-committee meetings, I might actually be capable of producing a printable report, one that steered clear of either libel or defamation while proving informative to the readership of the *Eastern Daily Press*, my sponsor and future employer. I was even taking pleasure in my fast-growing facility as both a touch-typist and a deployer of Mrs B's seemingly endless artillery of Teeline short forms. What I missed was any hint of what had lured me into journalism in the first place: glamour.

The intended highlight of the college week came early on, with our group attendance at the Monday evening meeting of the Cardiff Business Club. There, it was our task to listen to the guest speaker's address and produce, by the next morning, a usable news story to compare with that already filed and printed by whichever correspondent had represented the *Western Daily Mail*. We were exposed to captains of industry, police chiefs and trades unionists, medium-ranking politicians – no doubt solid citizens, all of them, but tanned, glamorous and sexy? Not in the least. And so it was no wonder that I was galvanized with excitement when it became known that the prime minister of the day, James Callaghan, would be calling in at the institute during a whirlwind visit to Cardiff. Obviously, it wasn't quite the same as if a pop or film star were dropping in from the heavens, but at least he was a household name.

Steve, who boasted of hard-left sympathies, refused to share my excitement. 'Shake his hand? Not me!' he sneered. 'I'm going to shout "Traitor" at him, 'cos that's what he is: a traitor to the spirit of true socialism.' As it was, the visit ran ahead of schedule and he was tucked up in a corner of the cafeteria with the *Guardian* and an all-day breakfast when the PM's party ambled along the main hallway. I myself, desperate to see, in the flesh, someone – anyone – I hadn't just seen in the papers but on a TV screen, was there in the front line. But what a let-down. No glamour. No star quality. Not even a hint of political hauteur. Instead, here was a big, grumpy-looking older man in a long black overcoat, surrounded by a gaggle of security men and local dignitaries. Ever hopeful, I looked to his wife, Audrey, following behind with a neutral expression, to save the day. But with sensible hair, sensible shoes and an outfit more Evans Outsizes than it was Yves Saint Laurent, she was no Jackie O. Disappointed and newly aware that I was hungry, I went off to seek comfort in a chicken and mushroom pasty and a side order of chips.

Later, back in the classroom, I felt myself edging further towards despondency, even though that afternoon's lecture was on a potentially exciting topic: the reporting of disasters. It was delivered by Sonia, a burly woman, passionate on the subjects of gender politics and community radio, whose bari-tone speaking voice I normally found fascinating. Today, I scarcely registered it. Was this the most I had to look forward to? I wondered, as she spoke excitedly of pulling her car off the road, pushing through a thick briar hedge and running across a series of wet ploughed fields to secure the first on-the-spot interview with the surviving pilot and passenger of a recently crashed light aircraft. 'I was torn and tattered at the end of it, but most of all I was proud,' her account concluded triumphantly. 'I'd done what every journalist dreams of doing: I'd got the story, and got it first.'

Perhaps we should have applauded. Instead, 'Blimey!' was the shocked exclamation that emanated from the chair next to mine. Sonia simpered unexpectedly, then blushed, unused to inspiring such urgency of feeling within her students. It was possibly the most heartfelt 'Blimey!' we would hear throughout the entire course. Noticing two sets of long, painted fingernails drumming agitatedly on the desk beside me, however, I sensed that it was triggered not by admiration or envy but by horror. Here was a slave to a particularly old-fashioned femininity. Anne had her jumble-sale finds, Heather her footless tights and hippie chic, but high heels and tight skirts were Carol's own particular trademark. As a consequence, her idea of a nightmare journey was any that involved climbing a flight or more of stairs. That she might be expected to shove through briars and brambles, then mud-wrestle her way to the site of a story did not bear contemplation. She and I sat side by side in preoccupied silence for the rest of that afternoon, each believing we had chosen the wrong career.

When college was through for the day, I fled to town to cheer myself up by buying a record. Not that, in my heart of hearts, I needed cheering up. Earlier in the week I had received my first communication in months from Christine; it was a calendar of Paul Klee paintings carrying the message, 'Delighted to hear you've started your course. Let me know how it's going. With love . . .' On the evidence of these few words, I allowed myself to believe that a *rapprochement* was attainable, if not inevitable, and my every spare moment was taken up contemplating this. Indeed, so sentimental was my mood that it seemed vital I should possess a copy of a particularly saccharine record much played at the time, 'Reunited' by Peaches & Herb. That I was now being nagged by doubts about my suitability for journalism and its suitability for me only made ownership of this single seem more crucial.

'What's that in your hand?' demanded Heather, catching me emerging furtively from a city store some time later.

'Er, the Pointer Sisters' new album,' I said defensively, drawing the plastic carrier bag I was holding closer to my body. 'They've done a great version of the Springsteen song "Fire". You might like it.'

'Unlikely,' replied Heather who, on the one occasion I'd been invited to her lodgings for tea, had played me something tune-free and turgid by a group called Pavlov's Dog. 'But let me see it. Come on! Are you hiding something in there?'

Having wrested the bag from me, she examined its contents. 'What's this you've bought as well? Peaches & Herb? Not even you could like that, surely? It's awful. So awful that you had to buy an LP as well just to distract attention from it. All your teeth will fall out if you play it. You know that, don't you?'

As we walked under darkening skies towards the suburbs, I tried to explain my fondness for the song and the import it had for me – I stopped short of quoting the memorable couplet 'We both got so excited/'Cos we're reunited, yey-ee-yey' however. Heather was tolerant of my frequent verbal meanderings on the theme of Christine, only objecting when they involved me getting up to put another soppy, though superior, ballad, 'The Closer I Get To You' by Roberta Flack and Donny Hathaway, on the jukebox of a pub where we frequently drank. This time, she was taking no prisoners. 'If it were me, I'd be horrified to find that a man who professed to love me could then allow our relationship to be summed up in the words of so trite and tragic a song,' she insisted, fuelled by the pints of lager for which we had stopped off. 'If you really loved Christine you'd . . . you'd just throw it away! Yes, that's what you'd do! As a romantic gesture.'

I was wavering under this onslaught. Just how well did I know women, after all? I had started out believing that unswerving devotion was what it took to inspire love in someone else, but I'd been wrong. Only now that I'd started to make an independent life for myself were the avenues of communication between Christine and me opening up again. So maybe my enthusiasm for Peaches & Herb did represent a retrograde step. Maybe she would recoil in horror if she knew I'd bought a record as glutinous and clichéd as 'Reunited'. Not wanting to take the chance, I decided to act on Heather's advice.

In one fluid movement, I slid the shiny plastic single from its sleeve and projected it at full strength, frisbee-style, towards the moon. A few seconds later a sharp rustle of leaves and the sudden, shocked appearance of a cat from over a nearby garden wall offered proof that it had made contact with the earth again.

'Don't you feel better for doing that?' asked Heather, uncharacteristically slipping her arm through mine as we walked on again. 'Now, tell me when you're going to write back to her and what you're planning to say.'

From then on, as if reassured she had taught me the difference between pop music that was simply regrettable – my entire record collection, for all intents and purposes – and that which was truly terrible – 'Reunited' seemed to represent the nadir – Heather took a more forgiving approach to my musical sins. She even consented to come with me when, in the very last days of our course, the then-emergent American singer-songwriter Billy Joel played at Bristol's Colston Hall. Nor did she laugh – at least, not audibly – when I turned up for the occasion dressed in imitation of him on the cover of his most recent LP, *52nd Street*.

We filed towards the door, Heather dressed in something multi-layered and flowing, me wearing jeans and sneakers, a checked sports jacket and white short. I'd even bought a thin black leather tie, just like Billy's, and had spent at least ten minutes knotting and unknotting it, until I'd achieved exactly the same don't-give-a-damn casualness as him. Luckily, I did retain some small sense of self-control – inexplicably for a pianist, the star was holding a trumpet in the photograph, but I knew that to do so myself in a public place would be just plain silly.

Fellow concertgoers were funnelling up the steps in front of the hall and into the foyer as we arrived. Heather and I were inching our way forward in the throng when a young male in front of and above us turned to survey the scene behind him and, suddenly noticing me, snorted with derision. 'Look!' he urged, tugging his mate's sleeve. 'Look at that total wanker who thinks he's Billy Joel.'

A lot of people looked. There have been more embarrassing moments in my life, but thankfully not too many – being asked, ''S'cuse me, but aren't you that Leo Sayer?' by a myopic pensioner on a rush-hour London bus came close. The horror and shame I felt as I slowly clawed the tie from my throat and stuffed it into my jacket pocket is almost as real to me now as it was then. The potential *Stars In Their Eyes* contestant within me went AWOL that night and, thankfully, has never, ever been seen or heard from since.

Recently, and almost for old time's sake, I requested an interview with Billy Joel, just after he'd made public his decision to retire from writing and performing popular music to concentrate instead on classical composition. We hadn't met before, and I found him in a somewhat testy mood at having been chivvied out of a dining room at The Dorchester by a young PR, purely to endure my questioning. Sensing the chill in the air, and hoping that it might amuse and flatter him, I shared with him my abiding memory of the night he played Bristol all those years ago. Unfortunately – and to the abject horror of the PR, sitting in – the pivotal line came out wrongly as, 'Look, he thinks he's that wanker Billy Joel!' Heather, always so much wiser than I, would doubtless have told me to stop before I'd even started.

The final Sunday morning in Cardiff, and my delayed arrival at the breakfast table caused Mrs Mullet – appearing several stones heavier than normal, for some inexplicable reason – to select from her vast armoury of facial expressions one of triumphant self-righteousness. As she paused briefly to let me admire its perfection, a dishevelled Steve shuffled into the room and, silently, took his place opposite me. Clearly, his hangover was even worse than mine. Mrs Mullet clucked briskly at this further evidence of debauchery, her eyebrows ascending skywards until they hovered meaningfully beneath the brim of a bunlike felt hat.

She wasn't one to undergild the lily, so felt it necessary to state the obvious: 'Out late last night, the two of you, and now you're paying for it,' she said. 'As I knew you would.' There was a further round of clucking and then she disappeared into the kitchen, reappearing instantly, two warmed-through plates of cooked breakfast projecting from her oven-mitted hands. 'Twelve minutes past three, it was, to be precise. I know because I was sitting up reading my Bible, and I checked with my bedside alarm.'

This late in our stay, we knew the litany off by heart. 'Not that I've minded you staying out at night. You've been free to come and go as you please, as well you've known. But I can't have you being late for your Sunday fry-up, not when I'm due at the Temple at ten thirty and the two of you are off for good this afternoon. And you've got me cutting it very fine indeed on this of all mornings, I'll have you know.' With this, Mrs Mullet popped the straining buttons of her overall, flung it free of her body and hooked it on to the back of a chair. In doing so, she revealed herself to have been wearing, all the while, a best tweed overcoat and neck scarf and, beneath them, a neat two-piece suit – her habitual winter Sunday best.

She had lost no time explaining that her faith was Pentecostal Evangelism, and the invitation to join her at the Temple had been extended on a near-daily basis. Steve and I went once, motivated both by curiosity and our affection for her, but on the way home we made much of our respective loyalties to the Catholic Church. The evangelical aspect of the service – its raucous, almost showbizzy nature – was appealing to me, but it didn't have the same transportive effect as it had on Mrs Mullet. 'Our dear pastor's better than folk you get on television' was her frequent claim, and the rapt, adoring expression she wore throughout his address was remarkable to behold. He and his community brought structure and relief to Mrs Mullet's life in what I now realize must have been the raw, early weeks of widowhood. At twenty-two, I found her devotion – not only did she attend Temple each evening Monday to Saturday, but a full three times on Sundays – comically obsessive, pitiable even. Two decades later, I wish I'd been slower to judge.

'Say a prayer for my guts to get better,' called Steve, but he was too late. And as the front door slammed, he pushed his untouched plate into the middle of the table and sank his head onto his folded arms. It was a condition with which I could sympathize. Although I could remember little of the later hours of our end-of-course celebrations, I knew that we'd entered into them with total enthusiasm. After a valedictory meal, this had involved pogoing to the Sex Pistol's 'Anarchy In The U.K.' at a university disco, then dancing to Chic's 'Good Times' in a cheesy city-centre club. 'I thought you and Heather were never going to leave the dance floor,' said a mouth contorted by contact with the tablecloth. 'Whoever would have thought she knew all the Gloria Gaynor arm movements for "I Will Survive"? And you! You seemed to think you were starring in *Saturday Night Fever!*'

'Do you know the Teeline for fuck off?' I countered, horrified to be reminded that I had publicly unveiled dance steps only previously demonstrated in the privacy of my own room, and without a partner. 'Now give me that plate so we can hide this food in the bin before Mrs Mullet gets back. You know what she's like about wasting things.' We both did. Just a week before, she'd told us to consider the poor, starving children of Africa when we expressed uncertainty about the batch of rock buns she had made in her pressure cooker. I hadn't been chastized in that way since I was in short trousers and being lectured to by the nuns at primary school.

Back in my room, I got on with packing, closing my case only after fitting in the newly washed pile of pants and socks that had been waiting in the hall when I made my descent earlier. I put the Paul Klee calendar and the small bundle of letters amassed from Christine in recent weeks into my hold-all, in case I needed reassurance on my onward journey. Then, swinging my feet up onto the counterpane, I lay back in the hollow made by the late Mr Mullet and indulged in a mental review of my journalistic career to date. Touch-typing was now no problem, and I was capable of accurately recording Anytown Council's meetings at a speed of 110 words per minute. Academic and practical work seemed to be less of a problem than I'd anticipated: to my genuine surprise, I had come top of the class in the concluding set of exams. Congratulating me on this, tutor Peter had clapped me on the back with such force that I'd dropped the coffee cup I was holding. 'Blimey! Leave it out!' Carol had said, one final, glorious time. Its contents had just landed in the open mouth of her cosmetics-stuffed handbag.

At this point I must have drifted into a restorative sleep for my next memory is being shaken awake by a returned Mrs Mullet. 'Wakey-wakey,' she chided fondly, 'and get yourself downstairs toot sweet! I've done a nice farewell lunch, and it'll be on the table in five minutes. Shake a leg now!'

I did, pausing only to reclaim from on top of the vast mahogany wardrobe – given her terrier instincts, hiding any-thing in my room was all but impossible – the china figurine I'd chosen on Steve's and my behalf as a leaving present. It was hardly an inspired selection: there were four variations of the same young-maid-with-a-big-skirt-and-mob-cap theme in her front parlour already. At least we could feel confident she'd like it.

Tears sprang to her eyes as she lifted it from its box. 'You boys, spoiling your old Mrs M.,' she said, pulling first Steve's and then my face towards her for a kiss. 'Wait till I show Phyllis next door. She'll be spitting pips. The same lodger for three years now and nothing more from him than a box of Maltesers at Christmas – and she with all her troubles!

'Now then, knowing the bad habits you two have, I've an extra treat laid on. A bottle of plonk. Just a half-sized one, mind. I'm not going to be to blame for the pair of you being tipsy when you catch your trains this afternoon.'

So it was with the dull throb of the previous night's hang-over and a glass each of warm, sweet white wine that we enjoyed our last, baby-soft, pressure-cooked-for-speed Mrs Mullet lunch – a goo of brown to signify meat, beige for potatoes, green and orange for the accompanying vegetables. 'Here's to the both of you, Alan and The Rip!' she said, toasting us with a beaker of tea. 'I hope to be as proud of you one day as I am of my Graham; he's a big cheese in the biscuit world, as I've no doubt told you. When you're rich and famous, I'll be saying to people, "They were my boys once, you know! They had my first-floor back bedroom and my de luxe *en suite*!" Now, let's get these pots washed and the two of you on your ways. I'm due back at the Temple by three, as you well know.'

My last words to her before closing the taxi door were, 'I promise to keep in touch.' I meant it, and believed I'd do so. After the first postcard and Christmas card, I didn't, though. It's only when you get older yourself that you realize how casually cruel you can be when you're young.

3

Returning to the newspaper office after watching a local pub landlord fail in his attempt to break the world record for downing pickled eggs, I found Odette adding to her already impressive gallery of pointing pictures. 'Look at this one. It's a corker,' she said cheerfully, standing back to admire the shiny 10 x 8 newly pinned to the noticeboard above her desk. 'How many pointing anglers does it take to draw a reader's attention to one very large fish? Twenty-six, if our Les has anything to do with it. And he's surpassed himself with the caption; one of his longest ever, almost as deep as the photo itself. Every single bloke in the line-up's been named.'

Les was an institution. As resident photographer for the weekly *Mercury* – of which I was now the junior member of staff – and its parent morning and evening papers in Norwich, he had chronicled the minutiae of life in this seaside town for close on fifty years. He'd been there for all the big things – Second World War bombings, floods, a wide variety of maritime disasters – but also all the little things. There could be no society or organization within the area, no matter how humble its business, that hadn't experienced his quavering, mumbled call of, 'Just one more, ladies and gentlemen. Just one more.' Forever grumbling at his workload, but so convinced of his indispensability that he rarely took a day off, he had recorded each cheque presentation, each mayoral visit, each new sporting line-up, year in, year out. And quite a proportion of these involved people pointing.

Odette's display of the most extreme examples said little about compositional technique but everything about the role of a local newspaper in serving its community. Here, we saw a thin, tired-looking mother, baby on hip, pointing at the vast patches of damp blossoming on the inside walls of her council flat. There, a local councillor pointed at the poorly maintained footpath, inadequately signposted bend or waterlogged playing field that he or she was making it their business to bring to public attention. And, this being Les's particular speciality, crowding into these and hundreds of other, similar pictures were large numbers of other people all pointing at the self-same thing.

'Don't you two have anything better to do than smirk over what are perfectly competent and legitimate photographs?' demanded our chief reporter – let's call him Barry – bustling into the room in one of his galaxy of different-coloured velvet jackets. 'Because if you haven't, I can very quickly find you something. There's an advertising feature here needs doing, for a start. Shopping in the historic Rows. Why it beats London's best in terms of convenience, quality and choice. "From corsetry to car parts, from rug-making kits to the latest record releases . . ." Any takers? Who's at a loose end, then?'

He was answered by an outbreak of fast and furious typing. Teetotal, and a stalwart of various religious, civic and amateur-dramatic groups, Barry was friendly, fair-minded, but also wearingly cheerful, a devoted fan of Cliff Richard, and able to make Mary Whitehouse look lax with his keenly censorious attitude towards all matters of an adult nature. Worse still, he had the sole, unchallenged power to commission. Get on his wrong side and you could find yourself writing ad features for weeks on end.

I continued to type noisily until he'd left the room again, by now wearing a purposeful expression and carrying a copy of the *Daily Telegraph*. When the door closed behind him, I turned back towards Odette. Queen of the women's page, Feminine Line, she was really a Rebecca but had once confided to me that, as a child, she'd longed to be known as Odette. Instantly, I renamed her in my mind. A blonde and sunny presence in my working life, she was also kindly fulfilling the role of my one-woman finishing school, in culinary terms at least. 'You mean, you've never even heard of taramasalata?' she would say to me, incredulous, as we grocery-shopped together in our lunch hour. Or, 'I don't believe you've not tasted avocado. You're the one who doesn't come from Norfolk. It's us down here who are supposed to be backward.' And now, once again, my appeal to her superior knowledge was to be food-related.

'Christine's coming up from London for the weekend,' I told her. 'Can you think of anything simple but nice that I could make, and which doesn't require more than two hot plates and an oven that's about nine inches square?'

As Odette wrinkled her brow and consulted her extensive library of for-review cookbooks, I pondered on my recently effected escape from the world of live-in landlords and ladies. On being dispatched to the coast, I'd been happy to accept an offer to lodge with the mother of my female predecessor, who'd been promoted to head office in Norwich. Eve was no Mrs Mullet, being some twenty-five years younger and of a glamorous-granny ilk; she put on make-up and high, strappy shoes even to visit the corner shop. Also, she was fine about me sharing my single bed with Christine on the weekends I didn't drive down to London, her new place of work. But unfortunately, and for reasons I never quite understood, Eve was living in a housing-association flat intended for occupation specifically by a single person or married couple of a pensionable age. Even alone, she didn't fit the bill. With me resident in her spare bedroom, she became the subject of gossip and speculation. It was only a matter of time before some curtain-twitcher rang the association. Inevitably, and with regret, we had to go our separate ways.

It was at a Divorced and Separated Club Annual Barn Dance, which Eve had pleaded with Christine and I to accompany her to, that I was introduced to her successor. A butcher by day and a bouncer by night, Jumbo was nearly as big as his name suggested. But more disconcerting than his size was the fact that his eyes looked out at the world in different directions. Hence, when talking to him, I found myself swaying this way and that, never quite sure when I was safely in his field of vision. He was a kind man. Hearing from Eve that I was in need of new lodgings, he offered me a spare room. I was glad to take it. What I didn't realize, until I became resident, was that he already had three other young male tenants, all of them working on the ferries. As a result, the household was a friendly but chaotic one – empty beer cans everywhere, cigarettes stubbed out on dirty plates or in the discarded takeaway cartons that littered the kitchen, porn magazines stacked high in the bathroom. I lasted only a couple of months, then summoned up courage to sway in front of Jumbo and tell him I had to leave.

And now I was in the process of settling into what was, in effect, little more than a bedsit. It was the first-ever home of my own, though, and I loved it. So much so that I even found myself wanting to make meals in what must surely have been the world's smallest kitchen, with the world's smallest cooker.

'OK, what about this?' asked Odette, passing me a book, opened at a picture of a rich, autumnal-coloured ratatouille. 'You'll need onions, red peppers, aubergines, courgettes . . . Oh dear, you're wearing your puzzled look again, aren't you? And tomatoes. You'll need tomatoes. Please tell me you've heard of tomatoes.'

Norfolk is famed for a small variety of things: its flatness, its Broads, its coypus and, latterly, the presence of saintly television cook Delia Smith on the board of Norwich City Football Club. It is not, however, famed as the sort of territory in which you are constantly bothered by visiting superstars. Day-trippers, tourists and the occasional influx of scooter riders, yes. Superstars, no. And in the three and a half years of my residency there, nothing happened to challenge this hard-won reputation for relentless normality.

I encountered the occasional cabaret act or minor TV star. I once even saw Des O'Connor there, eating a packet of crisps. But not once did I, or anyone I knew, have cause to formulate a sentence like, 'No, Miss Streisand, you turn left, not right, at the top of King Street if you want to find Sainsbury's.' Indeed, my quick thinking and local knowledge was never, ever called upon by a celebrity of any calibre, let alone a megastar. 'A petrol station that will still be open at this hour? Let me see, Mr Springsteen – because it is you, isn't it? – Nearly half eleven? You'd be best heading across the bridge into Southtown Road. There's an all-nighter there, a quarter of a mile down and on the left.' Sadly, it remained advice I was qualified, but never called upon, to give.

Despite my romantic leanings, I have a practical nature, and because famous people of the first, second or even fourth or fifth rank failed to present themselves to me during my Norfolk years, I set about creating alternatives from those around me. It took me some time to convince ever-so-busy Barry that an elderly councillor, whom I shall call Freddie Hiller, was a worthy subject for in-depth profiling, but eventually – to shut me up, I imagine – he came round to my way of thinking. 'If you must,' he sighed. 'But nothing too party political.'

Old Freddie, beady and suspicious, had been a stalwart of the local Labour Party all his adult life, and could bore for Britain on the subjects of poorly heated council flats, irresponsible dog ownership and – his cause célèbre – the need for twenty-four-hour public conveniences along the prom. With a younger, presumably smaller and Scottish, companion, Wee Angus, Freddie ran a bed and breakfast establishment just off the seafront and close to several of the town's most popular, boisterous pubs. This made him a particular authority on the paucity of existing toilet facilities.

Senior colleagues at the *Mercury* swore he'd once brought chaos to a debate of the environmental sub-committee with the declaration, 'Young men have been urinating up my back passage for years, and it's high time someone put a stop to it.' I had no way of knowing whether or not this rumour was true, and was too respectful to ask when finally he submitted to the Alan Jackson interview experience. Nor did I think to question him about his unique ability to cycle at no miles per hour without ever toppling over. I often saw him and his pushbike make their pained, wobbling progress along the road outside my rented flat, while being overtaken on the adjoining pavement by even the elderly and infirm. This seemed to me worthy of a TV talent show appearance: 'Folks, I'd like you to give a nice, warm Opportunity Knocks-type welcome to Freddie "Mr Motionless" Hiller! He started out a week last Thursday, so we're expecting him here at the studio some time in the year 2022!'

But respect where respect is due. Overlooking these more eccentric aspects of his character, my relentlessly upbeat profile concentrated instead on his years of public service and a reputation – one or two jealous fellow councillors claimed I'd invented it – as a tireless champion of the rights of the downtrodden; a St George forever battling the bureaucratic dragon. In grudging gratitude for this unexpected exercise in image-enhancement – on Odette's behalf, I even got him to pose for the photographer while pointing at a block of council flats, the upgrading of which he had fought for – old Freddie rewarded me with the tip-off that he would be delivering a bona-fide celebrity to the following weekend's fundraiser at a local arts centre he was involved with.

'Come on, Freddie, give me a clue,' I pleaded, excited despite my suspicion of him. 'Is it a he or a she? And how famous are they? Please?'

Eventually, having enjoyed stretching my curiosity to breaking point, he made a concession. 'It's a very famous film actress, with a well-known leaning to the Left. A bit controversial, you might say,' he told me, tapping his nose confidentially. 'And no, of course she's not from these parts. She's travelling up from beyond London especially. Now, that's all I'm going to be persuaded to say, other than that you won't be disappointed, and that I may need you to act as

67

her host for a bit, while I perform my official duties.'

Old Freddie having departed for supper with Wee Angus, I sat alone in the bar of the Labour Club and pondered the various possibilities. Had we been in America, of course, just about all of Hollywood's leading ladies would be under suspicion: Jane Fonda, Shirley Maclaine, Goldie Hawn, the lot. But in Britain? Vanessa Redgrave? Or Susannah York? But then, what about – yes, surely! – Glenda Jackson? Controversial? Certainly. No-one more so at the time. So that had to be it. I was going to meet – more than that, I was going to act as walker to – the wonderful Glenda, my illustrious namesake.

The following day, and in order of accomplishment, I alerted the news and picture desks to this impending visitation, had a lunchtime haircut and bought myself a new shirt and tie. That evening, I started swatting from a Halliwell film guide. *The Music Lovers*, *A Touch Of Class*, and *The Romantic Englishwoman*, I was fine with, but I needed to be sure I could make informed chit-chat about those others of her films I hadn't yet seen. It was a test, but one I felt sure I could pass. My byline on a story about Glenda Jackson. What a breakthrough that would be. 'You might even get her pointing, if there's anything other than old Freddie for her to point at,' suggested Odette hopefully.

When Saturday dragged around, I made sure I was scrubbed, polished and pressed to within an inch of my life – and also on duty at the arts centre at least half an hour earlier than was necessary. So it was with a combination of relief and surging trepidation that, on stepping outside the converted church for the umpteenth time, I saw a minicab pull up by the curb. As I stepped smartly towards it, old Freddie began to make his exit from its farther side. Then, decisively, the nearside passenger door opened and out stepped . . . not Glenda Jackson but a woman in, perhaps, her late sixties, smartly suited and with the bright, professional smile of the political consort. I struggled to make my facial muscles project a heartfelt welcome to her, whoever she was, then shot a fuck-right-off-you-misleading-old-git look at Freddie. He, all the while, was beetling round the Cortina's grubby boot in my direction, a triumphant Albert Steptoe but in a better suit.

Rosamund John was, I learned from recent obituaries carried in the broadsheets, one of the most popular British actresses of the 1940s. This, of course, explained Mr Motionless's palpable excitement in her presence; she was an icon of his era, and luring her to the seaside from her home south of London on a Saturday afternoon was, to him, as great a coup as producing the Miss Jackson I had been expecting. Celebrated especially for her appearances in the wartime dramas *The First Of The Few* and *The Way To The Stars* – artistic achievements far exceeding the demands of propaganda, according to *The Times* – she had later sacrificed her career to support that of her second husband, prominent Labour MP of the time John Silkin. 'You've no idea at all who you've just been landed with, have you?' she said to me, smiling, as I followed old Freddie's instructions to find her a cup of tea and keep her amused while he prepared to make a welcoming speech. 'Don't worry. You're far too young to have heard my name about the place.'

I sensed that it was better, and less insulting, not to deny the fact. And Miss John responded by being excellent company for the thirty or so minutes we spent together. She was someone with a sharp perspective on the work that had brought her to the nation's attention. 'My daughter caught one of the old films on TV the other afternoon and said, "But,

Mummy, you were all so wooden!" And do you know, we were, no doubt about it. I watch TV or go to the cinema now and it's like another world – all this naturalistic stuff, the recreation of real life. In my day it was all stereotypes, stiff upper lips and pretending.'

At which point, just as I was beginning to enjoy myself, old Freddie clambered onto the stage, tapped a microphone repeatedly, and then invited his guest to step up and declare the proceedings well and truly open. Miss John did so, both to the disgust of the *Mercury* photographer, who had just arrived expecting to capture Glenda Jackson in full flight, and to the clear delight of that small number of septuagenarian gentlemen huddled immediately below her.

What a trooper, I thought afterwards. Less than ten minutes later I was back where I wanted to be, but she had Yarmouth to Norwich and Norwich to Liverpool Street to accomplish by rail, then a tube or taxi ride across London, followed by who knows what other onward journey before her day was over. And for nothing more than basic expenses and the temporary diversion of a thin crowd, half of which, myself included, didn't even know who she was. All because Freddie Hiller, her ancient fan, wanted to prove he could pull a celebrity out of the hat, and she was good enough to oblige.

Had I not been in such a rush to play the Donna Summer compilation I'd bought on the way home, I might usefully have pursued this line of thought further. After all, this was my first intimation of how relatively short-lived fame could be. At one time in your life, you might be the toast of the film world, watched by millions; at another, you could be just another stranger on a train, unremarked upon by your fellow passengers, all but invisible. Not that any such realization would have undermined my intention to doggedly pursue

70

those who, to my eyes at least, were currently famous. My only problem was an old problem: they weren't to be found anywhere in Norfolk.

Undeterred, I honed my would-be colour-supplement prose on less elevated subjects. For example, there was my memorable profile of the wife of the incumbent mayor. 'Irene Webb has a cold,' it began daringly. And of the cast of an end-of-the-pier show for the senior-citizen coach parties brought in on the cusp of each new season to air the hoteliers' beds. 'They call me The Little Girl With The Big Voice,' lisped its featured female vocalist, and I solemnly recorded the fact in my notebook.

Neither of these assignments were properly fulfilling, of course: the names in question were celebrated nowhere beyond their immediate family and friends. But then there came news that an actual recording star, a Texan country-and-western singer of uncertain age and provenance called Jean Shepard, would be visiting the town and was available for interview. Again, Barry had to bear the weight of my vaunting ambitions.

'This Nashville legend!' I repeated, whenever I had his ear, and despite the fact that I'd never heard of her. She was to appear at the ABC Theatre as support act to the late Boxcar Willie, America's self-styled Singing Hobo. He had already been interviewed by phone for a preview piece, making Jean my only hope. But who was she? A homely looking woman in her early fifties, I was to discover, on sitting through her set on the night, and one with the alarming habit of launching into a full-throated yodel whenever one of her songs gathered pace.

Later, as we sat knee-to-knee in a cupboard-like dressing room, I did my best to disguise my total ignorance of her life and career with the blandest, most leading of questions – 'I imagine it must have been a very proud moment, the first time you appeared before an audience at the Grand Old Opry . . .' – and an ingratiating politeness – 'Would you think me very rude if I asked when that first appearance was, and how old you were?' Ironically, subsequent interviews with American country stars here and in Nashville have taught me that this is exactly the kind of interview technique they are used to and feel most comfortable with. Certainly, Jean seemed happy enough. 'Such a little gentleman,' she said of me, patting my hand when her husband looked in to see that all was well.

That even an artist of such specific and limited celebrity felt herself under the pressure not only of personal standards, but also of public expectation was made clear the moment our photographer knocked on the door. 'Just a minute,' Jean called out to him, alarmed and scrabbling urgently in a capacious handbag. From it she extracted a fork and, to my horror, began to drive it repeatedly into the soft, powdered, beige-coloured skin either side of her mouth. 'Don't look so worried, hon,' she chuckled, patting my hand again. 'It's just to get the colour up in my cheeks – make 'em nice 'n' rosy for the picture.' Hasn't this woman ever heard of blusher? I wondered to myself, finally obeying an instruction to open the door.

'A yodelling country singer? Not very rock 'n' roll, is it?' commented Ian, when I found him in the Oakwood towards the end of the evening. 'Joy Division, The Slits, Echo and the Bunnymen, they're the sort of acts we ought to be writing about, not Jean "Yodel-ay-ee-ho" Shepard, whoever she is.'

Chastened, I sipped my pint. OK, so Ian couldn't be arsed to pass his shorthand. And he might not, as Barry so frequently and embarrassingly pointed out, be able to cover a council meeting as comprehensively as I could, but he was still indisputably the office's Mr Cool. He liked all the right bands, wore all the right clothes, looked more like an actor than a local newspaper journalist and had girls falling at his feet wherever he went. He even flouted office policy to the extent of living not in the town, but in swinging, sinful Norwich, some twenty miles away. To the older locals I'd encountered, such a journey was the kind you made once or twice a year. Ian travelled back and forth daily. I wished I was more like him, but sensed I never would be. That was why I'd passed my shorthand. That was why I stayed awake and was able to take accurate notes in the council chamber. But still, I had my ambitions. And, while Jean Shepard was hardly at the cutting edge of pop, at least she'd actually made a record or two. Every would-be celebrity interviewer has to start somewhere.

Odette was a happy woman. With two celebratory flicks of her hair, she marched back across the room to her desk, seized her handbag and exited, smiling, towards the ladies'. Barry, sporting a previously unseen pale-blue safari suit, looked a little shell-shocked. He was in the process of delegating the week's assignments, and had hoped to persuade his woman's editor that an interview with a leading figure from the am-dram world in which he moved would make the perfect Feminine Line lead feature. But Odette, tired of doling out recipes, free puffs for beauty products and advice on safe tanning and how best to flatter a fuller figure, had prepared her own agenda. Intent on injecting a little excitement and controversy into her page, she'd suggested carrying out a vox pop on attitudes to the top-shelf magazine *Playgirl*.

Suggested? More accurately, she had first charmed, then all

but bludgeoned Barry into submission. 'There's legitimate news interest in seeing how they react to pictures of suntanned north American male limbs, particularly unclothed ones,' she had said, warming to her theme. 'After all, Suffolk County Council are planning to create a nudist beach just a few miles down the coast from here. Does all of this represent a healthy advance in social attitudes towards the human body, or is it evidence of a slide into moral turpitude? Let's hear what the ordinary woman in the street thinks. It's an important issue. Please?'

After first collapsing under the weight of the entire office's enthusiasm for the idea, Barry had rallied cleverly. No, he absolutely would not sanction the addition of *Playgirl* to the delivery-list of national dailies made by our local newsagent. She would have to buy her own copy. Naturally, she could charge it to expenses, but only if she got a receipt. 'And surely that's an important element of the so-called story,' he had added sweetly: 'the question of how easy it is for a woman to go into a shop and actually purchase such a title.' Won round to the idea, Odette had left to retouch her make-up in preparation for what might well be an ordeal.

I felt little other than bored, having been handed my usual dull selection of items from the office diary. First, there was the coroner's court, for which I was felt to have a special aptitude – a sympathetic expression, an ability to look neither too ghoulishly interested in, nor too physically repulsed by, details of the more unusual deaths in the town. It was my least-favourite job, apart from evening council meetings, but I took some comfort from the fact that Mrs B back in Cardiff would be proud to know I'd invented my own Teeline short form for the entire sentence, 'I would, of course, like to offer my most sincere and heartfelt condolences to the family and

74

friends here present on the occasion of this unfortunate death.' It was the phrase with which the youngish, but rather earnest and moist-lipped coroner began each summing up, and was, I felt, represented nicely by a round, Homepride-flour-grader-type face with the smile inverted and a tear running down its cheek. I was rather proud of this innovation, and would happily have passed it on to my fellow reporters, should they have been interested. Unfortunately, they weren't. They were counting on the likelihood that only I would have cause to use it.

There was the magistrates' court for me, too, and a couple of visits to the town hall, to cover council meetings big or small. 'Because you're good at them, Alan! It's a compliment!' Barry had said in his usual, bulldozingly positive way. 'One or two people round here would do well to read and learn from your account of last month's highways sub-committee. A model of local-government reporting, it was.' There had been muffled groans from all around me, and a sly but effective poke in the ribs from Ian. I'd landed the week's advertorial, too, this time for a DIY store. I was already writing in my mind: 'Within what is undoubtedly an Aladdin's cave for the home-improvement fan, you can be sure of finding everything from loft lagging to lawnmowers, screws to stepladders, and all at the keenest prices, too. The friendly and efficient staff will make it their business to ensure . . .' Reviewing this heady cocktail of assignments, it occurred to me, and not for the first time, that conscientiousness and efficiency are punished as often as they are rewarded.

Lying ahead would have been an entirely ordinary week but – and it was a big, almost glamorous, almost glittering, almost showbusiness but – for the last-minute job that had, apparently, arisen only minutes earlier. Barry had called me back to his desk to reveal that the soft-porn actress Fiona Richmond, headlining at the town's Windmill Theatre the following week in 'the sci-fi sex romp' *Space In My Pyjamas*, was making herself available for interview during the afternoon. Her brand of entertainment was hardly his cup of tea, he felt sure I appreciated, but still the show, and her presence in town, needed the *Mercury*'s acknowledgement. But only in a sensitive and responsible way, mind you. 'No leering. No innuendo. No smut. Got it?' I nodded my head eagerly to signal that I had. Yes! Yes! Yes! I thought, mentally preparing my list of questions. At last, the smell of the greasepaint and the roar of the crowd!

'Fiona will be with you as soon as she can,' said a brisk woman, clipboard in hand and a biro behind her ear, when I presented myself at the Windmill's stage door some hours later. 'She's in her dressing room right now, dying her pubic hair blue. Shouldn't be more than a few minutes.'

'Of course. Thank you. Yes, I'm more than happy to wait.' I hoped my pitch and delivery were smooth. More than that, I hoped they implied that this was information I received on a regular basis, part and parcel of my constant and close engagement with the celebrity world. Shocked? Heavens no, not me. Blue, red, green – I hear it all the time. And right on cue, as if to buttress the intended air of urbanity and experience my tone implied, a record began to play in my head. Damn! It was one of Cilla Black's, and in an idiot, childish, pleased-with-herself way she was cooing the lyrics to 'I Can Sing A Rainbow'.

'Well, hello! And who have we here?' The words issuing from Miss Richmond's lips, though superficially innocent, were so ripe and loaded with fruitfulness that they could have been bottled as jam.

'Alan. Alan Jackson. From the *Mercury*.' I struggled to look directly into two vast, saucer-like eyes, mocking me from beneath the fringe of a Cleopatra-style wig, perhaps not un-coincidentally blue-coloured also, and not at two magnificently upstanding breasts, also mocking me from behind their wholly inadequate, gauzy covering. 'I'm here to talk about the space in my . . . I mean, the space in *your* . . . Pyjamas, that is. What I'm trying to say is that I'm here because of your opening. In the sci-fi sex romp. You must be very exciting. Excited. Aren't you?'

Miss Richmond's eyes remained wide and unblinking, but her lips pursed slightly in what I took to be amusement and her bosom – I admit it, my gaze had wavered – rose, then fell, then rose again, as if bored with remaining still. 'Oh yes,' she purred. 'Very. That's the thing about openings. They always sets hearts beating a little faster, I find.'

At which point there was a thin, snapping sound. Instantly self-conscious, I looked down and saw the notebook occupying the space between us trembling in the air. Upon it I found an explanation for the small, dull ping. In my nervousness, I'd pressed down so hard on my nib that it had broken. 'A young gentleman of the press with no lead in his pencil. What a predicament,' breathed Miss Richmond, batting her eyelashes coolly. 'Luckily, I believe I have the very solution in my handbag. So if you'd care to follow me . . .'

Back at the office, I recounted my adventure. 'She was ever so nice, really,' I insisted, fending off all argument in the Pornography – albeit soft-core – Degrades Women debate with what a sceptical Odette clearly viewed as rather insubstantial ammunition: the fact that the blue-hued Fiona had bequeathed me her very own appropriately blue-inked Papermate, and so was clearly a fundamentally kind, good-hearted and generous

77

person. 'She didn't even want it back. She said she couldn't bear to think of me leaving the theatre with an essential tool of my trade not in full working order. She said I should take better care of my equipment. Anyway, you needn't get on your high horse about nudity. You're the woman who's spent her afternoon flashing a copy of *Playgirl* at unsuspecting shoppers.'

Odette tossed her hair dismissively to signal that I needn't think I'd come out on top in the Fiona Richmond debate, then reached inside the top drawer of her desk. 'This was possibly the single most embarrassing purchase of my life, and certainly in my history as a customer of John Menzies,' she said, opening up the magazine. 'I won't be going in that store again. Anyway, this is what I had to show them. Have a look.'

I looked. And saw a photospread of a handsome, grinning blond man with a big, floppy fringe and a big, floppy . . . In fact, there was something of a theme, for a big, floppy dog was frolicking with him in those few pictures that didn't involve his lounging carelessly on red satin sheets. 'You'd think his knees had fallen out with each other,' I said, unsure of how else to respond. 'How did our womenfolk react, anyway? Were they enraged and appalled, or rendered weak-kneed and breathless with lust?'

'Let's see,' said Odette, riffling back through her notebook. 'Amy Osborne, retired catering manageress, sixty-four, said, "Oh no, love. I put all that behind me long ago. I'd rather have a nice cup of tea and give my feet a soak." Then there was Phyllis Johnston, office cleaner, who wouldn't tell me her age but must have been in her mid to late fifties. She said, "Chitterlings and jot – I've seen it all before," and then cackled a lot. I'm not entirely sure what chitterlings and jot were, although she did say her husband worked in an abattoir. That means it's probably some term she's learned off him – the official term for a bullock's bits, or whatever.'

'Sounds like they were underwhelmed, despite the fact that it says here, "Scorpio Jeff is six feet two of what makes Canada great – and we're not talking about any giant redwood." Didn't anyone get excited by him?'

'A couple of fifth formers bunking off school saw me showing the magazine to one woman and tried to grab the whole thing out of my hands and run off with it.' Odette shrugged, pushing back her typewriter and pulling on her coat. 'But other than that, no, not really. Either I got a mis-representative sample of women, or they were too shy to say what they really felt, or they really and truly thought it was all just a load of chitterlings and jot.'

'And you?' I asked, handing back Jeff in all his spreadeagled glory. 'What do you make of him?'

'Nice eyes, but otherwise far too pleased with himself,' she said, shoving him roughly back into her drawer. 'Whatever, that's another fabulous Feminine Line feature finished with. Tomorrow I'm off on the trail of the girl's brigade leader who's also a committed nudist. Barry reckons parents are up in arms – or will be. Are you going over?'

I was, to the Oakwood, a not particularly inviting pub, but one historically established as the office local. It was happy hour, and pushing open its door we joined the usual scatter-ing of early-evening drinkers sitting glumly in corners or at the bar, nursing glasses. 'So, what about Ian, then?' asked Odette, returning from having rung her solicitor boyfriend, Ron, to ask if he fancied joining us. 'Jammy dodger or what? He hasn't even passed his hundred-words-per-minute. Barry looked sicker than when he found out we'd all gone on an office outing to see *Caligula* at the Three-In-One and hadn't told him.'

I sighed in sympathy. In line with company policy, Ian had been warned he'd be sacked if he didn't get his hallowed shorthand qualification – this at the fourth or fifth attempt – and clearly they viewed him as unemployable without it. Wrong. It was true that Ian hadn't passed the exam, and that the day upon which he would be reunited with his P45 had been named and was looming. But instead of looking chastened or defeated, as Barry doubtless expected him to, he had arrived at work that day looking defiantly smug and demob-happy. He'd got another job, and one outside Norfolk, too. He was going to London to be a feature writer on the rock weekly *Melody Maker*, a publication that was – Odette and I could hardly bring ourselves to say the words – available nationwide, and not just in Norfolk. It was going to be him who got to meet all the famous people, him who got invited to all the great parties . . .

'Shit, piss and buggery!' I said out loud, surprising myself as much as Odette.

'And jolly nice to see you, too, old boy,' said a pinstriped Ron, settling his briefcase down beside us. 'Want another pint, do you? Get that one down your neck, then. Happy hour's almost up.'

Ian did leave. And from time to time he'd call me from an office in which rock music or jazz blared and phones rang, forever unanswered. 'I'm just off to interview Hall and Oates,' he'd say, or, 'You'd like this new band, ABC. Their first album's not out for another three months, but I've got a tape of it here. Shall I send it up? Anyway, what's going on with you?' And I'd tell him some tale about the rural parish council meeting I'd covered the night before – 'all these Nimbies objecting to the opening of a pub restaurant in their village, saying things like, "Frankly, we don't want the smell of beef-burgers wafting across our back gardens of a summer's evening."' – so causing him to wince and sigh.

'God,' Ian would say. 'I'd forgotten just what it was like.'

God, I'd think. Will I ever get the chance to forget?

I did leave, a little more than a year later. I wanted to be among the bright lights. I wanted to live with Christine, now working in the capital, too. And so, after much deliberation and debate, I handed in my notice and began in earnest to apply for every London job I saw advertised and for which I wasn't totally ineligible. Eventually, I got one. It wasn't exactly Showbiz Central – minion in the overseas reporting unit of an obscure civil-service department – but at least it was based there. That had to be progress.

When the time came there was a collection on my behalf and, keen to continue the broadening of my culinary horizons, Odette suggested its proceeds be used to buy me a wok. This was duly presented to me at the leaving party held in a colleague's flat – lots of people drinking too much, squabbling about what music should be played and generally having a good time. At one point I went and sat in a spare bedroom among all the discarded coats, to try to sort out how I felt about leaving the people I'd worked with for over three years and who had been so good to me. Just as I was starting to feel tearful, Ron made an entrance. 'Get back out here and have another drink, Whacko. Who do you think you are? Jay Gatsby?'

The next morning I left for London, my small car piled to its roof with what constituted my worldly possessions, the shiny new wok in pride of place on the passenger seat beside me. 'A very sophisticated area, I don't need to remind you,' the letting agency had said of Bayswater, where Christine and I had found a flat big enough for two in a cul-de-sac opposite Hyde Park. On moving in, we came across a week-old copy of the *Evening Standard*, with a news item on the third page helpfully highlighted by the previous tenant in lime-green marker pen. It seemed that a police surveillance team had witnessed the comings and goings at a bondage parlour in a basement apartment just three doors away, 'within an area well-known for prostitution', the report said. 'Men, some elderly, were seen leaving in obvious physical pain.' An Old Bailey court case was underway. Sophisticated indeed.

Monday morning saw me heading out the door to my first-ever job in the metropolis. Was I to be surrounded by thrusting, sexy, go-ahead types, ruthless in their pursuit of money, pleasure and power? Erm, not really. Rather, it seemed I had stumbled onto the set of Alan Bennett's *A Woman Of No Importance*. A step or two away from the Bakerloo line, and behind a façade of greying net curtains – I supposed this to be a deliberately suburban touch, but in fact they were intended to contain splintered glass in the event of a terrorist attack – was an eccentric world such as I had never imagined could still exist in late-twentieth-century London. The young Muriel Spark would have recognized its more self-aggrandizing inhabitants; she might even have created them. The late Barbara Pym would have found herself at home amid its archaic practices. And yes, you really could ruin someone's day if, unwittingly and while edging up the canteen counter, you claimed that last Ski yogurt being eyed up by one of your elders and incremental-pay-structure betters further back in the queue.

The man identified as my section head was on the phone,

extolling the virtues of a forthcoming am-dram musical to a contact on some local weekly paper newsdesk when I arrived. Instantly, I felt as if I'd ricocheted back in time. Was I to trail this culture around with me like a ball and chain? I wondered. 'Welcome aboard the happy sh-sh-ship et cetera et cetera,' he said, covering the telephone mouthpiece with a confidential hand for a moment. 'You don't have to be mad to work here but it helps, and all that stuff. But see, the point is, old chap, that I've got a spot of extra-curricular business to deal with here, so grab yourself a seat, why don't you? Sh-sh-shouldn't be long.'

I duly sat on a tubular steel chair, the cushion of which was covered in a nylon fabric surely designed in the early 1970s by someone off their face on drugs, and listened as a man of late middle age with a Bobby Charlton-style flick-over and a grubby brown suit pulled off an equally grubby soft sell. 'As you know, upcoming is our sp-sp-spring production of *Guys And Dolls*,' he was saying. 'Now, I've got some lovely publicity shots of our leading lady – my eldest daughter, Faye, as a matter of fact – and I think you're going to find they're right up your particular *rue*, as they say in France. Scantily clad, she is. Pop them right in the post? Of course I will. Needless to say, any publicity you can give to our little production will be most gratefully received.'

Meanwhile, 'Horden!' announced a Donald Sinden-like voice, in introduction. 'Happy ship? The *Titanic*, more like, given the dimwits crewing this particular office. Can't even address a letter properly, most of them. Look at this. Tell me what's wrong here – that is, if you're not completely mentally deficient yourself.'

I looked first at the A4 manilla envelope being thrust towards me, then at the bearded, hook-nosed Horden himself. Like everyone else I could see in the long, poorly lit, low-ceilinged room, he was of late middle age and essentially grey-looking. 'Well?' he demanded. 'Care to give us the benefit of your no-doubt-profound knowledge of the lost art of letter-writing?'

Unsure quite why I was being set this test, I did my best to respond. 'There are full stops where there should be commas,' I offered hopefully. 'Look, here and here. And . . . and whoever addressed this hasn't bothered to use the postcode.' With that I stopped. I could think of nothing else to say.

'Precisely, dear boy! Precisely!' Horden took my right hand in his and pumped it vigorously. 'Music to my ears. Postcodes are a vital weapon in the modern correspondent's armoury. Always, always use the postcode. Which I'm sure you do. Delighted to make your acquaintance, Mr Jackson.'

And to Mr Section-Head, newly released from the telephone, he added, 'At last, a ray of intelligence has been sent to illuminate your desk. Here's a young man who recognizes the importance of postcodes. In my mind, he could come with no higher recommendation. Meanwhile, I believe this is one of your missives, and a personal one, too, if I'm not mistaken. If you have to waste public funds on publicizing your private endeavours, the least you could do is make sure you address them properly.'

'Hand that over right now! Honestly!' My new boss snatched back the offending envelope and directed a hearty V-sign at the departing Horden. 'Wretched man spends all his time looking through other people's mail and banging on about it being wrongly addressed. He's on the line to the post-code advisory service all day bloody long. Whichever poor sod is on the other end of it must be suicidal at the very thought of coming in to work.'

I smiled in a noncommittal fashion as my leader draped a matey arm across my shoulder. 'Luv-verly to have you with us,' he was saying. 'You'll find us a very happy team. All for one and one for all! Oh, dear Lord! Here comes the Queen of Sheba! I'm off, pronto. Head her off at the pass, will you, there's a good lad?'

Unexpectedly fleet in a pair of beige, pasty-shaped lace-ups, he then grabbed a tabloid from his desk and fled the room. Meanwhile, I turned in time to see a commanding figure with a tanned face and a pink bow tie bearing down on me at speed from the other end of the long, open-plan office.

'I see your illustrious leader has skipped off in his sew-'em-yourself shoes and urine-stained suit for a quick leaf through the racing news and a spot of self-abuse,' this unexpectedly colourful figure declaimed. 'Well, let me just say that it's nice to see someone walk into this room without the aid of a Zimmer. Perhaps you can bring a spark of creativity to what must be the dreariest department in the whole of the British civil service. God knows it needs it. Even Mother Theresa would fall victim to Tourette's syndrome if she read some of the stories your colleagues here churn out. It's my unlucky lot in life to have to process them – or not. Which is why, when Chatterton returns from tugging at his tired old todger, you can tell him I've rejected last Friday afternoon's pathetic output in its entirety.'

So saying, he tossed a sheaf of pages into the air, as if it were confetti. Dipping back into my psychedelically upholstered seat, I tried to remember what it was I was supposed to be doing here. What had they said at my interview? That the department's function was to supply British embassies around the world with news items showing our nation in a positive light. These would then be distributed by the various press attachés to local media outlets for, hopefully, publication. From interviewing a soft-core porn star to becoming a soft-core propagandist. It wasn't quite what I'd had in mind for myself in the big city.

'The thing is', I said to Ian, when we met for a drink near the *Melody Maker* offices behind Waterloo station, 'that nearly everyone I work with is a head case. Just this lunchtime, some bloke asked if he could join me at my table in the canteen, saying he'd heard I was interested in music. I told him to sit down – I mean, he was fifty if he was a day, but I thought there was a chance he might not be certifiable. So, "Yeah," I said, "I love it. And you? What sort of stuff are you into?"

'Well, he tells me he's Buddy Rich's biggest fan and that he likes nothing better of an evening than to put on one of the great man's albums, sit down at his drum kit and bang along. The trouble is, his wife can't stand the racket.

'"So what does she do about it?" I ask him.

'"Turns up the central heating until it's too hot for me to keep up," he replies.

'So I ask, "And then what do you do? Pack up?" and he answers, "Not on your life! I strip down to my vest and Y-fronts and keep on drumming, just to spite the old cow!" I mean, what sort of working universe am I inhabiting?'

Ian shuddered and reached for his drink. 'Maybe you ought to be making plans to get out of there, before you start turning weird yourself,' he suggested.

'But the thing is, I find the work really easy and I'm good at it,' I told him. 'It's not like the *Mercury*, where you have to work really hard because everyone else does. There, I'm the youngest person by about thirty years. I could coast and still they'd think they had Clark Kent in their midst. But I don't coast. I try hard, because it makes the day pass quicker, and because, well . . . just because.

'Last week they sent me to the Royal Show at Stoneleigh, looking for British agricultural innovations that might benefit the Third World. Sixty-eight stories, I sent back, over the course of three days. "Top-quality bull semen from the Bolton area of north-west Britain could soon be benefiting farmers from the eastern province of who-knows-where," and stuff like that. When I got back into the office I asked my section-head how many my counterpart had filed last year. "Oh, fifteen or sixteen," he said. "You did sp-sp-specially well."'

'You've got to get out,' said Ian.

'But no-one ever has, not back into the world of proper journalism,' I told him. 'I asked. So it looks like I've rendered myself unemployable in the real world. Meanwhile, I've just been offered a promotion. Deputy diplomatic correspondent, travelling back and forth to the EC with the likes of the foreign secretary. Pinstripe suits-a-go-go and, apparently, a pension to die for. I'm so depressed.'

'I've just been offered a promotion, too,' said Ian. 'Or at least another job. I'm going to be editor of the *NME*. So, I was wondering, would you like to come and work for me? There's a staff job going, if you want it.'

'Fuck!' I said, uncomprehending.

'I take it that's a yes, then,' said Ian, comprehending only too well.

4

In the arrivals hall of Los Angeles International airport, the figure holding up a flag of card with my name on it was as square-jawed and broad-shouldered as a Burton's window dummy. 'Welcome to the City of Angels. Now, let me take that for you,' he said, relieving me of the grubby canvas bag that had been part of my father's post-war demob kit, and then striding off with it through the early evening crowds. Trotting behind him, new kid on the block at the *NME* and already on a mission to meet my all-time musical heroine, I registered with surprise that what had appeared from the front to be a short, slicked-back hairstyle actually incorporated a considerable but tightly bound ponytail. And that though darkly besuited, he was wearing Cuban-heeled boots, not shoes. Mr Regular in the middle, an LA dude at either end. Clearly, there was more to the man who had introduced himself to me merely as Tom than first met the eye.

Following in his wake, it occurred to me that, actually, I knew nothing about him at all – who he was, or what he did. Three weeks after joining the staff of my new workplace, here

I was in California for the first time, alone, and *en route* to interviewing Joni Mitchell, the woman who had given melancholics everywhere something to play on their stereos in the difficult years before Morrissey was invented. And, already, a man with a sartorial split personality had requisitioned my one, sad-looking piece of luggage, and was leading me towards who knew where? Nobody back in London had indicated that I was to be met, so I had no idea quite who Tom was. An employee of the record company representing Joni at the time, perhaps, one who was kindly stopping off on his way home to deliver me to my destination? I had no idea.

My uncertainty evaporated the moment we arrived at his bay in the parking lot. Tom was a chauffeur, on a part-time basis at least, and this long, black and rather ridiculous piece of machinery was what he drove for a living. It was a stretch limousine and, as such, represented a terrible mix-up, some about-to-be-discovered case of mistaken identity. There had been another, very important Alan Jackson on my incoming flight, and right now he was tapping the toe of his Gucci loafer in irritation, while giving phone hell to someone somewhere about the non-appearance of his ride, the ride that I, in all innocence, was in the process of stealing.

But not so. Tom signalled his certainty that no error had been made with a shake of his very large head. 'The BA flight from London. Alan Jackson. Going to the Sunset Marquis. There's no mistake. Truly. Let me help you into the car.' And so saying, he gently lowered my bag onto the expensive carpet lining the Cadillac's vast boot – I imagine it was the carpet he was being protective of, not my bag – pressed shut the lid and ushered me through the rear passenger door into the room-on-wheels within. And oh, the foolish luxury I was confronted with: cut-glass decanters and a full bar, a television set and telephone, not one but two arrangements of silk-petalled flowers. My first visit to the city and I was arriving, albeit self-consciously, in a Dynasty-like approximation of elegance and style.

For several minutes, I sat in awkward isolation, still troubled by the thought that an essential error had taken place – one which would result in my eventually being ejected on some lonely street corner and left to fend for myself – and thus I was slow to appreciate that remarks were now being addressed to me. Perhaps sensing my vulnerability, the man with two hair-styles had depressed the smoked-glass screen separating us and was moving in for the kill. 'So, I guess you must be in the music biz,' he was saying. 'I'm a songwriter myself, y'know. Just do this driving stuff part-time. Wanna hear a track or two? It'd be no trouble; I got the tape right here. No, don't say a word. I know you're gonna love it. First number's called "Baby, We Can Make It". Wrote it during a bad scene with a lady I was dating. We ended up splitting but, well, hey! *C'est la vie!* The second's called "I Don't Need Nobody". Be honest now! Don't be afraid to tell me what you think!'

Thus it was to the loud accompaniment of Tom's grim home-studio power-balladeering that we left the airport environs and headed downtown. I had learned an important lesson, though, and early on in my visit, too: in this of all cities, no-one is quite what they seem. Meanwhile, if you're reading this, Tom, despite any encouraging noises I may have made at the time, let me be emboldened by a distance of thirteen years and 6,000 miles to say, finally and with all due apology, that your songs . . . well, Tom, that they were shite.

The scenery unravelled like a series of movie sets as we drove along, Tom attempting to harmonize with his tape-recorded voice and beating time on the steering wheel with his fingers; me lolling, disorientated and drowsy, behind him. Soon the scrubland and oil derricks were replaced by the gas stations, mini-malls and fast-food drive-thrus that line the route in through the southern suburbs. Then, finally, we were driving along Santa Monica Boulevard and through West Hollywood, towards the hotel that had been booked for me.

Situated on North Alta Loma Road, a short, largely residential street running downhill from the famous boulevard from which it takes its name, the Sunset Marquis is something of a best-kept secret within the recording industry. Low-rise, understated and relatively small, it's the choice of stars who want privacy and comfort, without the impersonality or, alternately, undue ceremony of larger, more celebrated establishments, and of civilians hoping for a little gilt by association. All these years later, the music business continues to provide the hotel's core clientele, as I was reminded recently by a full-page advertisement in the American trade magazine *Billboard*. 'Hotel rooms even a rock star doesn't have the heart to trash', read the copyline accompanying a photograph of a cool, sexily lit living area.

The main accommodation block of the Marquis is relatively unprepossessing, built around a central pool area, and with additional bungalow-style villas set within the grounds to its rear. If designed with anything in mind, it seems to have been a diversion of attention away from itself. Indeed, the only ostentatious feature, externally at least, is the profusion of white fairy lights twinkling in the trees lining the route to the lobby door. They made me think of Christmas as I clambered out of the Cadillac, reassuring Tom that I could carry my own bag inside and didn't need help. 'Well, I'm assigned to you for the evening, so whenever you're ready to head out again, you'll find me waiting right here,' he said, surprising me yet again. Little did I realize, meanwhile, that as I walked indoors and towards the front desk, I did so effectively naked – not without clothes but, far more alarmingly, without a US credit rating.

These days, I wouldn't dream of leaving the country without my American Express card, knowing from experience how essential plastic is to a smooth passage around the world. At the time, though, I neither owned nor saw the need for any kind of charge card, and so could offer anxious hotel staff no guarantee for my potential spend. It was a big mistake, as I was about to learn.

'Always a pleasure to welcome you back to the Sunset Marquis, Mr . . . Jackson!' said the duty manager as, with the self-congratulatory flourish of the magician producing a rabbit from his hat, he pulled confirmation of my booking from among the sheaf of papers within his file. '*Voila!* I see that the cost of your room and breakfast are to be billed back to CBS Records in London. So, how would you like to settle your extras?'

My mind worked furiously to keep up. Extras? What did he mean? The cost of that reassuring phone call home to my mum? Or, this being a rock 'n' roll establishment, that of a round-the-clock supply of call girls and cocaine. Hardly daring to imagine, I ventured, 'Er, with cash, please.'

'Cash?' He repeated the word, but with a new inflection, one that suggested he must surely have misheard.

'Yes. Isn't that OK?'

'You wouldn't prefer to use a credit card?'

'I'm afraid I don't have one.'

'I see,' he said, all too ominously, leaning forward a little to take in more of the curious specimen before him – this rather small, rather crumpled-looking Englishman with the unfortunate item of luggage and, yet more unfortunately, no credit card. 'Well, I'm afraid I shall have to ask you for a deposit of, say, two hundred dollars.'

Embarrassed, I reached for my wallet. Then, the transaction duly concluded – noticing how little money this left me with, I began to fear for my ability to survive the trip – I asked if I might have an iron sent up to my room. 'I have to go out again shortly and I need to press a suit,' I added, imagining an explanation was due.

'Why-certainly-Mr-Jackson. No-problem-at-all,' replied the duty manager who, I was discovering, had the idiosyncratic habit of eliding all his words into one continuous, melodic stream. He put through the necessary call to Housekeeping, then asked if he might take, a-hem, the liberty – I imagine I was correct in reading this as 'the massive favour' – of ordering a cab for me.

'Thanks, but I don't need one. I've got a car waiting for me outside,' I told him, at which point another member of staff, previously standing silently behind me, moved forward to address his superior.

'It's the stretch right out front,' I heard him say, *sotto voce*.

'Ah. Thank you,' the duty manager replied in a similarly hushed tone, then turned back to me and offered a newly dazzling smile. 'As I said, it's always-a-pleasure-to-welcome-you-back-to-the-Sunset-Marquis, Mr-Jackson. No help with your bag? Fine. The lifts are just there. We-hope-you-have-a-most-enjoyable-stay.'

Newly showered and besuited – 'Why, Mr Jackson, what-a-transformation!' my new friend exclaimed upon my reappearance in the lobby. 'Look, everyone. Doesn't-Mr-Jackson-look-smart?' – I rejoined Tom and his dream-home-on-wheels. My destination was the James Corcoran Gallery on Santa Monica Boulevard, where a gala opening of an exhibition of Joni Mitchell's paintings was being held, nominally as a fundraiser for the city's Museum of Contemporary Art, but mainly as a launch party for her forth-coming album, *Dog Eat Dog*. It was to be my chance to meet and greet, to make initial contact with the singer-songwriter, newly gaining attention as a painter, and her representatives, but also to gather a little background colour for my feature.

Wrongly assuming us to be some distance away, and lulled into a false sense of security by Tom's not having yet slipped another of his compositions on to the sound system, I settled back into the deep white leather upholstery and tried to enjoy my brief experience of a rich-and-famous lifestyle. But what was that happening further down the street? TV cameramen, photographers and banks of associated lights. A red carpet running all the way down to the roadside, with velvet ropes suspended at each side to keep out passers-by. A huddle of onlookers waiting to see who and what all the fuss was about. Suddenly, realization dawned.

But before I could tap on the smoked-glass screen and alert Tom to the fact that I wanted to get out, here and now, he'd swung the limousine in an arc and pulled up right beside the red carpet. He then moved swiftly around the car and opened the door for me, with what I had just enough time to foresee would be ego-deflating results. The camera crews and photographers, the star-spotters and the just-happened-to-be-passings all pressed forward, awaiting the emergence of whichever celebrity might be inside this splendid, ridiculous car. There was an anticipatory intake of breath and, a moment

or two later, a colossal exhalation. For it was only me –
unknown and, hence, uninteresting, even when wearing my
best suit.

The assembled masses sank back into their waiting pos-
itions, and I decided to tip and send home early an astonished
and delighted Tom. 'Wow, man! Are you sure? What a dude!
Listen, you gotta take the tape. It's got my number on it. Call
any time. And, like, wow! Thanks a lot! I could use the free
time. Those songs, you've gotta live with 'em a while to really
catch their power. Well, be seein' ya, then. *Ciao.*'

As a man who, at the time, drove a Ford Escort, I felt
uncomfortable with the size and status-implications of his
loaned car, and also the fact that he would have to wait indefinitely near by for my eventual re-emergence, merely to
transfer me the quarter of a mile back to the hotel. Easier
for both of us, I thought, if I walked or caught a cab. And so,
dutifully, I pocketed the proffered cassette and waved goodbye.
And that I had made the right decision was confirmed the
instant Tom climbed back into the driver's seat and switched
on the ignition. Within seconds, audible even above the
engine noise, came the sound of a duplicate tape playing
the terrible 'Baby, We Can Make It' and his accompanying
live vocal.

Suddenly alone, I ran the gauntlet of disappointed and
disinterested onlookers, and flashed the necessary invitation to
secure entry to the inner sanctum. But what to do once inside?
Unsure of what facial expression to adopt, I attempted an
enigmatic half-smile and, having practised it, moved from one
large, cool, white room to the next, all the while wanting to
look closely at Joni's big, bold, semi-abstract canvases, but
constantly being prevented from doing so by clusters of
excitable young women saying things like, 'Oh-my-God!

95

Don't look now, but Jack's just three people behind you now. No, make that two! Barbi Benton just moved. God, who'd have thought she'd still look that good? Oh, Jack! Look at me! Look at me! Look at me!'

Moving forward continually for no other reason than that to stand still would involve acknowledging the fact that I knew no-one, I accepted a glass of champagne from one of the constantly passing coterie of waiters – in typical LA fashion, and in spite of whatever greater excesses they might indulge in at home, most other guests were flamboyantly drinking Perrier – and tried to pick up the chit-chat above the sound of Joni's about-to-be-released album being played on continuous loop. Who, I wondered, was this Jack all the women were giggling about? At that very same moment the answer was revealed to me – yes, I'm at the same party as Jack Nicholson! – I rounded a corner and came chin-to-chin with a blessedly familiar face.

Here was a trap I'd fallen into only once before: the unexpected encounter with someone so well known that you're momentarily tricked into thinking they're a long-lost friend. I had come to think of that first experience as my Lunchbreak Shame. I had just returned, sandwich in hand, to the foyer of the *Mercury* office, only to discover the tanned, short-wearing TV presenter Judith Chalmers occupying one of its two well-worn, moquette-covered easy chairs. Was she in town to film a segment for a new travel show, a *Wish You Weren't Here?* To my regret, I didn't stop to ponder, and, instead, let fly with a cheery, totally spontaneous greeting: 'Hi! Great to see you! It's been ages! What on earth are you doing here?'

Presumably because this happens to television personalities all the time – it couldn't possibly be that she was equally as suggestible as me – she was generous enough to reply in kind.

'Hi! You, too! Yes, hasn't it! Oh, the usual! Well, see you!'

It was only later, safely at my desk, that the incident replayed itself in my head and I correctly self-diagnosed False Memory Syndrome. Oh, the total, terrible shame of it. And now I was about to make the same mistake again.

'What on earth are you doing here?'

'I was invited,' replied Sheena Easton. 'What about you? In fact, who are you?'

A reasonable enough question, and there was no need for her tone to be as friendly or amused as it was. Before I could expand, though, the singer who had gone from being patronized by Esther Rantzen to working with Prince in four short years was being whisked away by someone saying, 'Joni would like to meet you. She's over here.' At which this small, beautiful, spiky-haired woman, scarcely recognizable from her first incarnation on the BBC's a-star-is-born documentary series *The Big Time*, turned on her spike heels and walked off to meet someone who, I later discovered, she idolized, too.

No-one very much wanted to meet me, alas, and soon my facial muscles were aching from the strain of trying to look interested and interesting, rather than merely glum and glummer. After a while, two young women – gallery employees – took pity on me and came over to make conversation. Or so I thought. In fact, they were in competition with each other to see who could engage Mr Nicholson in conversation for the longest period of time, and needed an independent adjudicator to wield the stopwatch. First, though, they had to wait for the strawberry blonde currently holding his attention to clear out of the way.

In order that they should be well placed to pounce, I consented to join the sideways shuffle that would bring us nearer to their prey. Quick to learn and eager to please, I too opened and closed my mouth at frequent intervals to simulate an animated conversation. Except that we all remained silent, our mission being to eavesdrop on the on-going dialogue.

Strawberry blonde, coquettishly: 'Oh, Jack, you've had such a great life.'

Jack, smiling lazily while surveying the horizon: 'Great? It's been fucking amazing.'

Strawberry blonde, making a fatal mistake: 'Perhaps I could just freshen my drink?'

Jack, scarcely needing to play barman to get a date: 'Sure. See you around.'

One suitor's rejection is the next's golden opportunity, of course, and Gallery Assistant Number One was filling the vacant square metre of floor space in front of him within two seconds flat. To acknowledge her sudden appearance, Jack merely raised one piratical eyebrow in what I judged to be benign amusement and then smiled that Jack-like smile.

The subsequent sales pitch – a garbled gush about his performance in *Five Easy Pieces* – can't have been either original or compelling enough, though, and she was back beside us, blushing, before a full minute had ticked by. Gallery Assistant Number Two had better luck – the offer of a personal tour of the exhibition at a quieter time, should he be interested, was at least imaginative, and had the added benefit of implicit sexual innuendo – but she still managed no more than ninety seconds. Hugging each other, they reclaimed their watch and chorused their goodbyes, leaving me to stare in bemusement as yet another pair of heels clicked forward to replace them, magnetized by the challenge of the irresistible Jack. It was time, I felt, to head back to the hotel. But only after satisfying my curiosity with a glimpse of the woman I was really here to meet.

And there she was, Joni, all high cheekbones, black beret and cigarette smoke, being interviewed by a Japanese TV crew. Having waited half my life for the opportunity to encounter her, I decided that it was safe and wise to let anticipation continue to build over the course of one more night. So, having confirmed the arrangements for the next day with an employee of her record company, I sought directions back to the Sunset Marquis.

It was late evening now and, though the red carpet and velvet ropes were still in place, the thrill-seekers had long since gone home. Suddenly, what seemed, due to their presence, to be a supremely glamorous location was revealed as just another shopping street, inhabited by liquor marts, dry-cleaners, adult book stores and a 7-Eleven. Feeling suddenly too drunk with tiredness to absorb, let alone process, this information, I began to walk.

And I had not got far when something that looked worryingly like a police car pulled up alongside me, and someone who looked terrifyingly like a policeman climbed out and asked me to produce some ID. Confused and fearful, I handed over my passport and a card confirming my residency at the hotel. 'British, huh?' said the cop, as if that were all the explanation he needed for what he clearly viewed as an act of wanton stupidity. 'Y'know, you might as well have a sign pinned to your back saying, "Mug Me", parading round in a suit and tie at this time of night. Get in. I'll give you a ride.'

Which is how I came to leave my temporary home in a stretch limo and return in a squad car driven by Jerry, 200 pounds of law-enforcement muscle with a blind spot where Joni Mitchell was concerned, but with a distinct weakness for Eighties rock star Pat Benatar. 'Never mind that "Big Yellow Taxi" shit, man. Have you seen the video for "Love Is A Battlefield"? God, that chick's foxy. You wanna get yourself an appointment with her, never mind some so-called sensitive . . .'

But by that time we were back in North Alta Loma Road, where I offered profuse thanks to Jerry for his kindness – my gratitude seemed only to compound his earlier verdict that I was mentally challenged – and quickly sidled past the Marquis' twinkling tree lights into its deserted foyer, intent on escaping the duty manager's attention at all costs. Eureka! His back was turned.

But, 'Why, Mr Jackson! A smaller car than you left in, but this time with a pretty blue light on top,' came the unmistakable voice, as I waited, heart pounding, for the lift to arrive. 'Well-you've-obviously-had-a-much-more-exciting-evening-than-little-old-me!' Smiling, despite my blushes, I stepped through the newly opened doors and looked forward to being beamed up to my bed.

At a maddeningly early hour, I awoke within the cerise- and pistachio-coloured world that was my first-floor mini-suite. Switching on the TV, I zapped expectantly through fifty-seven channels of evangelism, aerobic workouts, cookery demonstrations, vintage sitcoms, and stock-market analysis, then fell despondently back onto my pillow. I tried to sleep again, but remained resolutely conscious. Finally accepting defeat, I dressed in my trunks and complimentary fluffy white robe and went down to the pool, where my lone companion – doing an urgent, scarily Jaws-reminiscent front crawl – was, I felt sure, the actor Roy Scheider. The fact of his presence in the water was unnerving. Feeling that, at any second, a shark might surface at the deep end, I found myself breast-stroking at twice the normal speed. Twenty laps and I was exhausted. Mr Scheider, meanwhile, just kept on swimming. 'Look out behind you!' I wanted to call, as I clambered out, wheezing. He was moving too fast to have heard me.

Back in my room, I ordered and ate a room-service breakfast, delivered on a cart the size of a hospital trolley, then looked at my watch to discover it was still only half-past eight. By 9 a.m., I was showered, shaved to within a millimetre of total chin removal and ready for Joni. The only drawback was that my interview wouldn't take place until 4 p.m.

Another seven and a half hours to fill. Plenty of time, in fact, to develop a personality disorder. Locked in the bathroom – there was a telephone on the wall next to the toilet. What self-respecting, lapsed-Catholic boy could talk to anyone while sitting there? – I changed and rechanged clothes in a hopeless, pointless bid to imagine What Joni Might Like Best. This process caused my self-confidence to plummet and my level of general neurosis to soar. As if she'd care or notice, or even be able to tell the difference between one sports shirt or another just like it – particularly when it was all but hidden beneath this jacket or the other one, its twin in almost every detail. Dispirited, over-heated and still with six hours to kill, I lay down on my king-sized bed and fell deeply, mercifully asleep.

I woke up again with very little time to spare. It was now 2.45 p.m., and I had no idea how far away was the address I had to reach, nor how long it would take me to get there. An exploratory call to the front desk reunited me with my special friend, back on duty and eager to be helpful. 'Just a walk away? Oh, I think not, Mr Jackson. Do you have a, ahem, car at your disposal today? No? Oh. Well, let's see. I'd be only too happy to arrange for our complimentary limousine service to transport you to your destination. No really. Just doing my job. Oh, you're sweet. Now, I would suggest three fifteen, to be on the safe side. Truly, think nothing of it, Mr Jackson. Always-a-pleasure-to-have-you-with-us-at-the-Sunset-Marquis! Bye-bye!'

I showered again, and dressed in one or other unmemorable variation on my core, essentially nondescript travelling wardrobe: I daren't wear my best suit again, lest, beyond fiction, Joni had noticed it the previous evening and should conclude it was the only item of clothing I owned. Then, all but making the sign of the cross to arm myself for the encounter, I prepared to face not her, but the duty manager. 'An all-important business meeting this afternoon, Mr Jackson?' he ventured smoothly, upon my appearance in the lobby. 'Well, may I say that I hope it proceeds to your entire satisfaction?'

With which I walked off towards yet another long, self-important car, on yet another pitiably short, unimportant ride. But not before a final observation could reach me from behind the front desk: 'The casual look suits you very well, sir, if I may be so bold.'

Deposited outside the offices of the all-too-near Peter Asher Management – yes, the orange-haired half of the Sixties British singing duo Peter and Gordon – at a time all-too-far from my appointed hour, I considered how best I might deal with being stuck beside a four-lane highway in oppressive heat, with a full forty minutes to kill. The options seemed limited: run around in the traffic like a madman and risk being killed or stay still and concentrate on absorbing as little carbon monoxide as possible. I plumped for the latter, encouraged by the presence of a bus stop and attendant bench just yards away.

It was served, I discovered, by only two different routes. 'D'you want this one, honey, 'cos I don't?' remarked my sole companion, an elderly black woman who, seemingly oblivious to the heat, was wearing a buttoned-up coat and tennis shoes, when, minutes later, a first bus approached. Shortly afterwards, her own preferred ride followed and she got to her feet. 'So, you must want this one,' she declared, but I told her no. 'Well, if you didn't want that one and you don't want this one,' she said, climbing slowly aboard and shaking her head theatrically, 'I guess you ain't goin' nowhere.' My fear entirely.

For the next twenty-five minutes I sat in solitary splendour, watching the speeding cars and trucks go by and trying my best not to sweat. Finally, it was time for me to approach the doorway that had been opposite all the while, just metres away, across in Doheny Drive. 'Aha, the man from the bus stop!' exclaimed the receptionist triumphantly when I announced myself to her. 'And to think that we imagined that we had our first stalker. It didn't occur to us you might be Joni's next interviewer!'

And you have a nice day, too, I thought, wretched at having the last shred of international sophistication stripped from me. But I was being too harsh on her, me and the entire human race. For before either of us could say another word, my idol's arm linked itself through mine, and an amused, Canadian-inflected voice spoke winningly in my ear. 'Come and have some tea, Alan. Tea, as in cucumber sandwiches with the crusts cut off, and scones with jam and cream. It's been brought all the way from Malibu from some fancy English caterers. How much more at home could we make you feel?' Hello and I love you, Joni Mitchell. Truly, truly I do.

The special occasion was not, obviously, our meeting, but

the birthday of Peter Asher's PA, like him a British exile. And so it was that I joined the small office party already underway, one at which about a dozen people picked at food more English than anything we in England would ever eat. Among them all, pouring me tea and wondering if I needed milk or sugar, was the woman whose very best albums – *Blue, Court and Spark, Hejira* and my special favourite, *The Hissing Of Summer Lawns* – I had played a thousand times, and whose facility for self-expression had both humbled me and made me aspire to be some kind of writer myself. Even today, I hope that she interpreted my mute staring as a sign of devotion, not mere vacancy. I imagine that she did. She certainly laughed kindly at the blank but encouraging head-nodding with which I responded to her eventual declaration of needing to go pee before any kind of interview could begin.

To spend an hour asking questions of someone whose work you love, respect and know intimately is, I find, a thrilling thing, even today. It's an experience that reminds me why I do my job. Thankfully, I'm better at it now than I was back then. The printed results of our interview are before me now, within the yellow-edged pages of a twelve-year-old copy of the *NME* and, though it is neither definitive nor particularly accomplished, it's still a kind of personal milestone, an ambition fulfilled, a dream realized.

With a small shock I note she was forty-one years old when we met – my age as I write these words. She was beautiful – and still is today – with a Dunaway-like bone structure. She had dressed expensively, in a mannish grey flannel suit and a heavy, lustrous silk shirt. It was her manner to hold back her upper body and head, and to fix me with a cool, appraising look whenever I spoke. Instead of being intimidating, though, this scrutiny felt oddly flattering – such undivided attention, and directed at me, too. More flattering still was the consideration with which she rewarded each question or observation, and the deliberate way in which she leaned forward, jabbing at the air with a cigarette as she ventured her response.

At that point in her life, Joni had already experienced the vagaries of fame and critical acclaim – their first lavish bestowal, and then the sudden harsh reeling-in and disavowal. Her early- to mid-period LPs – romantic and confessional in subject matter and with their musical roots firmly in the folk tradition – had been both critically and commercially well received, establishing her reputation and allowing her to live in some considerable style outside Los Angeles and on the remote coastline of Saskatchewan in her native Canada.

Her growing interest in jazz, and a move away from the personal subject matter of the aforementioned records – the songs on *Dog Eat Dog* were almost exclusively concerned with the ills and inequalities of Gordon-Gekko-era America – troubled critics and core fans alike. Anyone who achieves longevity in a public career learns to accept that such judgements are cyclical. Although it wouldn't happen for a further decade, Joni has since been welcomed back in from the cold, with a wealth of younger artists hailing her as a key influence, or covering her material, and lifetime achievement awards coming at her from every side. What I was unable to understand, though, was why *The Hissing Of Summer Lawns*, a ground-breaking album, which I still play today with pleasure and awe, had been so reviled – voted worst release of its year, 1976, by critics on the then-influential US rock magazine *Rolling Stone*.

'Oh, well, that's fame for you,' said its maker, drawing deeply on one of the cigarettes she chain-smoked throughout the afternoon. 'I remember that afterwards I got a telegram from Paul and Linda McCartney, saying, "We really liked it." It was the only really good review it got, and then it was almost motivated by sympathy. That album was destroyed on so many levels, and I admit it really hurt. There's no way, just on a level of craftsmanship, you could say it was the worst record made that year. If they'd just said they hated it, I could have taken it . . . But to say it was the worst?'

She held out her cigarette and paused for a moment, then took another deep drag. 'Stay as you are and bore us, or change and betray us.' She shrugged, with a thin, pale smile. 'That's your choice these days, as an artist.'

The description most often applied to Joni's style of song-writing is 'confessional'. Devotees have poured over her lyrics as guiltily as if reading her bedside diaries, looking for clues to her mental and emotional state. Generally, they haven't had to look too hard. 'I never thought of myself in that way, particularly,' she told me. 'But in order that my work should have vitality, I felt I should write in my own blood. The closer it was to my direct experience, the less it was going to be hearsay, and the more poignancy it should have. My job, as I see it, is to be a witness. I am a witness to my times. The world had become mysterious to those of us looking from the vantage point of the Sixties and Seventies. There was disillusionment – the killing of the president, the stain of the Vietnam War. It was a natural thing that we should then look in on ourselves. So what followed was a period of soul-searching. The dream – everything that America stood for – was broken, and people broke a little along with the dream. Where else was there to go but inside?'

I knew other people of Joni's age who felt alienated from the children who'd achieved adulthood in their wake. She – almost the official spokesperson for Woodstockian liberals

– understood that alienation, yet managed to be sanguine, too.

'This current generation kind of resembles that of my parents,' she observed. 'They're like a throwback, which often happens. Their aim is to get a job and hold it, because they came up in a depression. Not one as severe as that of the 1930s, of course, but still one that put them under similar pressures. Whereas we grew up in the greatest pocket of affluence there has been, post Second World War. The country was rich. The economy was in good shape. We were raised on certain philosophies – spare the rod, and yes, do spoil the child. So there is a sense in which we never really reached proper adulthood. We were a kind of freaky, self-centred generation as a rule. Both in bad ways and in good.'

It's a widely held view that the best art comes from pain, heartache and personal struggle. To a degree, Joni's work supports this theory. *Dog Eats Dog*, within which critiques of contemporary American culture and mores replaced more familiar, introspective themes, was one of her least-accomplished albums, although I was, at the time, too starstruck to recognize the fact. Two years earlier, she had made a late second marriage to the record producer Larry Klein; it would later end in divorce. Did the onset of personal happiness, even if not long-lived, necessarily carry with it the prospect of a creative decline?

'It took me a long time to find a partner again,' she acknowledged. 'But then, what am I expected to do now? Torture myself? Sit there and reminisce about the past? It would be bad for me, bad for my marriage. So, with that taken care of, you start to look around you. It's a natural sociological phenomenon, you know?'

Over our tea and scones, we talked on into the late afternoon. I was every bit as charmed and impressed as I'd hoped to be. And when, eventually, after being hugged a final goodbye, I set off slowly on my way, I felt suffused with a Ready-Brek glow. It was an inner warmth generated by my joy at having met and not been disappointed by a woman whose work and personality had been central to my life for at least fifteen years. And she'd actually put her arms around me, too. Oblivious to the noise and fumes of the traffic, and too exhilarated to consider that I might once again attract police attention, I zig-zagged my way back through the tea-time streets towards the Sunset Marquis, outside which the fairy-lit trees were already sparkling. Once past them and indoors, I wished for someone, anyone, with whom to share the details of my encounter. There was no-one. Even my friend at the front desk was now off-duty. So, instead, feeling suddenly dead with tiredness, I lay down on my bed and instantly sank into sleep.

When I woke, a couple of hours later, it was with the remainder of a long and empty evening stretching ahead of me. Slow consideration of the room-service menu took up some time, the waiting for and eating of my order a little more. At which point, distractedly leafing through the list of hotel amenities, I noticed mention of an outdoor spa area. With my trunks rolled up inside a towel, I went to investigate, and found there, amongst the trees and satellite bungalows, a big, empty jacuzzi. The closest I had ever come to one thus far was via the adverts for whirlpool baths at the back of the Sunday supplements. Here was my chance to actually test the foaming water.

Emerging from the changing area, I climbed warily in and, after a minute or two of nothing happening, noticed and duly pressed a large button on the side. First-time experiences are meant to feel sinful or sybaritic, but this felt merely silly.

Here I was, a grown man, sitting in a bubble bath in someone else's garden. They didn't do that in Norfolk. Gradually, though, the warmth reactivated my jet lag and I began to feel pleasantly sleepy. Teetering on the brink of dreamland, I congratulated myself on carrying the day. I'd met an idol, and not disgraced myself. Perhaps I was up to the demands of this jet-setting, star-spangled lifestyle, after all.

Suffused with smugness, and with my eyes closed and arms extended, I had been relaxing there for perhaps five minutes when I became aware of a secondary presence. 'D'you mind if I join you?' asked a lookalike for *Dallas* beauty Pammy with, inexplicably, a ghetto-blaster in hand. Before I could muster up a reply, she let her robe fall from first one shoulder, then the other, and stepped out of her high-heeled mules.

'Er . . . No. Please. As in not-at-all,' I managed, my face contorting in the effort not to stare at her low-necked swim-suit, full make-up and carefully styled hair.

She rewarded me with a smile, said, 'You're kind,' and made something of a performance of sinking into position directly opposite me. There then passed an awkward silence, during which she stretched and flexed her neck and elab-orately cleared her throat. Finally, she spoke again: 'Let me ask you something else. Do you like music?'

'Of course,' I replied, guardedly.

'So, you won't mind if I put on a tape?'

'Er . . . no. Go right ahead,' I managed, my heart sinking at the possibility that it might feature some of her own com-positions. 'Be my guest.'

'Thanks. I hoped you'd say that.'

And, with one flick of a switch, she filled the air with the sound of an orchestra playing the introduction to a familiar carol.

'I'm in a choir, you see,' she offered. 'We're getting ready for the festive season.'

'Right!'

As I tried unsuccessfully to distract myself by calculating how many shopping days remained for those lucky souls who had credit cards at their disposal, she threw back her head, drew in a deep breath and began to sing in a rich, pure contralto: 'God rest ye, merry gentlemen, let nothing you dismay. For Jesus Christ, our saviour, was born on Christmas Day . . .'

Taken aback by this unexpected development, I struggled to maintain some semblance of composure. How best, and when, to make my excuses and leave? My facial muscles stricken by a rictus which, I hoped, suggested appreciation of a sublime talent, I forced myself to wait for the carol to end. Then, in the short pause before the orchestra resumed its playing, I clambered out and grabbed my clothes from the changing cabin. 'Meeting a friend for dinner,' I blustered, hastily recovering a dropped shoe from the shrubbery as the opening bars of 'I Saw Three Ships' unfurled. So, I had begun to feel at home in Los Angeles, had I? Maybe East Anglia was where I belonged, after all.

Leaving an increasingly faint trail of wet footprints, I hurried indoors and along a network of carpeted corridors, across the lobby – thank God he was off-duty! – and up the service stairs, then along to the haven of my suite. I burst into the bedroom, clothes clutched to my chest, as if I were some character in a farce, to find that my bed had been turned down for the night, and that a small box of chocolates had been placed on the pillow. Tucked under the imitation red rose that decorated its lid was a hand-inscribed card, reading, 'We trust you have enjoyed your stay at the Sunset Marquis,' and reminding me of the various ways in which I could settle my account before leaving.

Had I enjoyed it? Do we ever enjoy having change forced upon us? It may seem strange to refer to a two-night stop-over in a comfortable hotel as a life-altering experience, but I genuinely felt I would never be quite the same again. I was either going to have to rise to the challenges of the fast lane, or retreat not even to London, but to the quieter roads of Norfolk. Leave the world of international travel and famous names that I had lusted after for so long? Go back to sitting on the press bench in the council chamber and at the magistrates' court? I would have to be mad. Feeling suddenly sleepy, but somehow triumphant, I weighed up the evidence and concluded that I was, that I had to be, able to cope with the future which had been made available to me. There could be no turning back. And as the pillow welcomed my head, a strangely familiar voice rang in my head. 'Why, Mr Jackson!' it said encouragingly. 'What-a-transformation!'

5

The swinging London scene, newspaper reports of which had so entranced me as a child, had been centred on London's Carnaby Street. Some twenty years after the show had moved on elsewhere, I had found myself walking its length in search of the *NME* offices, then situated above a noisy, glittery street-fashion and souvenir shop. Once inside, I was accused instantly of being an estate agent by the skinhead Swells, contributor to the paper and part-time ranting poet. 'Ey up,' he'd exclaimed, shocked to walk in from the gents and find someone who was not only wearing a suit, but was also actually answering a telephone, rather than allowing it to ring indefinitely. 'I've got a bone to pick. The state of those bogs is bloody appalling. You should be ashamed.'

I had cut a bit of an odd figure on my first day there. So steeped was I in provincial-newspaper and civil-service culture that, for at least two years after leaving it behind, I couldn't leave the house on a weekday morning without a tie around my neck. And though such a dull, conventional personal style was at odds with the way my new colleagues dressed – some didn't care about clothes at all, but others cared deeply, affecting highly individual looks that included Goth, designer-casual and pretend heroin-chic – I hadn't the confidence to reinvent myself with a whole new working wardrobe. How would I know who to be, for a start? Far safer to look like someone you could harangue about a dysfunctional flushing system.

Thus attired, I began the process of assimilating myself into the culture of a paper I'd been reading for over half my life. It wasn't easy, and not just because of how I dressed. Any new boss creates a climate of unease, intentionally or otherwise. So far, the jury was out on Ian. While his staff waited to make up their minds about him, and he about them, along came me, not just his first appointee, but also his friend. Not good. We'd anticipated this, of course, and had agreed that I might be accepted most easily if I were introduced in some particularly appealing capacity. Not quite as the toilet-unblocker, but almost. Although employed as chief feature writer and also put in charge of the opening bits-and-pieces magazine section, Thrills, I would also be the lowest of the low: live reviews editor.

It was a job no-one wanted. You had to talk to a hundred press officers a week, all desperate to get their artists reviewed in a paper highly influential in its sphere. A further hundred or more unsigned acts pursued you, too, with news of gigs happening – usually on that same night – at youth clubs, pubs and clubs all over the country. Daily you would hear variations on the theme, 'If you wanna hear a band that's really cooking, get yourself down to the Dying Stoat tonight at ten.' No matter that the Stoat was somewhere near Carlisle, you were in central London and it was already 5 p.m. 'If you get a train now, you'll make it with time to spare,' one lead guitarist pleaded with me, early into my tenure. 'My mum says she'll cook some tea for you, 'cos you're bound to be hungry from the journey and there'll be nowhere left open by the time we get off stage.' Did I go? I didn't, although the offer of a home-cooked meal was no small temptation.

Groups, their PRs, their managers, their fans, their mothers – all of them called the reviews desk. Not to mention all the wannabe-reviewers calling from sad places like, er, Norfolk, who, because of my provincial background, I felt it was my duty to offer advice to and encourage. All in all, being editor of this particular section was not unlike being the man at the other end of a telephone helpline: I cared, I counselled, I adopted a non-threatening, non-judgemental speaking voice. Even so, I was more than glad to be there, and keen to give it my very best shot. Which was why, having introduced myself to all of the regular freelances who drifted in and out of the office to collect their pay cheques, mail and simply to shoot the breeze, I began ringing round my inherited list of provincial stringers.

'Hi! Alan Jackson here. I've just taken over on the live reviews desk here at the *NME*. I wanted both to introduce myself and to find out a little bit about you and the sort of stuff you're interested in covering for us.' This little open-ing speech worked well enough when I dialled Edinburgh, Glasgow, Manchester, Birmingham, Cardiff, Bristol, Brighton and Norwich. But a city somewhere in the middle of them all . . .

''Ello?' said a suspicious voice. I took a deep breath and began my introduction. Freelance From Hell, the charmer, interrupted. 'New live reviews editor! No-one told me the job was going. And I've never even heard of you, so how come it's you that's got it? Fucking hell. I'm gobsmacked!'

So was I and, on putting down the receiver a couple of minutes later, scratched my head in wonderment. But at the very moment I turned and looked for a colleague to repeat the exchange to, my phone rang again.

'Hello, Alan Jackson speaking, live reviews editor—'

'I don't care what your name is or what you do. You're a cunt!'

'Sorry? Who is this? And why am I a—'

'Cunt? Because of this review in today's paper. "Marc Almond is the Dorothy Squires of rock," it finishes up. Well, this is Stevo, his manager, and you're a total—'

'Yes, yes. But I didn't write it. I didn't even commission it. I only took over here yesterday and—'

'I don't fucking care. All I care about is letting you know that you're a cunt. Now fuck off!'

Crash! He'd put the receiver down, so I did, too. Sinking back onto my chair, I reran the two conversations I'd just had, and tried to assess their implications for my future. Was this how it was going to be? So OK, I had escaped both local-newspaper journalism and the unfragrant backwaters of the civil service, but instead of doing so in order to rub shoulders with pop's glitterati, it looked as if it might just be to field abuse from their representatives and those who wished to write about them.

In fact, the Freelance From Hell and Stevo had done me a kind of favour, indirectly: they had won me some sympathy among my new colleagues. There were spirited denunciations of both from various quarters, and then, almost as an after-thought, a casual invitation to join the straggling line of writers heading out for an early lunch. Delighted at being included, I got my coat. And it wouldn't take me long to realize that these outings, to any one of a small number of favoured Italian eateries, were as vital to the smooth running of the *NME* as its official Tuesday morning meetings.

Once the topic of football had been dispensed with – this took some considerable time and I, having nothing to contribute, remained mute throughout – the real business of the paper would come up for discussion. Like all music titles, we received a daily avalanche of product from the record companies. And of this generous daily postbag, the most important items were the advance tapes, sent out to specific journalists, of forthcoming releases by their artists, whether long established or as yet unheard of. These cassettes were essential to the shaping of future issues of the paper, and provided endless opportunity for debate. Who had received and listened to what? Was the new Prince LP seminal, average or disappointing? And what about the Style Council's latest? Which was to be the next breakthrough indie band or imported dance act? Or, as was the subject under discussion on one of my early ventures into caff society, who would be the next soap-star-turned-pop-hopeful to follow in the footsteps of Jason Donovan and Kylie Minogue?

'You live in Islington, don't you?' remarked Danny, the deputy editor, a forkful of spaghetti vongole in hand. I did, Christine and I having recently moved from Notting Hill Gate to a first-ever home of our own, a tiny two-bedroom flat. 'Well, one of your neighbours is putting out a single.' It was the theme tune to a forthcoming TV programme and, though irredeemably naff, was highly likely to be a hit. 'Maybe there's a Thrills piece in it,' he continued. 'What do you think?'

The actress Su Pollard is best known to most of us as Peggy, dizzy chalet maid at a 1950s holiday camp in the BBC's sitcom *Hi-De-Hi!* To Danny's Irish mum, another Islingtonian, she was better known as a fellow worshipper at the local Catholic church. I didn't know this, my faith having lapsed to the extent that I hadn't even been there. I was aware that she lived near by, however. Each morning, on my way to work, I would call at Patel's Convenience Store and Newsagent, only a zebra crossing away from my front door, to buy a paper. And, frequently, Miss Pollard would be there, too.

Dressed in one or other of a series of velour jogging suits, and with toning plastic bows or grips in her hair, she would delight whichever other customers were in the shop by rushing to and fro amid the cartons of milk, boxes of Mr Kipling cakes and rolls of black bin liners, assembling her intended purchases. Mr Patel and the rest of his clientele seemed to adore her.

'Sure,' I told Danny, remembering the not-so-far-off Yarmouth days when I was grateful even to profile old Freddie Hiller or the mayor's wife. 'Of course I'll talk to her. Just tell me who I need to call.'

At the time of the release of the song 'Starting Together', its title that of a prototype docusoap about the institution of marriage, Su was starring in a West End production of the stage musical *Me And My Girl*. I met her in her dressing room above the Strand on a Wednesday afternoon, in between her matinée and evening performances. 'Ooh, I'm knackered, me,' she said cheerfully, inviting me to sit on a low chair opposite the day bed onto which she threw herself. Clearly, it was to be an informal meeting, she newly off-stage, barefoot and wrapped in a belted trenchcoat, me keen but nervous in the face of her stream-of-consciousness chat. And so I sat back and prepared to drink in her observations, about the musical, the single, whatever.

As she talked, the hyperactive Su folded and unfolded her legs repeatedly, rather in the style of the late Kenny Everett's comic invention Cupid Stunt. Sitting those few crucial inches below her, I soon came to feel that I was getting to know the actress more intimately than was absolutely necessary for a short article in the Thrills section. 'You've been very generous with your time,' I said, struggling to my feet after several minutes of looking at the ceiling, the walls and anywhere else but the pair of legs directly in front of me. 'I think I've got everything I need now. Thanks very much indeed.'

'Don't need any biographical info? I suppose not,' said Su, as I slunk towards the door. 'Everybody knows that I come from Nottingham and that I got beaten by a singing dog on a talent show.' I stopped short, turned round and reluctantly returned to my seat. I didn't know these two basic facts, but clearly I should.

'Well, love,' she began, in her breathy, confiding way. 'It was a big deal for me, and I'd got on this lovely velvet maxi-skirt from M&S. I did "I'm Just A Girl Who Can't Say No", and I seemed to go down really, really well. But who was I up against other than this guy and his incredible singing Jack Russell? I didn't stand a chance. His big number was "Oh, What A Beautiful Morning," and every time he'd get to the bridge, the dog would go, "Ah-oooh!" A technician said afterwards they'd only won because the bloke had his finger up the dog's bum to make it sing . . .'

A couple of Mondays after the piece was published, Danny entered the office with a mischievous smile and headed straight towards my desk. 'Best thing you've written for us so far, that Su Pollard piece,' he said. 'It's just a shame she doesn't think so. My mum saw her at church yesterday and said she's livid about it. Claims that she was grossly misrepresented and that the next time she catches you in Mr Patel's . . .'

My phone was ringing. It was Christine. 'Yeah, yeah,' I interrupted, barely hearing whatever it was she had to say to me. 'Meanwhile, I think it's time we moved to a different part of London.'

On my return from the trip to meet Joni Mitchell, Danny had asked how my time in Los Angeles had been. 'There were just so many famous people at the reception I went to,' I reported, before launching into a list of all the household names. 'Oh, and Sheena Easton was there, too,' I concluded, suspecting she was hardly the kind of artist to inflame passions at the *NME*. 'Actually, I mistook her for somebody I knew and asked what she was doing there. She was really nice about it. Seemed to think it was funny. Then she got whisked off because Joni wanted to talk to her.'

'You met Sheena Easton and you didn't ask her for an interview?' Danny was incredulous. Clearly, the Glasgow drama student turned pop singer turned Transatlantic temptress had a status with him that I hadn't anticipated.

'Well, yes. Did we want one?'

'We've been requesting an interview for about a year now and keep getting blanked. You know she's been working with Prince, don't you? And that her new album is going to be produced by Nile Rogers. We'd love to talk to Sheena Easton. I can't believe you didn't ask her.'

Tail between my legs, I went back to my desk. Not for the first time, I realized I didn't yet have the lie of the land. At those Tuesday morning meetings, artists whom I imagined everyone would judge worthy of interview were regularly dismissed as yesterday's news. Similarly, the mere mention of others so mainstream that my mum might have heard of them could cause excitement . . . because they had ironic appeal, were ripe for revisionist critique, were redefining their image by collaborating with younger, hipper talents, whatever. Sheena, it seemed, fell into this category. I determined to redeem myself in Danny's eyes by somehow getting that interview.

The PR responsible for her British releases had good and bad news. Yes, the new LP was imminent and she would be coming to the UK to promote it – the very next week, in fact. But no, I couldn't talk to her. Sheena and the *NME* were incompatible. She'd had a mauling from the paper in the recent past and, not being a masochist, wouldn't be in a hurry to recreate the experience. Sorry, but there it was.

I brooded on this for a day or two, then tried again. 'I met Sheena the other week in LA, at a party for Joni Mitchell,' I began this time, instantly amazed at how easily the sentence slipped off my tongue. 'She seemed very friendly. Are you sure you couldn't just ask if she'll talk to me?' The PR sighed heavily, but listened as I explained that Sheena was a huge fan of Joni's, and that she might be interested in reading a copy of my interview with her heroine. If I got it round to EMI with a covering letter, would they at least promise to pass it on?

There was a further heavy sigh, to make me doubly aware that I was being a nuisance. However, I was a nuisance who might just be indulged. 'I suppose so, but it probably won't do any good,' I was warned. 'She's someone who never, ever goes back on her word, and I know she's sworn not to deal with the *NME* again.' Even so, I dropped an envelope in at EMI's reception desk and, on the very day the singer arrived in London, was rewarded with a phone call. 'I don't know what you put in that letter, but she's said yes, she'll see you,' the PR told me. 'No-one here can believe it, but anyway. Tomorrow morning at eleven. The Meridien Hotel in Piccadilly.'

I dressed with care the following day. I didn't own any tartan, but I did have what I believed to be the next best thing. 'I've put this on especially for you,' I said, drawing attention to — perhaps handing out a pair of sunglasses would have been the kinder option — my loudly checked purple and blue sports jacket, recently bought in Liberty. 'If you think that's remotely Scottish, you must be on drugs.' She grinned, raising a hand to shield her eyes. Encouraged, I set about my business with a bland remark about how difficult it was for a mainstream artist, particularly a female one, to escape stereotyping. Even when you repositioned yourself in the marketplace, as she'd clearly done, it could be just a case of exchanging one stereotype for another, and—

'That's something I've had to face since I first came into this business and opened up a newspaper,' the star responded hotly. 'People say to me, "Sheena, define yourself. What are you?" I say, "I'm a pop singer. You can tell me what I am when I read the article tomorrow." That's the media. It's, "Let's categorize people. Let's put them in this box. And now, let's move them into that box." It's, "So, Sting, you've gone from being a rock artist to being a jazz artist, have you?" I can see the look on his face right now.'

Shuffling uncomfortably in my seat, I acknowledged yet again what I'd realized was my professional weakness. From the very first time I'd talked to a fake Anytown council representative in that Cardiff classroom, I had wanted the people I was interviewing to like me. Worse still, if I really liked the person I was interviewing — as I liked Sheena — then I really,

really wanted them to like me. And yet here she was, getting heated up beneath her mock-ocelot waistcoat, her dark eyes appraising me with what seemed to be withering contempt.

'I don't even try to defend myself against that kind of thinking any more. I don't waste my breath,' she continued. 'Whatever you see me as, that's what I am to you. I know what I am to me, and that's a multi-faceted artist. To me, I'm not a stereotype of anything, other than that I'm a female pop singer. I don't know. Is that a stereotype? Well, you're a male journalist. That must be a stereotype, too!'

And so it went on for the remainder of the hour. God, I thought, leaping to my feet the moment the PR entered the room to say my time was up, she really hates me. Which is why I blanched the moment Sheena was asked the inevitable question: 'So, how did it go?'

'Great,' she replied. 'I really enjoyed it, which is something I never say about interviews. Some good questions. One or two dumb ones, too. It was fun.'

Then she turned and shook my hand. 'And I really enjoyed your piece on Joni, too. Thanks for getting it to me. I hope we meet again sometime.'

I exited the hotel's revolving doors feeling confused but ten feet tall. I was still feeling enervated when coincidence had me walk back through them just days later, this time to interview the former Eagles drummer, Don Henley, by then established with a successful solo career. On entering his suite, I found him sprawled across a deeply upholstered sofa, feet crossed and resting on an occasional table. At once, I was struck by the fact that he was wearing sheepskin moccasins. They were a rock 'n' roll substitute for carpet slippers, I assumed, for standing empty on the floor near by was a particularly fine pair of cowboy boots, their leather the rich mahogany colour of a newly fallen conker. I had grown up in the pre-trainer age, when a new pair of slippers was something you could very well expect to be given on Christmas morning. I'd hated the very idea of them. If an unexpected visitor came to the house when I was wearing them, I'd rush to change into my outdoor shoes or, if that was impossible, would determinedly hide my feet from view. Slippers seemed to me silly and unmanly; they put you at a disadvantage with the world. And that Don, too, was not entirely at ease in such comfortable footwear was made clear the moment an apologetic PR put her head round the door and announced that she needed to borrow him for a brief photo session.

Instantly, he looked at his feet and then at the magnificent, ludicrous pair of cowboy boots that stood to attention close by. And for the briefest moment, indecision was written all across his blandly handsome face.

'Full–length or portrait?' he demanded.

'Portrait, definitely,' she replied.

Thus reassured, the singer padded out of the room in his moccasins, pausing at the door only to bid me to help myself to a drink while he was away. 'So sorry,' smoothed the PR. 'I'll have him back to you in just a few minutes.'

From amid a small armoury of bottles, I extracted some mineral water. I sat. I sipped. I looked at my watch. At least half a minute had passed. I sat some more, mentally reviewing my list of questions, then flicked through the pages of a nearby directory of the world's most luxurious hotels. Another look at the watch. A further ninety seconds had been used up. And all the time they sat there like magnets, exerting a strange, seductive power over me – those totally foolish, totally fascinating cowboy boots, chestnut–hued and smug.

I twitched. I scratched my head. I crossed the room to the

window and peered out through the fog of thick net drapes. And eventually, with a covert look at the door, I succumbed to temptation and walked back towards them. Yes, I had been correct! By placing a foot next to the right boot, I was able to confirm my suspicion that Don and I were approximately the same shoe size – the same cowboy-boot size! Scooting back to my seat, I tried to reject the obvious next question, but found myself powerless to do so. How would it feel to actually wear them?

The angel on my right shoulder was insistent: it would be madness; the singer might reappear at any moment. How would he react if he found his splendid, beloved boots gracing his interviewer's feet, and my own wholly unremarkable pair of shoes sitting neatly, vacantly, in their place? Did I think he wouldn't notice? Did I think he might say, 'Hey, great swap, man! I'd been admiring those Saxone lace-ups from the moment you walked in the room. Now I'll get to see what it's like to actually wear 'em. Neat!'

The devil on my left shoulder was silkily persuasive, though: Go on, do it, he urged. You'll never have the chance again. What's the very worst that can happen? Who cares if you get caught?

Groggy with desire, I searched for a compromise. Perhaps I could just slide one empty boot inside the bottom of my trouser leg? That way, I'd get a sense of how they might look, but without actually taking my own shoe off and putting a foot inside. It seemed a workable solution. True, I'd looked a little like Rolf Harris performing 'Jake the Peg', but so what?

At which point, the door opened and Don re-entered the room. He found me rooted to my chair, hands clasping its arms for dear life, ostensibly the picture of innocence, yet feeling as guilty as if I had not just his boots on my feet, but his wallet in my pocket. Resuming his former position on the sofa, he swung his moccasins back up onto the table and asked cheerily, 'So, had a good root around in my luggage while I was gone, did you? I know what you British journos are like. If anything's missing, you'll be my number-one suspect, OK?'

'Yeah, OK,' I replied, grinning weakly. 'Amazing boots, by the way. Just my size. I've been dancing around in them while you've been off having your photo taken. If you'd come back thirty seconds earlier, you'd have caught me still wearing them.'

'Like, right, sure,' said Don, grinning. 'Or you thought you'd maybe try and steal them from me, leaving your own shoes in their place. Hey, you're one funny guy.'

The great thing about working for a national title, I soon discovered, is that it gives you potential access to almost anyone it's your heart's desire to meet. Well, not quite anyone: I knew better than to suggest a critical reappraisal of Petula Clark. I also learned that, as in the manner of Sheena Easton, there was a small army of established mainstream stars – Peter Gabriel, Annie Lennox and Sting among them – who were reluctant, unwilling or, in some cases, simply wise enough not to want to talk to a paper that had roughed them up in the past. I could only pick up such information as I went along. Meanwhile, I found it wonderfully invigorating to pick up the phone, ask to meet with whoever, and actually stand a chance of doing so. Not that anyone seemed able to understand why I'd want to meet Angela Bofill or Phyllis Hyman. No-one else seemed to even know who they were.

Some weeks after my arrival there, the *NME* was pitched into a state of blissfully contented head-scratching by Danny's decision to poll his writers on the one hundred best albums of all time. This provided a heaven-sent task for a group of people who took their role as arbiters of taste with total seriousness. For a week or more, the atmosphere in the office was so intense that a visitor might have imagined we were each labouring over our last will and testament. I was flattered even to be given a form to fill in, and duly chewed my pen top while deliberating as to whether *Kind Of Blue* by Miles Davis should rank above the early Smiths releases, and how many of Joni Mitchell's albums I should place in my personal Top 10. But in amongst this list of fairly un-controversial names were two others, those of Angela and Phyllis.

'Never heard of them,' was a widespread response. 'You're joking?' was that of those who had. Not that the two women weren't great singers. Bofill's lower- and middle-range voice has an astringent edge to it, while her upper register is beauti-fully sweet and clear. Hyman's, meanwhile, was smoky and smooth. Both had learned from the interpretative skills of the great female jazz vocalists. But both were also signed to Arista, the label founded and run by a legendary figure in the American recording industry, Clive Davis. His reputation was that of a controlling figure, someone who decided what direction an artist should take – around this time, he was preparing to launch Whitney Houston – and pushed them that way relentlessly. He had decided that Angela and Phyllis were not jazz or R & B singers, but glossy soul divas. As a result, their Arista releases comprised either splashy ballads or formulaic dance tracks. Both would end up parting company with the label before the decade was out.

The rest of the *NME* was quite right to judge them unworthy of inclusion in any Top 100, let alone a Top 10. Great voices, certainly. But the records in question were, I realize now, only average. Even I haven't played them in years. That I ranked them so highly on my list only confirmed the general suspicion that the mate imported by editor Ian had seriously dodgy taste. Only Cath, a freelance who would go on to make her own LP for Factory Records, had let the side down more spectacularly – though at least she had humour on her side. Her nomination for the greatest album in the history of pop was the double-album vinyl accompaniment to the first of Jane Fonda's aerobic workouts. As I was to discover in time, this was an LP that these two particular singing heroines of mine would have done well to introduce into their own collections.

I admit that I'd bought my first Angela Bofill LP for no other reason than that she looked so beautiful on its cover. Happily, I found that I liked the record, too, and that I loved her voice. Whenever I came across the cover of *Something About You* while looking for something else, I would pause momentarily to admire again the slender neck, proud cheek-bones and vast, imperious eyes. Cuban-American, she looked like some latter-day Carmen; for months after buying the album in Norfolk, I'd kept its cover propped up on my desk. Over the course of subsequent releases, however, I noticed that line drawings of the singer's face or, in one case, a picture so soft focus that it appeared to have been taken in a Victorian pea-souper, had become the norm. I wasn't suspicious. I fondly imagined Angela to be the same slight, haughty beauty I'd first fallen in love with. But I was wrong.

Exactly how wrong was only made clear to me when the singer made her first-ever appearance in Britain some months later. Learning that she was to perform at London's Hammersmith Apollo as part of a jazz-fusion bill, I entered a state of high excitement. Not only could I go and hear her sing, but I could commission myself to interview her for the Thrills section, too – the stuff of dreams in Norfolk was now about to become true. Just a phone call or two and I could arrange to be in the very same room as the lovely Angela. I felt enormously happy.

The singer's record-company PR, on confirming the details for our rendezvous, mentioned that it would be the first time her charge had travelled abroad since starting a family. Naturally, it would be a wrench, she said. But the child was now two, apparently, and thus old enough to be left with its father for a few days. I found myself thinking of this as I drove towards Hammersmith the following afternoon, and so I made a detour to find a toy shop. Aware that I was probably being silly, but enjoying myself all the same, I chose a chunky little train set, with an engine and succession of linked carriages hand-carved out of blond wood. I imagined myself giving it to her with a little speech about how much her music had meant to me, and how I'd bought this present for her son as a token of thanks. I imagined her smiling in response, and grinned to myself in the traffic as I did so.

'Angela's on good form,' said the PR, guiding me through the hotel lobby and into the restaurant, where the singer was grabbing a quick bite. 'A little tired from the flight, and missing her daughter like mad, but otherwise fine. And she's a complete darling. You'll love her.'

Before I had time to register my mistake, I saw a roly-poly woman in a fuchsia-pink pants suit push back her chair and rise to her feet, all the while dabbing at the corners of her mouth with a napkin.

'Alan, Angela. Angela, Alan,' said the PR. 'Now, I'll just leave you to talk. Back in forty minutes or so. Anything you want to eat or drink, just add it to the tab.'

'You wanna order something, babe?' asked the goddess from the sleeve of *Something About You*, falling heavily back into her seat and looking daggers at the barely touched bowl of salad before her. 'The burgers look pretty good. I'm desperate for one myself, but . . .' She gestured with a plump, pink-nailed hand at her silk-upholstered frame and raised two despairing eyebrows. 'I'm on rabbit food morning, noon and night, trying to lose this weight. I so don't wanna spend the rest of my life as Big Mama Blues. It doesn't seem to be working, though, does it? On second thoughts, don't have a burger. I don't think I could bear to sit here and watch you eat it.'

Though initially surprised to find her once, twice, almost three times the lady I'd been expecting, I enjoyed our meeting more than I could have hoped. I even confessed to the mistake I had made, delivering my awkward little speech and pushing the train set into her hands in spite of it. 'But she'll just love this!' exclaimed Angela, rising again, this time to envelop me in her warm, fragrant embrace. 'She's not some prissy little missy, my daughter. She'll have a ball throwing this around and about. Thank you! If I'd've known that coming over here meant having nice young Englishmen making puppy-dog eyes and giving you train sets, I wouldn't have left it so long. You sure you're not hungry? Now, did I tell you my husband's into organic farming? We've got this place outside Los Angeles and . . .'

I left the hotel dazed but happy, with the singer's parting message ringing in my ears. 'Remember, always be careful in the fresh-produce section. Our vegetables are being zapped by gamma rays!' And she was wonderful on stage at Hammersmith that night; I imagine she's as wonderful now. Certainly, she seems to be as big. I know this because a good friend, Len, was in New York recently and, leafing through the *Village Voice*, found an advert for a concert she was doing there. Floating above the usual details of place, time, date and ticketing was the balloon-like head of a woman, Angela, looking as if it had just burst free from some off-camera bicycle pump. 'Shoehorned into another venue . . . !' he had written in the margin. Fondly, I pinned the cutting to the wall above my desk where it, and not the cover of *Something About You*, remains today.

And Phyllis? I met her not too long afterwards, and this time saw the goddess of her album-cover shots being built up from scratch, before my very eyes. For the woman who greeted me in her dressing room at the very same Hammersmith theatre was not the luxuriant-haired, painted and begowned creature I had seen on television, or who had starred on Broadway in the Duke Ellington review *Sophisticated Ladies*. Instead, she was a Gauguinesque work in progress. Over six feet tall in her bare feet, and wearing an old towelling robe, she crunched my right hand in hers while running her left across the close-cropped top of her skull. 'I'm behind schedule, hon,' she said, directing me to a seat. 'You ask away, I'll answer. But in between, I gotta get busy with the paintbrush.'

At which she disappeared behind the pink plastic hand mirror she'd extracted from within a multi-drawed make-up box on the floor beside her. It was to this, and the big, spatulate fingers grasping it lollipop-style, that I addressed my questions. In turn, she replied from behind it, her other hand moving constantly across the canvas of her face, smoothing on foundation, painting in cheekbones and lips, blotting and highlighting, gluing on lashes and teasing them out with mascara. The only time she dropped her little shield, enabling me to meet her newly vast, exaggerated eyes, was when I mentioned Clive Davis, her former label boss. 'I don't like to hear that name,' she said, suddenly fierce, making as if to spit contemptuously on the carpet. 'We had a falling out about who Phyllis Hyman is and what kind of records she should make. Now, pass me that box over there, could you? We're almost there.'

From within it, she produced a wig, then turned her back to me. 'I'd give it a saucer of milk if there was time, but it's gotta go straight onto my head,' she said, pressing it down against her temples with the palms of her hands. '*Voila!*' She turned again in my direction, hands on hips, her glossy lips moving in a parody of seduction, waves of synthetic hair spreading across the towelling of her shoulders. 'Kinda more like what you were expecting, I guess, heh?'

Because I couldn't think of anything better to do or say, I gave a little round of applause. She made a regal gesture of acceptance with one hand, grabbed my shoulder and swivelled me round to face the door with the other. 'Now, the interview's over,' she said, propelling me firmly towards it. 'I gotta stick my nails on and get dressed. So, enjoy the show, and just make very sure you've got your superlatives down and dusted. When I see you at dinner afterwards, I expect to hear how totally, unbelievably fabulous I was. Or else. You got me?'

I had. But it was all right, because she was. And she not only looked a million dollars, but a million miles high, too, stalking about the stage in vertiginous shoes, a long, milky slither of a gown and a matching bishop's mitre of a hat. All of which she was still wearing when, close to midnight at Julie's, off Holland Park, she made an entrance compromised only by the celebrated basement restaurant's necessarily low ceilings. 'I want him sitting next to me, here,' she ordered, pointing at me and causing instant revision of the seating arrangements made by her new label, EMI, our hosts for the evening. Meekly, I changed seats with a red-faced record-company executive, and at once had thrust upon me the floor-length cream cashmere coat she'd travelled in. It felt twice as tall as me, and as rich and sinful as if it belonged to Cruella De Vil. 'So,' said Phyllis, running a false nail across my cheek, as I struggled to stow its bulk on a vacant chair. 'How wonderful was I? Just utterly and completely to die for, or can you come up with something more poetic?'

It's the custom, whenever an artist arrives in an overseas territory for TV appearances, concerts or other forms of promotion, for such a dinner to be held in their honour. The venues will range from expensive to astronomically expensive, depending on the selling-power of that artist. And the guest list will include their manager and key members of their entourage, senior executives from the label itself and, if there's still room, known fans within the media – myself, in this instance. Normally, they are stilted, awkward affairs, regarded as a chore by all parties. Perhaps this was entirely the same. The only thing that makes me think otherwise is that Phyllis herself was the life and soul, touching everybody with her energy and spirit. 'And you've all got to have your picture taken with me, individually,' she insisted, when a photographer arrived to record the occasion for the trade papers.

When it was my turn to pose for his camera, I leaned in awkwardly beside her chair, Kermit entering the court of Miss Piggy. Phyllis responded by snaking a hand around my neck and forcing my cheek hard against her own. 'Smile, hon,' she purred, posing professionally herself. 'Now, about this piece you're writing. It'd better be nice. Otherwise, I'll be back to break your fuckin' legs. OK?'

She was joking. She must have been, for the sad fact was that I never wrote up the interview: there was no space for it in the paper, and no real interest there beyond my own. From time to time, though, I would wonder whatever happened to Phyllis and pull one of her old albums out and play it. There was the occasional, subsequent LP release for smaller American labels, and then nothing. I had heard no news of her in years until the day that, nearly a decade later, Christine and I found ourselves waiting at Antigua's airport, on our way to a holiday on nearby Nevis. Having exhausted what reading material we had left London with, I went in search of something new. At a news-stand on the tiny concourse, and despite initially baulking at its exalted price, I bought a two-week-old issue of the American magazine *People*. It was midway through our island-hopping flight that I reached its equivalent of a births, marriages and deaths page. And there it was, in black-and-white.

Aged forty-five, and on the eve of a comeback performance at Harlem's famed Apollo Theater, Phyllis Hyman had been found dead in her Manhattan apartment. The assumed cause was suicide. I felt sick. Not because of the jilting, lurching cigar tube in which we were travelling. Because of the fact that, in my mind, she would live forever as the half-joking, semi-threatening, self-assembled creature I had met that day. The one who was part cover image, part reality, and who sang so beautifully. Didn't she know that out there, somewhere, were people who loved her, whose lives she had touched? Had we all been too busy, or looking the other way, when she needed us? We had. We had let her down.

It was a prior arrangement within my travel plans that I would return via New York to interview Whitney Houston. She was still busy with a Japanese film crew when I arrived at the hotel floor seconded for her promotional duties, and so I settled in to wait among members of her staff in a nearby room. Among them were the female aide who was running the record label Whitney had newly set up, and one of its signings, a then-fifteen-year-old girl singer. We chit-chatted about this and that – recent records we liked, who we'd seen in concert. And then, because we were talking specifically about black music, I mentioned my sadness at Phyllis's death.

'A great loss,' the aide agreed, extracting a perfect strawberry from amid an enormous plate of fresh fruit. Then, to the teenager, she added, 'Are you listening to what we're saying?'

Bored, the girl looked up, unsure of what it was that she'd missed. The statement was then repeated for her benefit. 'Phyllis Hyman was a great singer who died way too young. A wonderful talent. We should all mourn her passing.'

Swallowing the strawberry, Whitney's assistant stood up. 'You know?' she observed to me, in a detached, gossipy tone, 'I heard that she'd gotten so fat she couldn't even bend down to tie her own shoelaces.' So saying, she allowed herself a reassuring glance down at her own perfect waistline and sent the fingers of her right hand flickering elegantly out across the display of food. They returned, empty, to her side. There was nothing there to tempt her. The girl, meanwhile, continued to stare blankly at the floor.

My phone rang again the second I'd fended off the previous call, as it so often does. Be polite but firm, I said to myself. Polite but firm. And then, 'I'm sorry. Even if it is urgent, I can't talk to you now. I should have left for an interview ten minutes ago. I'll call you tomorrow.'

'So, who're you on your way to see, then?' demanded my scourge, FFH, or the Freelance From Hell.

'Dusty Springfield. She's making a sort of comeback. There's a new single and she's doing her first interviews in ages and—'

'On the cutting edge, as always, I see. I don't know how it is that some people just waltz in and start writing features, when others of us . . . Anyway, never mind that. And never mind tomorrow, either. Call as soon as you're back. There's something important I want to tell you.'

In a cab heading north, and much as it pained me to do so, I found myself wondering if West Yorkshire's own Henry Kissinger might not actually be right to express cynicism about the wondrous Dusty's newsworthiness. After all, though an icon of the British showbusiness scene, it had been a good fifteen years since she'd had a major hit. In purely commercial terms, she was history. In another couple of years, the Pet Shop Boys would rescue her from oblivion and put her back up in the charts, but I had no way of knowing that then. Even so, I decided no, his viewpoint didn't bear consideration. And to distract myself from it, I thought instead about assertiveness-training courses, and whether I'd ever be able to overcome my background and nature sufficiently to tell the awful FFH simply to take a hike. Thus absorbed, I forgot to worry about the passage of time until we pulled up outside a small mews house close to Regent's Park. Normally early for any appointment, I was now fifteen minutes late.

The woman PR who opened the door to me was dressed head to toe in black and wearing dark glasses, even though it was an overcast day, and inside all the curtains were drawn. 'Don't worry. We're running late anyway,' she said, staunching my flow of apologies and drawing urgently on a cigarette. 'Dusty's still upstairs getting ready. Make yourself comfortable. I'm sure she'll be down before too long. At least, I hope she will be.'

I sat in the peachy sunset of a small room which had been lamplit to compensate for the lack of daylight. And sat and sat and sat. Above me, intermittently, I heard restless footsteps moving back and forth across a bedroom floor. The PR, re-entering the room every now and then to flash me an apologetic smile, seemed increasingly on edge, despite her carefully cultivated Snow-White-skin-and-scarlet-lipsticked brand of Soho cool. Counting the blooms on the flowered curtains for the umpteenth time, I felt my enthusiasm and expectancy dribble away to nothing. I had been waiting for nearly an hour. Up above, there was only silence. And a man-mountain of a photographer from a Sunday tabloid – the publication scheduled to interview Dusty after me – had just arrived. The room seemed too small to hold us all, he laden as he was with assorted bags and cases of equipment.

Suddenly there came a small, apologetic cough from the doorway of the room. There, silhouetted against the hall light, was the singer herself, hands holding something to her breast. 'I'm so terribly sorry to have kept everyone waiting for so long,' she began, adding vaguely, 'Jet lag . . .' Then she stepped into the room and held out for us to see the two tiny kittens she'd been cradling. 'Aren't they beautiful, the darling babies?'

I was happy to agree that the photographs be taken first. That way, what might be a tense interview could unfold without the additional handicap of a looming figure sitting next door, but still in earshot, sighing loudly each time he looked at this watch. 'Pray, be gentle with the lady, for she hath had too little sleep,' said Dusty, curtsying to him in mock-medieval fashion. Standing to the side, I groaned inwardly – not for her, but for the rest of us, who were all apparently making her feel this awful pressure. Firstly, all the angst and preparation upstairs. Then not just the eventual descent with the calculated diversion of the kittens, but also the fact that she'd felt obliged to make such a total presentation of herself: the colour of the dress toning with that of the shoes, the eye shadow, the lipstick, the nail lacquer. If only she could just have walked into the room and said, 'Hello, I'm Dusty.' Didn't she realize that we knew every fantastic record she'd made, and loved her for them? Couldn't she have gained the necessary courage from that? If only life were that simple.

I don't remember what questions I started off asking. I probably didn't get far beyond grinning a lot and telling Dusty she was wonderful. What I do remember is that less than fifteen minutes into our eventual chat, the woman journalist companion of the tabloid photographer arrived. And insisted that, no, she absolutely could not be made to wait. I could have fought my corner, but felt the eventual result would be better if I didn't. An impatient photographer eavesdropping from the adjoining room would have been bad enough; to have had his journalistic sidekick there as well would have been worse. Dusty squeezed my hand and asked if I'd mind. How could I? I walked around the park for the best part of an hour, then returned to pick up the pieces of my interview.

The PR was looking more white-faced than ever. 'That went really badly,' she whispered in the hallway. 'All the usual old stuff. "Do you have a boyfriend? No? Well, how about a girlfriend? No? Well, would you like to settle the issue of your sexuality once and for all?" You know the kind of thing.' As a result, Dusty herself had further disintegrated into an unhappy-looking mismatch of party clothes, teased and lacquered hair and frayed nerves. 'I'm sorry,' she announced not long after we'd sat down together again. 'I'd forgotten quite how unhappy an experience it could be, meeting the Great British Press. Not you, love. But I'm feeling really tired right now, and while I know I've wasted your afternoon, if you wouldn't mind so very much . . .'

A minute later, I was walking towards Camden Town, without a printable interview, and with a heavy heart instead. My first professional encounter with someone who had been famous for as long as I'd been cognizant, and I'd blown it. Not only that. I had left the woman whose hit records had played on the radio throughout my early childhood looking hollow, unhappy and as vulnerable as a child. The very same woman who had sung 'Goin' Back' and 'The Look Of Love' and 'How Can I Be Sure' so perfectly. The woman who had recorded the sublime *Dusty In Memphis* album. This wasn't how I'd imagined things at all.

The central London streets were dark and full of the homeward-bound by the time I reached the office. Climbing the stairs, I gave myself a quick talking to: You're lucky to be here. Lucky to have the opportunity to meet these people, even if it doesn't always go as planned. It's what you've said you've always wanted. All of which was true. So, arriving back at my desk and looking at the long list of calls to be returned, I decided to signal my gratitude by tackling the worst one first. I duly dialled the necessary number and asked, 'So, what was that important news, then?'

I played diplomat. Devil's advocate. I tried persuasion – 'I know I can guarantee you more work if you stay where you are,' – flattery – 'It's so important to us to have someone we value up in Yorkshire,' – and veiled threats – 'We're over-run with freelances down here, and you'll have thrown away your unique selling point,' – all to no avail. Eventually, I replaced the receiver and announced my news to what was left of the office.

'Honestly, I've tried to talk him out of it, but he's dead set on it. Our Freelance From Hell is moving to London.'

6

The estate was the size of a public park, and climbed by means of a series of terraces to meet the lower slopes of the uncultivated, scrub-covered hillside above. Sited on it were two low-rise but still-imposing homes. I parked as I'd been told to, outside the upper one, a U-shaped building with large picture windows. And it was there, with the mid-morning sun pressing heavily down upon me, that I stood and waited for something to happen down at the other, lower house. In the air, a bright counterpoint to the dull hum of distant traffic, was a sound of birdsong so busy and insistent that I wondered if it might not be a taped effect. Here and there on the lawns around me, gardeners clipped or raked, moving slowly and deliberately because of the heat, their faces shielded by long-visored caps. To pass the time, and to keep my spirits up, I sang to myself an old and favourite song by the artist I was waiting to meet. 'It's ecstasy, yeah, when you're laying down ne-ext to me, ooh yeah . . .' Odd how different it sounded when delivered not in the sexually charged tones of its originator, but in the vanilla squeak of a nine-and-a-half-stone Englishman.

Presently, a broad-shouldered man emerged from under the portico below, and was ushered by a chauffeur into the white Rolls-Royce parked close by. I could see a second, smaller man, too, fussing and circling at his heels like a small dog, and climbing in a second before the driver pulled off. So began a journey which lasted, oh, all of thirty seconds. Inevitably, and as if in slow motion, the big, heavy car moved up towards me, then stopped by my side. Automatically, I stepped forward and opened the offside rear door. And Barry White, vast and imposing enough to be the head of state of a far-off country, let alone an icon of soul music, manoeuvred himself out. Somehow he managed to do so without dislodging the velvet-collared, camel cashmere overcoat that, despite the brilliant sunshine, hung from his considerable shoulders. I opened my mouth to speak, but was interrupted by the other man coming scampering around the car to where I stood, hand extended.

'Gotta be Alan from London, England!' he said, insinuating himself in between myself and the great Barry. 'Gotta know we're just so damn pleased you could meet us here. Oh, London Town. What a be-yoo-tiful place! My brother works there as a DJ, so I know it really well. Buckingham Palace! The Changing of the Guards! Harrods! Terrific! Anyway, we've got ourselves a great day here today. And the vibes are good, too. So, I kinda just know that this interview is going to go—'

There was a deep, significant cough. A Barry cough. For a brief second, the world stood still.

'Alan Jackson, from the *New Musical Express*,' I said, rallying.

'Sho'isguraseeya,' he responded, basso profundo, causing me to panic.

'Barry wants you to know that it sure is good to see you,' interpreted the smaller man, wringing his hands in Uriah Heep fashion.

'Always a pleasure,' continued the singer, in a tarmac-melting tone, and proceeding to shake my hand as if it were a pump handle and he was in need of water.

'It's very good of you to invite me here. I appreciate it.'

'Like I said, always a pleasure. England's been very kind to Barry White. And Barry White never forgets a kindness.'

With this, he shrugged off his coat and handed it to his assistant, who accepted it with a reverence more suited to handling the Turin Shroud. Then, with a majestic wave of his hand, Barry signalled his desire for the two of us to be left alone. 'My personal press adviser,' Barry rumbled in explanation, as his aide climbed reluctantly into the back of the departing Rolls. 'Gets a little excitable, but his instincts are good. Now, you wanna come inside? You wanna see where Barry White makes his music?'

I certainly did. This, it emerged, was the point to having two homes on the same site. One was for living in, the other housed a recording studio. And both, I would soon discover, had been styled and furnished a decade and a half earlier, in the early 1970s, at a time when he was enjoying his greatest commercial success. This was *Shaft*-era black chic, on a scale to make social historians drool. As I followed the singer along the hallway, past side rooms filled with musical instruments and related equipment, towards a main entertaining area, I found myself hacking through lush pastures of shagpile – chocolate brown, then olive green, then the inevitable used-to-be-creamy-white. 'And here', announced Barry, making a sweeping, proprietorial gesture, 'we have the White Room!'

It was a large, central space of polar-hued splendour, its outer wall dominated by a vast, curving picture window, which looked down across the gardens, but which, sadly, was in need of a liberal application of Windolene and elbow grease. At one end stood a white grand piano. An L-shaped sofa of airport-lounge proportions filled the rest of the floor area, its back and sides and each individual cushion form-fitted with a protective casing of polythene so hard and shiny that it reflected the giant chandelier hanging above. But when I paused to peer through the foggy glass of an ornamental fish tank, Barry placed a giant hand on my back and steered me forward. 'Here is where I really love to be,' he said, propelling me into a control room containing a mixing desk and two revolving seats. 'Here, everything is peaceful. Here, there's no hunger, no bombs, no gangs, no tricks. Here, there's nothing but pure, raw honesty.'

I gulped, sat down as bidden on one of the stools, and riffled the suddenly empty filing cabinet of my brain for an intelligent first question, some incisive opening remark. 'I really like your new record,' my ears heard my mouth saying. OK, there was a more than half-decent comeback album in the shops, but still, how banal could you get? I looked down shamefacedly and, realizing that I'd begun spinning round slowly, pointed my toes in an effort to make contact with the floor and halt my rotation.

'Sho'isgurrahearit!' said Barry, punching me on the knee in a way that set me spinning again, but faster. 'You think it's a good record? Sho' you right! I *know* it's a good record!'

I felt as if I were conducting my interview in a foreign language, one packed with unfamiliar vocabulary and strange, semi-musical cadences of speech. Soon a pattern established itself. I, through nervousness, disorientation and inexperience, would bat him easy-peasy questions about this or that. He would sigh heavily or harumph, then lean back in his seat and pontificate. And he was well qualified to do so. Having been around long enough to know that fame can ebb and flow like the tide, he had achieved a certain perspective on the vagaries of success and was only too willing to share it with the wider world.

For instance, again and again I've heard artists speak of the frustration of completing an album while being championed by one particular individual or team of record-company executives, only to find that individual or team forced out in some staff shake-up before it could be released. The incoming replacement will have little or no interest in promoting their predecessor's pet projects, and so the work will be slipped out to the public with minimal or even no promotional budget. Worse still, it might be shelved entirely, never to see the light of day. White had met the former fate after moving from the small independent label 20th Century, with whom he'd enjoyed his greatest success, to the corporate major CBS. He exhaled massively, almost setting me spinning again, when I raised the subject.

'I signed a five-year contract. It was a huge, huge deal,' he said, rubbing his immaculately manicured beard reflectively. 'But it was all just paper. It didn't mean nothing. One thing I learned was that you cannot have a hit with a major if they don't want one. There were a lot of personnel changes. The guy who signed me left just after I got there, and the new guy didn't want to work with someone else's acts. But fortunately, I'm not as emotional as some artists, because I understand this is a business like any other. Once I've made a deal – whether it's a mistake or not – I live with it. So Barry White just delivered the stuff he was contracted to deliver, and then he left.'

But surely, I ventured, it must have been immensely frustrating for someone who had already sold tens of millions of records to have his new work greeted with apathy not just by the public, but by his own record company? After all, they're the ones who are supposed to be on your side.

'Frustrating, but not that frustrating,' he thundered. 'Let me tell you, I'm a wartime general when it comes to disappointments, let-downs, having people lie to me and deceive me. But I knew I could just bide my time and then move on. The associations I have with my fans will never diminish. Sure, other people came along in the meanwhile who were trying to borrow from Barry White's style, but that didn't bother me none. There are many clocks out there ticking, but there's only one Big Ben.'

At the singer's suggestion, we moved outside to a small, poolside area at the rear of the house, he settling himself majestically on a lounger, hands clasped across his vast green-suited belly and neat, loafer-shod feet extended, me sitting like an acolyte on a chair by his side. 'You know, I am probably one of the most blessed black artists on this planet,' he then noted. 'I can go anywhere in the world and play. Now, how does a man like me create music that people of every nationality love? What is it about my music? Well, I'll tell you. It's because the subject that I choose to talk about is lurve. Lurve . . .'

He paused, relishing the word, and inviting me to savour it, too, before continuing. 'No matter if you can't communicate by language. No matter if you don't eat the same food or wear the same clothes. We all like to make lurve, every last one of us. So it's a subject that people automatically migrate to.'

It seemed an appropriate moment to tell him that, when I was a teenager at school, even the heaviest rock fans in my class recognized the wisdom of turning up at a girlfriend's house when her parents were out with a bottle of something alcoholic and a Barry White album. In fact, such was their reputation – as a statement of intent, if not as an aphrodisiac – that a more responsible record company than 20th Century might have included condoms within the packaging. Barry chuckled so deeply at this observation that there was an alarming pinging noise from one of the rubberized slats of his lounger. In response, he pulled himself upright and swung his feet to the floor. Then, thus positioned, he leaned forward and, great hands clasped together, addressed me confidentially, big man to little man.

'Well, I can tell you that there's a great many Barry-inspired babies out there in this world,' he then reported. 'I've been introduced to a lot of little boy Barrys and little girl Barrys, and I'm very proud of it. People come up to me and say, "Barry, this is your baby! We conceived it to so-and-so record." Or you hear of them using your music to get married to. That, to me, is more important than any record-company deal that did or didn't go down right. That, to me, is the people talking.'

We were joined at this point by Mrs White, a statuesque and highly regal woman, whose astonishing, gold-painted nails extended at least four inches beyond the tips of her fingers. I had jumped to my feet and put a hand out in welcome the second I'd heard her heels clicking on the patio. I regretted doing so the instant I saw her talons, but felt it would be rude to withdraw. In self-protection, I began to stare at that hand as if it were a vile object that had somehow become attached to my arm. How did this get here?

I hoped my body language was shouting, Madame, you certainly wouldn't want to shake it. You never know where it's been.

'Honey, this is Alan, from London, England. Alan, this is Glodean, my very special lady,' boomed Barry, standing also.

'Delighted to make your acquaintance,' she said, vertically clawing the air between us in pantomime of a more traditional greeting. 'And let me say that I just love your London. Buckingham Palace! The Changing of the Guards! Harrods! We've had so many special times in your beautiful city.'

As she spoke, she rubbed her husband's shoulders in a fond but potentially shirt-slashing way, then announced that she was off to the city to shop. 'Don't spend all my money, honey,' he called to her departing, click-clacking form. The talons waved playfully, dismissively in response, before she disappeared. 'Ladies!' sighed Barry, settling back on his lounger again. 'Don't they just make the world go round? You married? No. Girlfriend? I'm glad to hear it, huh-huh-huh!'

Our interview drew to a close with a few incidental questions about life beyond music. For example, I was keen to know what Barry White – in my experience, black artists are especially prone to referring to themselves in the third person, and the habit can be catching – liked to do to relax?

'One thing Barry really likes to do is to scuba-dive,' he said, contentedly rubbing his stomach. 'And do you know why Barry likes scuba-diving so much?'

I couldn't answer. I was too busy contemplating that stomach, and trying to imagine it encased in black rubber. Perhaps that was how he'd won the nickname I knew he hated, but which I assumed was affectionately bestowed: the Walrus of Love. A big, questioning finger pointing directly at my nose effectively broke this pattern of idle thought.

'Because there ain't no phones on the bottom of the ocean,' he said, making me suddenly aware of the one which was ringing unanswered somewhere in the house. Barry lumbered to his feet, lounger pinging again, and went indoors to answer it. It seemed as good a time as any to call a halt.

A short while later, on driving out of the gates of the estate, I checked my rear-view mirror and saw that he was still standing in the doorway, where we'd said our goodbyes, one hand raised in sustained benediction. What a guy! I thought, hooting a final farewell as I pulled out onto the deserted, sunbaked street. But what was it about the name Barry and safari suits? First, my old chief reporter in Norfolk, now the great Mr White. I decided that I would have to make it my mission to meet Barry Manilow and see if he could provide me with a hat-trick.

Emerging from the revolving doors of the Royal Garden Hotel, Kensington, into the evening air, I saw them again. Four women, aged around thirty, they were chatting in the animated, jokey manner of people determinedly keeping their spirits up across a protracted period of time, and shifting constantly back and forth on their feet to ward off the cold. The PR had pointed them out to me on my arrival. 'Marie's fans,' she said, nodding in their direction through the lobby window. 'They've been here ever since she arrived yesterday. Once they'd got an autograph each I thought they'd go. But no. They just stand there, waiting for another glimpse whenever we go off for a radio or TV appearance. One of them said she'd taken time off work specially to be here. The others have put their kids with sitters. Odd what people do with their time off.'

I'd asked to interview Marie Osmond only because I was curious about her. It certainly wasn't that she was of vital importance to the *NME*. Indeed, Danny had raised a significant eyebrow when I'd announced my intention. 'It's OK,' I'd told him. 'It's only for a little Thrills piece.' And that was pushing it, I knew. Even in purely showbusiness terms, she wasn't significant enough to have ironic or even kitsch potential. No matter. Every other writer on the paper followed their own agenda. It just so happened that mine was frequently more unfashionable and less music-led than anyone else's. I wanted to meet her precisely because she used to be very famous, and must have had to adjust to the subsequent diminution in her status. I was intrigued to know how well or otherwise she had coped.

For a few years during my youth, the Osmond family members had been major stars. I thought they were awful: if forced to lend support to a ruthlessly packaged pop family, my money would have been with the Jackson Five. But for some reason that I couldn't then and still can't quite explain, Marie fascinated me. It certainly wasn't because of her records: it would drain anyone's reserves of charity to forgive the awful, lisping version of an old Anita Bryant song, 'Paper Roses', which was her first solo hit. But I suppose that, as both she and I grew up, I was seduced by the Vegas sheen she acquired, and which she demonstrated on a weekly TV import, *The Donny and Marie Show*. These days we're used to formerly homespun, duckling-like girl singers metamorphosing into swans before our very eyes. Back then, the process was new to me, and for a while I followed it avidly.

But by the time I got to meet her, more than a decade had passed since the time of the Osmonds' greatest success. That was why there were just four diehard fans buoying each other up among the arriving and departing taxis, not the screaming tens of thousands there had once been. In the interim, Marie had failed to update herself successfully as a pop star, but was enjoying what would be a shortlived and more localized popularity in the US as a rather unconvincing country act. She hadn't looked happy, even so, self-consciously arranged next to the window of a suite overlooking Kensington Gardens. The look was pure *Dallas*: the high heels, neat, short-skirted suit and clutch bag; the big, heavily lacquered dark hair and red lipstick; the sort of earrings that would have to be taken off to answer the phone. Pretty? Yes. Happy? No.

Thanks to the inhibiting presence of her manager, an older man wearing Western gear, the interview proceeded in a dismal fashion, with Marie unrelaxed and me increasingly awkward. Finally, blessedly, he was called away by a record-company PR wanting to discuss the remainder of their promotional schedule. Alone at last, I looked over at the array of hospitality beverages on a side table. Perhaps a drink would help break the ice.

'Could I pour you a coffee?' I asked, hopefully, guest turned host.

No, I couldn't.

'Or a soft drink? A Coke, maybe?'

'I'm Mormon,' replied Marie, glum behind a perfect application of make-up. 'I'm not allowed to drink either of those things.'

It was a statement of the absolute, blindingly obvious. She was a Mormon. I was a moron. How could you have been so stupid? I asked myself shortly afterwards, passing her brave quartet of loyal fans. Ask anyone in the world to name a

Mormon family, and they'll say the Osmonds. And what does absolutely everyone know about the Mormons? That they don't take coffee, Coke or other stimulants. What were you thinking of?

Walking past the lighted store-fronts towards the tube, it occurred to me that something was wrong with the picture of fame that was being painted for me. It was all too down-beat and muted; the colours were wrong. From back in Norfolk, the world I was now venturing into had seemed a bright, enticing alternative to a flat reality. Yes, I had a well-cultivated melancholic streak – I was on to my third vinyl copy of some of Joni Mitchell LPs by now – but that was no reason to deny the fact that, when most people encounter it for a first time, celebrity and success, even other people's, represent a dream come true, a running amok in the sweet-shop of adolescent fantasy. What I needed was to reconnect with that dream. Accordingly, I decided that I had to talk to Danny, to see if there wasn't some recently up-and-come act for me to interview. Someone who'd arrived at the top and was loving every minute of it.

Thus resolved, I re-entered the office to find my desk occupied by a tallish, blond male in a leather bomber jacket. His feet were resting in my in-tray, and he was mid-conversation on the phone. 'Oh yeah, feeling completely at home,' he was saying. 'I've been ringing around the record companies, letting them know I'm down here now. Settling-in stuff, you know?'

I was drawn aside for a moment by Danny. 'Tonight there is a new star in London's journalistic firmament,' he told me, his mouth moving in the exaggerated way of one forced regularly to communicate with the simple and slow-witted.

'And that star has decided to grace your humble workspace with his presence. I present the Freelance From Hell. Your problem, I think.'

Suddenly, I found that I didn't merely want to interview some current chart-topper; I wanted to interview them out of London, preferably several thousand miles away from my hijacked desk, and as soon as possible. Danny was accommodating, and less than a week later I found myself landing in Minneapolis, *en route* to meeting the Manchester band Simply Red, who were on a tour of America at the time and enjoying a number-one hit there with the track 'Holding Back The Years'.

'You must be really, really tired from your flight,' sympathized their American PR, a woman wearing a velvet Alice band, tartan skirt and cashmere twinset, on picking me and photographer Mike up at the airport. 'That's why I've arranged for you to get the work bit over straight away. Then you can get to your bed and crash out.'

I didn't understand her logic, but was too tired to protest, instead allowing myself to be nannied through the hotel check-in process, and then transported to meet the band's leader, Mick Hucknall. 'He loves to eat,' she explained, pulling up outside an Italian restaurant, Ciatti's. 'His interviews with men always go better when there's food involved. Good luck! Call me at the hotel if you need a ride home!' And with that, she was off.

There is a golden rule to the talking-over-lunch-or-dinner scenario: first establish who is picking up the bill. I didn't know this yet. Most PRs are the very soul of professionalism and discretion in this regard, on hand to see you to your table and effect the basic introductions, disappearing to who-knows-where while you simultaneously eat and carry out your interview, and then reappearing, as if by magic, as coffee is served in order to pick up the tab. But when there is no such PR on hand to provide this invaluable service, the waters are muddied. Some subjects delight in exploiting the situation. The assumption may be that the journalist can always claim back expenses, but that is not always true.

Once, by coincidence also in Minneapolis, the soul singer Alexander O'Neal asked me to meet him at a restaurant at a certain time, in order, I naively assumed, to have our talk. On arriving, I found that his party numbered twelve and that they had already arrived at dessert. I ordered a piece of apple pie for myself, but had to eat it alone. He and the entire table simply got up and left, leaving me to pay for their meal. A neat trick, but one that Ian's successor as editor at the *NME* did not appreciate when it came to submitting my expenses claims. It would be me who paid for dinner with Mick, too – 'Yours, I believe,' he said when the cheque arrived, sliding it across to my side of the table – but at least this time I got to sample all three courses. And at least it was fun. Mostly, we talked about sex. That is, he talked and I listened.

'I'm not a skirt-chaser, I'm a lover. I make love.' To underline this essential distinction, he jabbed the air with his fork, a piece of gnocchi balanced precariously upon it. 'The women I have relationships with understand the difference, and I have great times with them.'

Like the masseuse he'd met two shows back in Los Angeles, for example. She had suggested they take a drive in search of a quiet place where she could demonstrate her skills. They'd pulled over onto a deserted roadside. To set the mood, she selected a late-night station on the car radio and, in the glow of the side-lights, helped him take his shirt off. And then . . . a flat battery. 'Three miles out of town, and we had to leg it if I was to stand a chance of catching the tour bus,' he recalled, grinning. 'It was all right for her because she was dead fit. But I was stopping every few hundred yards and saying, "I'm not sure we need to be in quite such a rush."' The result, apparently, had been a missed connection, a night on a choppy waterbed and a morning flight out to catch up with the rest of the band in time for the next performance. The grin made it clear it had been an effort worth making.

'There's a classic Steve McQueen quote about a time when his wife confronted him about his infidelities,' Mick continued, warming to the theme of life on the road. 'He said that he had just got tired of saying no. Listen, if you find your-self in a situation where a beautiful woman is demanding to spend the night with you, you can only hold out for so long. In the end, you think, I'm lonely. I'm really lonely. I've not had any company since whenever . . .'

The conversation continued in this vein as we left the restaurant and went in search of a taxi. The following night, Simply Red were to play at a club in the city, First Avenue, and he was keen to check it out in advance. Just as I succeeded in hailing one, a small English sports car sped past, braked heavily and then reversed to where we stood at the kerb's edge.

'Aren't you the guy who sings "Holding Back The Years"?' asked its driver, a collegiate type whose blonde companion was smiling winningly from the passenger seat. 'D'you need a ride anywhere? We'd be glad to take you.'

'But what about this?' I asked, gesturing at the waiting cab.

'Are you man or mouse, Alan?' asked Mick. 'Don't you know that, sometimes, you've just got to go with the flow?'

So we went with it, at about sixty miles per hour in a thirty-mile-an-hour zone, he and I perched precariously on the car's sloping boot, our legs wedged in behind the two front seats. Already it seemed possible that the driver was in danger of losing his date's attentions. By the time Mick and I had spent ten minutes crushed up among them and the other drinkers at First Avenue, it seemed a veritable certainty. Intrigued by this group dynamic, but feeling suddenly paralysed with tiredness, I decided to remove myself to bed.

'Call yourself an *NME* journalist?' said Mick, incredulous, when I made my excuses. 'You're supposed to be able to party all night. I'm very unimpressed.'

Outside, the sharp night air intensified the effect of the wine and beers I'd drunk, and I was grateful to find a taxi straight away. 'Where to?' asked the driver, a young black guy with a radiant smile. I realized I didn't know. I had absolutely no idea. The whole checking-in process had been handled so speedily and efficiently on my behalf by the lady with the Alice band that I hadn't even noticed the name of my hotel. My registration documents were in my room. I'd handed in my key. I was sunk.

'Chill out,' said Jimmy, smiling his smile. 'I know all the hotels. What d'you remember about it?'

'Tall,' I answered with certainty. 'It was very tall.'

'They're all tall here, boy,' he laughed. 'We'll just have to go on a tour till you see the right one. So, you're a music journalist, are you? You wanna hear some fresh sounds while we drive? I'm in a band, and . . .'

He got me home and I slept until one. On entering a bar downstairs and meeting up with the rest of the band, I was told that not only had Mick brought company back to the hotel with him the previous night, but that he was currently on a lunch date with yet another girl he'd encountered. 'Keeps him sweet,' said one of the crew members, smiling and finishing up a beer. 'Irritable isn't the word if he's not getting his exercise every day.'

The gig that night was celebratory, and the mood backstage afterwards even more so. No Mick, of course. For much of the time he was on the tour bus, entertaining on a one-to-one basis. As a result, the Simply Red party was two hours late setting off on its overnight journey to Chicago and the next date of its tour.

It was fresh but sunny the following morning, as photographer Mike and I had breakfast. We made an odd couple, him tall and immaculately suited, me small and in my new *NME*-friendly uniform of jeans, T-shirt and trainers. Looking at him, all GQ-like in his soft Armani suit and perfect loafers, drinking caffe latte, I wondered if I was destined always to get it wrong. But mismatched as we were, we could at least agree to kill what time there was before we left for the airport by wandering around one of the city's many lakes. Climbing out of a cab amidst a landscape peopled by joggers and power-walkers, realization suddenly hit me – yes, this was the world of *The Mary Tyler Moore Show*. This was the city of her character, Mary Richards. The place where she worked as a television news journalist.

'You remember,' I encouraged Mike. 'They used to show it in the afternoons sometimes. In the opening credits you saw her shrugging in the supermarket and throwing some kind of sad meal-for-one into a trolley. Then you saw her striding out, around a lake just like this one. And finally you saw her spinning round on a city street corner and flinging her knitted beret in the air.'

He claimed amnesia.

'You must have seen it,' I protested. 'There was this so-bad-it-was-good theme song. "Who can turn the world on with her smile?" it went. "Who can take a nothing day, and suddenly make it all feel worthwhile?"'

Mike's look of horror made me realize how inappropriate this level of intimacy was. He usually took pictures for *Vogue* and the colour supplements, and had only accepted this assignment as a favour to the art editor, and because he'd worked with the group before. I barely knew him well enough to talk to, let alone sing to. And I couldn't possibly expect him to be interested in the daytime television habits of the northern working classes.

'Truly, I don't remember,' he insisted. 'I'm sure I never, ever saw *The Mary Tyler Moore Show*. But then, I was brought up in London. They probably only ever showed it in the regions. Here, d'you want some of this?'

Chastened, I sat down next to him, beneath a tree on the waterside. No, I didn't want a toke of his joint. 'It just makes me fall asleep,' I explained. 'I'd rather have a beer if we had any. Thanks, though.' He shrugged and lay back on the grass. We sat for a while in silence.

Why was it, I wondered to myself, that even when all the right ingredients were in place – America, sex, drugs and a sort of rock 'n' roll – I still felt and behaved like an imposter? Why was it that when anyone else would be jumping in at the deep end, relishing life in the fast lane, I was still saying, 'No, thank you,' and singing the theme tune to a 1970's sitcom which only the housebound and long-term unemployed would remember?

As I pondered these imponderables, I became aware of a gentle snoring sound emanating from the stretched-out body by my side. So, dope made other people fall asleep too, did it? Even people in Armani suits and perfect loafers. I found this revelation comforting and, feeling the sun on my shoulders while waiting for him to wake again, amused myself by picking at the peeling transfer of my *Meat Is Murder* T-shirt.

As for the man we'd been sent to meet . . . Was he furious about an *NME* cover that showed him emerging from a revolving door, the words, SIMPLY RANDY: MICK HUCKNALL MAKES IT IN AMERICA printed above his head? The next of my colleagues to interview the star certainly expected him to be so.

'Hi, I'm Alan Jackson,' he said, by way of joke introduction, then ducked, as if to dodge the punch that would follow.

'Don't you say anything against Alan,' Hucknall chided. 'He's a good lad. Give him my regards.'

And to me, years later, he added, 'It was you who first gave me this Lothario image, you know. I ought to thank you.'

Music-paper journalists are a pretty inward-looking bunch. Trainspotters, of a kind. And on the *NME* of the mid 1980s, we not only took ourselves very seriously, but were actively encouraged to do so. The weekly meetings, at which the newly published paper was debated and future issues planned, were as earnestly conducted – and, frequently, in similar need of arbitration – as any peace process. Pre-meetings would be held in nearby coffee bars by the various sparring factions – the champions of the then-emergent dance cultures hip-hop and house, say, or of world music or plain old indie rock. There, agendas and campaign strategies would be thrashed out over capuccinos. 'If they try and put the Housemartins on the cover, we point out that their new single is an Isley Jasper Isley cover, spell out the fact that all white pop is a rip-off of black culture, and weigh in with Trouble Funk, OK?' That sort of thing.

I've never been very good at confrontation. I like to look for the best in people, or at least try to find some aspect of their character with which I am in sympathy. Only if confronted with the likes of Pol Pot, Pinochet or, increasingly at that time, my Freelance From Hell, would my policy of It's Nice To Be Nice have been tested to breaking point. Thus I found the factionalism and tribal behaviour that dominated so much of the *NME*'s editorial business both fascinating and slightly scary. When tempers flared over whether Hüsker Dü's latest album or Ciccone Youth's new 12-inch single was better or worse than the last one, I found myself with nothing useful to contribute. I simply couldn't tell. I listened, learned and smiled a lot, and tried always to be polite on the phone to those PRs known to be scared of ringing a title whose staff had a well-cultivated reputation for abruptness, if not open hostility.

This, and the fact that I wanted to interview interesting people, not set myself up as an arbiter of musical taste, meant that, over time, I came to be a specialist writer of a kind. First, and like everyone else on the paper, I would put myself forward to interview those artists for whose music I felt a particular affinity – overweight female soul stars, for example, or the sensitive singer-songwritery types. And then there were all the bruised superstars, the big names who felt they'd been badly treated in the days of star *NME* writers like Tony Parsons and Julie Burchill, and who now wouldn't talk to us as a result.

Peter Gabriel was a first such scalp. In my commissioning role, I rang his record label to ask for reviewer's seats at a forthcoming London show, only to be told that they were under instructions never to furnish the paper with any of his product or to facilitate our attendance at any of his concerts. No, the PR couldn't remember what had so upset him, or when, but something had. Sorry.

Puzzled, I walked down to Shaftesbury Avenue in my lunch hour, bought two tickets for his performance from an agency there and duly sent someone along to offer their personal, unabridged twopenn'orth about it. The resultant review may not have been exactly glowing, but it certainly wasn't unfair, and I sent a copy of it to the singer, via his manager, with a covering letter. 'I don't know why it is that you feel so very anti-*NME*, but wouldn't it be healthy to talk about it?' it said. 'If you ever feel you want to, please don't hesitate to give me a call.' Within a few days, he did, and I went down to his studio, in a converted watermill in the Wiltshire countryside, where we had a perfectly civilized chat about South African politics and other, similarly worthy topics. I never found out what had upset him in the first place, but I was glad to have helped him consign it to the past. And perhaps he got his own back. Was it in subtle and belated revenge that he insisted on making me an alfalfa sprout sandwich – wholewheat, inches deep, very hard on the jaws – to eat on the journey back to London?

Interviews like that with Peter couldn't be expected to excite the paper's self-appointed style police. But when, shortly afterwards, I was approached with the offer of a face-to-face with Sting, at least there was a contemporary political element to mitigate their disapproval. The Conservative administration of the time had announced its intention to amend the Local Government Act so that it became an offence for individual authorities to do anything which could be interpreted as promoting homosexuality. Sting had spoken in opposition to this plan when accepting the Best British Album trophy at that year's British Phonographic Industry Awards for *Nothing Like The Sun*. When screened on TV the following night, his appearance was reduced to a grin, a handshake and a thank you. Purely due to time constraints, said the BBC. 'Censorship!' was a popular response among the right-on, not least at the *NME*.

Given that the purpose of my trip was a serious one – Sting was to be allowed his unvetted say on the matters of censorship and homophobia – I was ashamed to find myself having so much fun before even leaving Heathrow. Unexpectedly, I had become part of a posse. There was Paul from a glossy teen mag, Pete from a mid-market Sunday supplement, and, most especially, Lou from the *Daily Express* showbiz desk. To date, the only Fleet Street journalists I had met were scary figures with steely jaws and even steelier news agendas, forever hogging the limelight at press conferences with questions that began, 'So, you claim that . . .' But here was someone lovely – imagine Rosanna Arquette, but with a plait and a fierce passion for Crystal Palace Football Club – whose first words to me were 'Hi! Nice to meet you. Now, where's the bar?' This was the very acceptable face of tabloid pop journalism, and I was prepared to be enchanted by it.

We stayed at the Plaza Hotel, overlooking Central Park, with me in the biggest suite and with the biggest bed I've ever experienced: my entire flat would easily have slotted into it. And we were treated like visiting royalty, due largely to the fact that not just one but two of Sting's PRs had become competitively embroiled in our visit. 'Cocktails at six, chaps?' one might suggest. 'Hors d'oeuvres in the Oyster Bar at five forty-five?' the other would respond. 'Then dinner before we leave for Madison Square Garden and Sting's show.' For someone who, not so very long before, had been queuing with a melamine tray in a civil-service canteen, it was the high life indeed.

The interviews took place at the offices of Sting's manager, Miles Copeland, high above Broadway. Lou had been scheduled first. I arrived towards the end of her allotted time and, mindful of the fact that I had a full hour in which to talk to him, asked for directions to the men's lavatory. As I walked down a long corridor in search of it, I was aware of footsteps some way behind me, but didn't turn round. Instead, I entered what must have been one of the smallest rest rooms in all of New York City: somehow, a cubicle, a tiny sink, a roller towel and two urinals had all been crammed into a space little bigger than a cupboard. Predicting that to use the right of the two would be to risk being sent flying should anyone else come through the door, I approached the left, unbuttoned and began.

At which point the door opened, and the person who'd been following me down the corridor took his place beside me. An awful moment ensued. A quick sideways glance confirmed that, yes, it was Sting who was being forced to position himself so that our arms were actually touching. What on earth was the etiquette for dealing with such a situation? We'd spoken only for the briefest moment the previous evening, backstage and in a room packed with famous faces; I couldn't possibly expect him to remember who I was. But saying, 'Hello! Remember me? I'm Alan!' might sound overfamiliar in the circumstances. And if I turned my body by even the slightest degree to make eye contact, I'd be in danger of peeing in his urinal instead of my own or, worse still, down his leg. Anyway, surely the least courtesy you could afford a public figure was to respect his privacy at a time like this? To distract myself, I attempted to mentally whistle one of his hits. Inevitably and unhelpfully it was 'Don't Stand So Close To Me' that sprang to the fore.

For a few, awful, staring-up-at-the-ceiling moments, we remained shoulder to shoulder. Then, mercifully, I was able to shake, put away and, after the most cursory of hand-rinsing, disappear back outside.

A minute or so later, Sting sauntered back into Copeland's office, where his two competing PRs and Lou were hovering amid an assortment of passing staff members. 'So, not speaking to me today, eh, Alan?' he asked, pretending to punch my shoulder. Then, to the rest of the room, he explained, 'He and I were just in the Gents' together. He blanked me totally.'

I blushed. 'I didn't think you'd know who I was. And it didn't seem the right time or place to make an introduction. Sorry.'

Sting adopted a hurt expression and continued to play to the gallery. 'Anyway,' he said, 'I took the opportunity to cop a look and' – he motioned at my crotch, then made one of those the-one-that-got-away gestures that fishermen use – 'it's enormous! Truly! Just huge!' All eyes turned to meet mine and then dropped, as if respectfully, to my flies. I shuffled uncomfortably, my hands clasping and unclasping uselessly at my sides. Finally, I placed them together in front of me, like a football defender waiting for a penalty to be taken.

Our subsequent interview went well, with Sting answering questions as fluently and quotably as always. There was even another moment of toilet humour when, towards the end of our hour, his son Jake, then aged two, burst into the room. As the child flung his arms around his father's neck, I became aware of a pungent smell. Sting wrinkled his nose with distaste, then asked me, 'Have you just done a pooh?'

The little boy laughed delightedly. 'Jake's the culprit,' said his mother, Trudie Styler, entering in search of him. 'Or, at least, I would hope he is.'

When we had said our goodbyes, I went in search of the others. No sign. 'They've gone round the corner for something to eat; they want you to join them,' said the receptionist, smiling not at my face but at my trousers. 'Here, they left this note, telling you where they are.'

While waiting for the lift to arrive, I looked at the piece of paper in my hand. 'F.A.O. Chopper Jackson Esq.,' it said, and gave the name and location of a diner. 'Don't be too long – tho' we know you can't help it!' was the postscript. 'P.P.S. Will book an extra seat on the flight home for your python!'

Back at the *NME* two days later, I made the mistake of recounting this story to Danny. By the time it had gone the rounds of the office and reached James, compiler of the paper's gossip column, the details had become somewhat blurred. 'Right, straight into the sort of stuff that racy paperback novels are made of,' he wrote that week. 'Get ready for the raunchiest human-interest story to hit these pages yet. The scene is backstage at a Sting concert in New York. A post-gig party is in full swing, and our man-on-the-spot, Alan Jackson, has sneaked away from the exclusive company of Dennis Hopper, Suzanne Vega and numerous other very famous people to spend a penny – or is it a dollar?

'Anyway, midway through his pee, who should walk in and stand next to Alan but Sting himself? Now, although the two have met the day before, he fails to recognize our Al and no words are exchanged. But moments after the two have returned to the festivities, Sting's memory is jogged, he puts a name to the face, and finds himself so pleased to have urinated alongside such an esteemed member of the *NME* that he silences the party by screaming at the top of his voice, "I have just seen Alan Jackson's chopper! And I tell you, it's a whopper!"

'Of course, poor Alan is so stunned by this public outburst that he faints, returns to England, and then makes the mistake of spilling the beans – only to find himself swamped by a barrage of cheap jokes and smutty innuendo too base and immature to be repeated here . . .'

At least Sting looked good on the cover of the following week's issue, the word CENSORED stamped across his fore-head, and was eloquent across the centre pages, hitting out at homophobia in government policy. 'Very interesting,' said my mother when I next spoke to her on the phone. 'But your father and I were wondering, why does it say, "By Alan 'Chopper' Jackson" at the top?'

I had bigger things to worry about than that. Or smaller, perhaps I should say. For weeks afterwards, I always went up a floor or down a floor when I wanted to pee. Embarrassed, if a little flattered, though I was by the new respect shown to me by my colleagues, I didn't want to run the risk of being spotted in action. Because the problem with Sting's joke was that it was exactly that: a joke. I'm Mr Average, not Chopper Jackson at all.

7

Discontent was in the air when I returned to the *NME*, and the Freelance From Hell appeared to be the cause. Apparently, he was treating the office as a kind of social club-cum-drop-in centre, spending hours at a time on the phone there, either regaling friends back home with the details of his exciting new lifestyle, or blagging copies of the week's new releases from juniors in the various record-company press offices. All in all, it made my colleague Paolo's complaints seem petty.

'What does it for me is the fact that he's a fashion nightmare,' bemoaned the man whose dictums on when socks should be worn with loafers, and when they shouldn't, marked the changing seasons outside of *NME* Towers more precisely than any official calendar. 'The leather of that jacket looks like it comes from a rhinoceros. And what about those jumpers? But as for the things he wears on his feet . . . I'd give him money out of my own pocket, if only he'd promise to buy a decent pair of shoes. It hurts me just to look at the ones he's got on now.'

Shortly afterwards, an edict was handed down from on high. There was to be a rationalization of the freelance staff, and FFH was at the top of the list of those to be rationalized. The bad news for me was that, apparently, it was my job to tell him.

Some people enjoy wielding the scythe. I don't. Nor do I have much aptitude for it. So rather than coming out with a blunt, 'Do us all a favour and just clear off, will you?' I invited my victim for a spot of lunch the following day to discuss the situation.

'There's something I need to say to you,' I began, once the pizzas had been ordered and the bottles of Peroni poured. 'The thing is that—'

'You're going on holiday and you want me to stand in for you,' interrupted my guest. 'I'd need a guarantee of complete editorial independence, of course. But there are one or two ideas I'd like to try out in the Live Reviews section, and as for Thrills, well, I'd say a total rethink was the only—'

'I've been told I've got to halve the number of freelances I'm using. There are just far too many. So, in fairness, I wanted to alert you to the way the wind is blowing. And ask if, maybe, you'd thought of writing for one of the other papers? That way, you'd be getting out ahead of the pack. You'd save face, and you'd have a head start when it came to finding alternative work.'

FFH looked incredulous for a moment, then banged his fist down loudly on the table top. Cutlery scattered and fellow diners turned to stare. 'I don't believe it!' he said, unnecessarily. 'Why me? 'Cos if the paper's got too many free-lances, why not just have a clear-out of the ones who aren't any cop? Tell me that, eh? I could give you a list of names.'

'Look, I hate to say it, but as far as the editor's concerned, that category includes you. I'm really sorry. But that's why I'm encouraging you to defect now. To jump before you're pushed, so to speak.'

Incredulity turned to anger right before my eyes. 'You, you of all people, are telling me I can't write. I find that very ironic! There's a lot of people round here who think your feature-writing is a lorryload of shite!'

'The Capricciosa? The Napoletana with extra cheese and anchovies?' At exactly the wrong moment, our food had arrived. I looked up at the waitress in embarrassment. Across the table, two eyes continued to look daggers at me.

'You can stuff your bloody pizza up your arse!' FFH told me, shoving his chair back into that of the woman directly behind him and looming to his feet. 'You're right. I will be writing for someone else from now on. In fact, I wouldn't write for you again if you got down on your knees and begged me.' And with that, he turned on his heel and slammed out into the passing crowds of tourists and lunch-hour office workers.

It was the first and only time I have been abandoned in a restaurant, and the scenario proved every bit as excruciating as it's made to seem when happening to characters in books and films. 'Not the way I would have gone about it,' said Danny, when I recounted the incident to him, 'but at least you got the right result. And two pizzas to go. Now, how d'you fancy going to Paris to talk to Annie Lennox?'

Lou called on the very day that interview was published. 'You rotten old scumbag,' she said cheerfully. 'I've been trying to meet Annie for two years. Meanwhile, you just swan off to France, without even telling me. I don't suppose you've got any good quotes left over? 'Cos if you have, you could do a piece for us. Or maybe she'll agree to talk to you a second time. You know, you really ought to think about moving on to the nationals, before it's too late. Think of what the future holds if you don't. The wrong side of forty, pony-tailed and wearing leather trousers, a fixture at the bar in The Marquee, forever boring girls half your age with stories of how it was to hear The Clash for the first time . . . It won't be a pretty sight, I promise.'

Well, if she put it like that. Indecently soon afterwards, I made my first tentative step towards what was still then Fleet Street, dropping off a note to Paul, features editor on the *Sunday Express Magazine*, asking if he might be in need of freelance contributors and enclosing a wodge of photocopies of recent interviews I'd done. I'd met him socially for all of ninety seconds once, and had found him friendly and approachable, despite his man-in-a-desperate-hurry demeanour. 'Let's get together, matey,' he said, when I called to ask if he'd received my letter. 'Let's talk turkey. Bring some ideas with you. Tuesday do you? Three thirty, Gloriette's. Know it? Bahhh!'

Bahhh? I deduced later that this was 'bye' delivered at speed. Paul was a media lifestyle on two legs. Just back from lunch at Soho media haunt The Groucho when our meeting came round, he was returning to the office for two or three hours, then off for drinks and dinner somewhere else. 'Nah, nah, nah, nah and nah. Sorry, matey!' One by one, he dismissed the interview subjects I suggested. They were either too pop, too square, too left-field or too mainstream. And then he came to Sheena Easton's name. 'Too right, we'd be interested in her,' he said, draining a coffee and climbing down from his stool in the busy pâtisserie that was our meeting place. 'Won't talk to any of the Brit papers, these days. Been turned over too many times. So, if you can get

Sheena, we're in business, OK? Gotta go now! Bahhh!'

Paul gave the impression that his career was moving at a breakneck pace. Mine seemed reluctant to shift out of first gear, and my own natural reticence was probably to blame. Certainly, it felt like time to leave the *NME*. But another staff job, particularly one in Fleet Street? On my few incursions into the *Daily Express* offices to meet Lou, or indeed Christine, who was now working in advertisement sales for its parent group, I'd encountered a prevailing atmosphere so different to any I'd met previously that it unnerved me. Too many people seemed either boorish or a bag of jangling nerves. Section editors shouted abuse at all those under them. Everywhere, everyone chainsmoked and snatched at take-out coffees. Well, perhaps that was what the real world of work was actually like, I thought, staring into my cup following Paul's departure. Perhaps it was time for me to grow up and just get on board.

My conclusion was the same as always when I've had such internal debates. Compromise was the better option. Going freelance was the safer and only path. At home that night, I sat and composed a letter to Sheena. I reminded her of the interview I'd done with her two years earlier. I acknowledged that I was aware of her mistrust of the UK media and understood the grounds for it – she has had a consistently hostile press, particularly in her native Scotland, since moving to the US shortly after finding fame, as if to do so represented some kind of betrayal. I told her that I wasn't offering, should she grant me an interview, to produce some piece of hagiography, a rerun of one of her own press releases. I predicted also that she wouldn't want me to do so. What I was asking for, instead, was the chance to write something that was fair, accurate and unbiased. I was hoping to go freelance shortly, and I told her which publication I would like to place an interview with. What did she think?

Four weeks later, and immediately after New Year, I was on a plane to Los Angeles, business class. Sheena's manager, Harriet Wasserman, had called me to say the answer was yes. I'd called Paul, who had, in turn, invited me to his office on a dead, post-Christmas day for a last-minute pep talk, and to hand over a satisfyingly thick wad of dollars, the result of a per-diem calculation of what would be necessary to meet my basic expenses. 'Go steady with it, mind,' he warned, seeing my impressed expression. 'You're not obliged to spend it all. And make sure you get receipts for absolutely everything, otherwise the accounts department will want it all back again. Champagne, controlled substances and the personal services of resting actresses are not considered chargeable to the company. Other than that, I've nothing to say but good luck. Do this one well and there could be plenty more commissions for you in the future. OK?'

I felt very OK, sitting there miles above everything, clouds below me, assignment ahead. And I was OK, too, after reaching the other end, and taking up residence in a hotel room close to Universal Film Studios. I was still OK the next day, when I set out to have lunch with Harriet, after which I would meet Sheena and do my interview. I cut a stylish figure, carrying with me, as I did, a Sainsbury's carrier. It bulged with tins of Heinz baked beans and Cadbury's drinking chocolate and boxes of Smarties, the result of having asked if there were any items the singer particularly missed from Britain, which I could bring out to her as a thank-you for seeing me.

Through eagerness and ignorance of local geography, I was early. The cab I had asked to pick me up half an hour before my meeting duly dropped me off outside the appointed restaurant three short minutes later. Stepping out of its cool interior, back into the sunshine, I found myself staring across a blur of traffic at the high-rise hotel complex I had just left. Effectively, I'd just been driven to the other side of the six-lane highway. Looking not as if I were about to power-lunch, but as if I'd just passed through a supermarket checkout, I stood alone, with a further twenty-seven minutes to kill. I couldn't just stay there. Somewhere within the adjoining building above was Harriet's office. She might look out of her window at any moment, catch sight of me with my plastic bag and write me off as a hopeless loser. Right now, she might be on the phone to Sheena. 'Stay home. I'm going to cancel. He's just some dosser, not a journalist at all.' There was nothing else for it, I would have to take a walk.

Stepping around a succession of skeletal Christmas trees, lying discarded and awaiting collection by the roadside, I passed an office-supplies store, a dry-cleaners and a florist. All were closed. Then a copy shop, a pharmacy and a nail-extension parlour. The same. And as I walked, slowly so as not to melt in the heat, I became increasingly aware of a squeaking presence behind me. Should I turn and identify it? Before I could, there was a sudden tap on my elbow. I wheeled round, nervously. 'Whoops! Didn't mean to frighten you,' protested a Hispanic woman of indeterminate age, letting go of a shopping-trolley handle for long enough to raise her hands in I-mean-you-no-harm fashion. 'But here you are, a man in a nice suit, with what looks like a bag full of groceries. I couldn't resist taking the opportunity to intro-duce myself to you and your purchases. Don't suppose there's anything in there that might be going spare?'

She was, she told me, sleeping rough behind an Italian delicatessen. 'He's a nice guy that runs it, but he's been shut right across the holidays and nice ain't worth jack-shit when the "Closed" sign's down. Sorry, sorry, sorry. I'm getting ahead of myself, forgetting what's left of my manners. The name's Juanita. Ever-so-ever-so to meet you. What's your name? C'mon, I want to know all about you.'

I allowed her to steer me along the sidewalk towards a gas station, in the cabin of which you could buy hot and cold drinks to go. 'Coffee, white, with sugar, since you're asking,' she said, urging me through the door, but remaining outside herself, and thus able to stand guard over her cart full of plastic-wrapped possessions. I emerged with two drinks. She drained hers in three deep glugs, wiped her mouth and then reached for the second disposable cup. 'Thirsty,' she explained unnecessarily. 'Now, you were going to tell me all about yourself. You don't sound local. Are you just visiting? Tell Juanita who you are and what you're doin' here.'

We sat together on a low wall to the side of the forecourt; she moving the trolley gently back and forth, back and forth, as if it were a pram in which a baby was sleeping. 'I'm Alan,' I told her. 'I'm a journalist for a magazine in London, England, and I'm here to interview a British pop star who's very successful over here. Sheena Easton. Have you heard of her? She's—'

Juanita jumped to her feet, shimmied to the centre of the pavement, adjusted an imaginary microphone and then counted herself in. 'A-one, two, three, ooh . . . Strut, pout, put it out, that's what you want from women. Come on, baby, what ya' takin' me for? Strut, pout, put it out, all takin' and no givin'. Watch me, baby, as I walk out the door . . . !' As she sang, loudly and off-key, she sashayed this way and that, swinging her considerable hips and pointing the toes of her torn and grubby sneakers. Of course, I had to applaud.

In response, Juanita curtsied. 'I love that song, "Strut".' She grinned, sitting back down beside me again. 'You couldn't escape it last summer. Sheena's kickin'! And you're gonna meet her today. Well, you'd better be extra nice to her, or maybe it'll be your skinny English ass that she kicks!' She laughed, nudging me good-naturedly in the ribs. 'No offence meant. None taken, I hope.'

I gave Juanita two tins of baked beans – she promised me she had a can opener – some drinking chocolate, a box of Smarties, a $20 bill and a kiss on both cheeks. She wished me luck in my endeavours, and I returned the compliment. And then I headed back two blocks, along the boulevard to 3575, an office complex with a glass-fronted restaurant at street level. Harriet, power-dressed, no nonsense, businesslike but friendly, was already in place at a window table, considering the menu. We ordered quickly. 'No house dressing on my salad, thank you,' she instructed. 'Just bring me oil and vinegar on the side. I'd prefer to mix my own.'

The very first time I'd been taken out to a restaurant as a journalist, I had found it difficult even to eat. It was towards the end of my first week in Norfolk, and I'd been sent out to the wind-raked industrial estate to which a local firm of meat processors had just transferred, thus to record the occasion for the business pages. The two bluff, beaming proprietors clearly relished the opportunity to show off their shiny new premises to an interested third party. Back and forth we trailed, through a chilled forest of suspended animal carcasses, with them drawing my attention to this or that nicety of the storage process, and me taking notes with a cold-deadened hand, feeling increasingly queasy. Finally, one of the two clapped his hands together, rubbed them briskly and announced a special treat. 'Well, you've seen the very great care we take with our beef. Now, let's away and eat some. I guarantee you'll have tasted none finer.'

It was a generous gesture. But as I stared at the expanse of steak on my plate, I couldn't help but relate it to the great, dripping, marbled carcasses we'd been strolling among just minutes earlier. Further unsettling my stomach was the fact that I was due at the coroner's court within the hour, to record the forensic details of a successful overdose, a road-traffic-accident fatality and a pensioner who had died after falling off the toilet in an old people's home. Making my excuses and leaving the table, after which I threw up discreetly behind my car, I knew I'd been a major disappointment to my hosts. For what's that cliché about my chosen profession? Aren't journalists supposed to do anything, go anywhere, to bag a free lunch?

Sitting down to eat with strangers can be a fraught business. What I had learned in the interim is that, when in doubt, it's best to take a lead from those who are entertaining you. I'd assumed that the Los Angeles lunch experience would be a relatively straightforward one – don't appear to be hungry and, even if you are, don't eat much. But here, too, it seemed, there were potential pitfalls. Accepting house dressing on your organically grown salad leaves, as I had just done, might well be akin to announcing yourself a closet lard-ass, someone who couldn't wait to get back to their hotel room to pig out on Toblerone and tacos. Harriet's face was giving nothing away. Thank goodness I'd been smart enough not to accept her offer of wine. But was it a mistake to have ordered a sybaritic, non-diet Coke instead of her mineral water, twist of lemon, no ice.

Hang on a minute, I thought. This is someone whose client pines for baked beans, hot chocolate and Smarties. Relax. I tried to do so, and must have succeeded because, at first, I didn't notice the Jaguar saloon that had pulled up outside. Consequently, I was startled when there was a rap on the plate glass beside me and I turned to find a woman with horn-rimmed glasses and spiky auburn hair pulling faces at me. I jumped and dropped my cutlery. 'All for me? Wow! Christmas really has come late this year,' said Sheena, joining us at the table and rummaging through the contents of my hastily proffered plastic bag. Her eyes then took in the soggy green debris on my plate.

'Who's been intimidated by the calorie police?' she demanded. 'Harriet, this man has flown the Atlantic to be with us today. He's probably in desperate need of a cheese-burger with double fries. You should be ashamed of yourself, making him eat lawn trimmings. This is no way to treat a journalist, you rotten old bag.'

She grinned at me and I grinned right back. I continued to do so until my jawbone began to ache, then stopped and merely smiled instead. After all, I didn't want to give the impression that I was simple, or a push-over. Instinctively, though, I felt I'd made my first showbusiness friend.

Flying back to London in lonely luxury, I set about tran-scribing my interview. The upstairs cabin was all but empty, no distractions. Sheena's voice rang out through my head-phones, the accent as hard to place between the two continents as the plane in which I was travelling. Yes, she was acknowledging, the contrast in past and present lifestyles was enormous. 'Being brought up the way I was in Scotland, I saw hardship throughout my early years. My father died when I was ten, and my mother was left to raise six of us by herself. I was a selfish little teenager, going, "I've got to have a new dress and a pair of high heels for the school dance or everyone will laugh at me", but she always pulled through. Maybe my Christmas dress wouldn't be paid off until August, but still she never fell apart. Absolutely, she's my role model.'

The interview had been fun. And afterwards, Sheena had asked where I was staying and had offered me a lift back to my hotel. In the car, we'd chatted as any two people establishing common territory might – about recent films we'd seen and could recommend, records, books and TV programmes we liked, that sort of thing.

'What plans have you got for the rest of the day?' I'd asked, standing in the late-afternoon sunshine, looking down through the driver's window.

'I'll probably just take a walk in the park with my dogs. Then, because I haven't eaten yet today, I'll maybe pick up a takeaway,' she had said from behind the wheel. 'Mexican probably. I know a good one.'

There was a momentary pause before our respective thank-yous and goodbyes collided with each other. 'Enjoy yourself,' I called after her. It was only after the car had disappeared that I was struck by the obvious. I was there on my own, knowing no-one and with nothing to do before going home the next evening. Why hadn't I asked Sheena if I might go for a walk with her? Or pay for her takeaway? Why was it so hard to believe that famous people might want you to treat them as if they were ordinary?

Oh, well. Mindful of features editor Paul's words of guidance, the remainder of my LA trip passed off in parsimonious isolation. To stay in a hotel at someone else's expense was still a novelty to me, and I didn't want to take the piss. That night, because I didn't feel like sitting at a dining-room table all by myself, I ordered up a burger from room service. It was the cheapest main dish on the menu and I ate it to the accompaniment of beer and coffee, not wine, let alone champagne. Then, before turning in, I called down to reception with an enquiry. Yes, there was a bus service that connected the hotel with the airport. 'You're welcome, Mr Jackson. Now, be sure and sleep well.'

I was more than halfway through my mid-air transcript when I felt a hand on my shoulder. 'Hi, I'm Jinks, your flight attendant for the rest of the journey. Can I offer you some Dom Perignon? You know what they say about all work and no play . . . And your choice of entrée? Would you prefer the beef, the chicken or maybe the lobster?'

'Hi, Jinks,' I said, then blushed. 'I'm sorry. I wasn't thinking. You must get that all the time.'

Her look of momentary puzzlement suggested she didn't, but I was more than happy to accept the offer of something fizzing. 'We're so quiet up here tonight. Mind if I slip in next to you for a moment?' asked Jinks. 'Now, I'd hazard a guess that yours has been a work trip. So, how'd it go? Did you whip the other guy's ass? I bet you did. Wanna tell me all about it?' And I had thought business travel was all about seats for big arses and room for long legs. Was it really part of the service to have your ego massaged over a glass of non-vintage, too? Oh boy.

Back at home in London, on the telephone to the *Express* accounts department, I encountered bafflement. 'You want to return money to us? Sorry, I don't understand.'

'I'm freelance. I was given an advance for a trip to America to do an interview. I was told not to spend it all, and so I didn't. Which is why I'm calling. To ask how best to give the remainder back.'

There was silence at the other end of the line, and then the sound of a hurried consultation, conducted in whispers. 'Again, I have to say I'm sorry,' the voice said, 'but this genuinely is a first. We've never, ever had a journalist wanting to give money back to us before. Normally, they come back with a list of additional expenses as long as your arm. As a result, there's no procedure in place to deal with it. I'm afraid we're going to have to instruct editorial to deduct it from your payment. Apologies, and all that. Spend up next time, that's my advice. Everyone else does.'

Lou rang as soon as the piece was published. 'Lovely, but why didn't you do it for us? Do you want to have lunch? How's life at the *NME*? You've got to get out of there, you know. Yes, I know you think you like it, but . . .'

Again, she wanted me to make enquiries about interviewing Annie Lennox for the *Express*. This time I did. And, to my surprise, was told that yes, it was a definite possibility. A couple of weeks later, I was on my way back to Paris, to the same hotel in which I'd met the singer just three months earlier. Previously, we had talked face-to-face, like chess-players, across a table in an ante-room off the lobby. This time, a small suite had been booked for the purpose and I found Annie contemplating the view from the window when I arrived there. 'Such a lot of words, last time,' she exclaimed of our earlier encounter. 'God, but I felt sorry for you, reading the piece afterwards. Your poor ears!'

We talked about this, that, everything. She was living in Paris with her partner, and soon-to-be husband, an Israeli film-maker, Uri Fruchtmann. Were children an ambition? 'Oh yes, yes, absolutely. I'm not saying we're planning that right now, but definitely at some point . . . Chrissie Hynde and I talk about this a lot. She's someone who has tried to integrate being a performer with being a mother, and I know it hasn't been easy for her.

'As for me, I'm not predicting anything. But if it were to happen, then I would certainly feel my life were being enriched. At the same time, I'd want to keep on doing what I do. It's essential to me, music, you know? Otherwise, I feel like I die. Like I shrink a little inside.'

Lou and her bosses were thrilled. The only problem was what byline to give me. 'I can't be Alan Jackson, 'cos I'm still at the *NME*,' I pointed out. 'I'm not supposed to write for anyone else without permission. And having already asked for it once, doing Sheena for the *Sunday Express Magazine*, I'm a bit nervous about pushing my luck.'

An assumed name was the obvious answer. But who should I be? I considered various, unlikely options. The women's-page editor wasn't one to waste time, though. 'What's your middle name? Richard. Right, I'm giving you a choice. You can be Alan Richard, or you can be Richard Alan? Which is it? I haven't got all day.'

I bit the bullet, but quibbled about the spelling. And so began my very brief moonlighting career as Richard Allen.

A few months later I did leave the *NME*. The highlight of my Friday-night farewell party was a personal appearance by the Mancunian icon Frank Sidebottom, part human, part huge, grinning papier-mâché head. He sang the Kylie Minogue hit 'I Should Be So Lucky' in a falsetto voice, while playing the banjo and dressed in a very tight suit.

'We'd thought about putting a band together from people on the paper to do a medley of Sheena's hits, but then we thought better of it,' confided Danny. 'We weren't confident that any of the men here could carry off her saucepot-era persona with quite the necessary panache.'

I reassured him that I was thrilled with the way things had turned out. Frank was a particular favourite of mine, and I especially liked his sidekick, Little Frank, a two-dimensional puppet made of jointed cardboard. No-one heard a word of my farewell speech, because I wasn't able to master the art of talking into a microphone. It didn't help matters that, half-way through, I spotted what looked like a gang of football casuals bulk-ordering at the free bar. Everyone, Christine included, imagined that my incoherent gesticulations meant I was tired and emotional, and patted me encouragingly on the back. What I was trying to point out was that this bunch of chancing bastards was decimating my float.

The whole glittering, early-evening affair had taken place in a basement nightclub in Clerkenwell. A colleague had suggested the venue, and only afterwards did I learn that it was not only a dance club, but also the location for gay all-nighters and a host of other sybaritic revelries. I'd believed myself to be temporarily on the cutting edge, drinking beneath pavement level in the company of a man with a big paper-and-paste head. How very wrong I was. How hope-lessly tame and mundane that evening must have seemed to the seen-everything bar staff and bouncers.

The following morning, understandably, I had a hangover. Two mornings later, I woke with an anxiety attack. I was now freelance. As Christine got ready for work, I concen-trated on breathing normally and thinking positively. At least I had work lined up, although I wasn't in a position to be too proud about where I found it. Luckily, Lou, who seemed to have contacts everywhere, had introduced me not only to colleagues on the *Express*, but also to friends on TV-listings magazines and women's weeklies all over central

London. And, to my surprise, they'd begun to call up.

My first day of self-employment might well have been spent, directionless and depressed, in front of the TV. Instead, I was on my way to the studios of London Weekend Television. The first lady of country music, Tammy Wynette, was recording a segment for a variety show hosted by Jimmy Tarbuck, and I was to interview her during a break in rehearsals. I arrived wearing the nervous sweat of a man who has had to run half a mile because all the nearest carparks were full. That unmistakable voice was in full flight, singing 'Stand By Your Man' for the ten thousandth time as I rushed through to the backstage area. Rehearsals were already underway.

I was introduced to her – a small, candyfloss-haired woman, with a still-young but tired face – in a canteen overlooking the Thames. We sat across from each other at a plastic-topped table. Her fifth husband, George Richey, bearded and wearing a sharp, open-necked suit, sat at another, along with his wife's personal hairdresser-cum-make-up artist, and an LWT PR. They were less than two inches away from us. If I moved my arm just a little to the left, it would have brushed that of the protective George. How to get Tammy's undivided attention, let alone a decent interview? But I wasn't giving her credit for being a woman used to turning on the professional charm in circumstances many times more trying than those that we found ourselves in.

'Lovely to meet you,' I said, because it was. Smiling encouragingly, I leaned in towards her, willing her to concentrate on me and me alone. As a result, I felt as if I were a prison visitor, trying to make a private communication, despite our being watched over by warders and fellow inmates.

'And to meet you, too,' she replied, reaching forward and

covering my hand with her own. 'So sorry if you were kept waiting. But you know how it is with rehearsals. You've sung a song a million times, and still they want you to take it just once more, from the top.' She smiled a dazzling, confidential smile and leaned in, too. 'But I'm all yours now. Ask away.'

In preparation for our meeting, I had watched a BBC2 *Arena* documentary about Tammy's life. It had unreeled like some southern-states fiction. Born Virginia Wynette Pugh, near Tupelo, Mississippi, in May 1942, she was raised by her mother and grandparents, her father having died when she was just ten months old. From an early age she'd picked cotton, the family being poor by any standards. At seventeen, she had married the first of her five husbands, a construction worker called Euple Byrd, and began training as a beautician. It would be some years yet before she gave rein to her musical ambitions, leaving Byrd and moving to Nashville with their three young children. And throughout all of this, there had been persistent and protracted bouts of ill-health, some of them life-threatening. The TV cameras had shown her reflecting on all of this as she walked around what remained of her childhood home in Itawamba County. Unaffectedly, she had cried as she talked. 'I'm pleased to see you looking so well today, after all you've been through,' I said, this documentary footage in mind.

'Well, Alan, seventeen major operations in as many years; it hasn't been easy. So I appreciate your saying that. And I'm actually feeling well today, too. Life is good.'

The business of interviewing for a national newspaper, whatever its character, is very different to that of interviewing for a rock paper, I was quickly discovering. Although traditional news values were returning to the *NME* and its competitors, the legacy of the late 1970s and early 1980s meant that many young writers felt the celebrity profile to be a device for presenting themselves, not the actual subject, to readers. Botched encounters, forgotten questions, missing information could all be glossed over or disguised within such a format. The national-newspaper medium was far less forgiving. Don't ask the right questions, don't expect to see your interview printed. Botch one interview, don't expect to be commissioned to do another.

I thought back to my encounter with Dusty Springfield – she had been at ease for as long as I, a music journalist, asked about her music, but became frantic when someone from the tabloids grilled her about her private life – and I reminded myself that I was now working in this other, potentially fraught league. My hope was that I could remain the same person, let alone journalist, I had always been, and still get some kind of result. Tammy's openness and lack of guile, be it real or professionally adopted, made me think this was possible.

'I had gotten so dependent on painkillers that I was caught in a vicious circle,' she volunteered, in response to my benign remarks about her apparent good health. 'It had become a major issue. I'd arrive in a city to do a show, and would be in such horrible pain that I couldn't stand it. I had to do something to enable me to walk out and face those people with a smile on my face. But that way, it got to be an everyday thing, which was very scary.'

To deal with her addiction, Tammy had followed other high-profile individuals, such as Elizabeth Taylor and Mary Tyler Moore, by checking herself into America's Betty Ford Clinic. Her stay would coincide with that of Stevie Nicks, whom I was to meet a few months later, and, despite not having met before, they took comfort from their shared situations. Two famous women whose celebrity suddenly meant nothing as they scrubbed floors, attended Narcotics Anonymous meetings and worked out alongside other female addicts who were unknown beyond an immediate circle of family and friends.

'It's real frightening when you first get there,' Tammy told me. 'Your loved ones can't call or visit you for the first five days, so suddenly I found myself totally alone.

'I was in a building with about twenty other women, and we had these group-therapy sessions, which could be very painful. But that way they got us to really open up, and the first thing it taught us was the importance of the self. You're there for you, and you have to do what makes you feel better. That's why it's such a great programme, because when you're feeling good about yourself, then you can be so much better for all the other people in your life, too.'

Ironically, her stay was brought to a premature end by a recurrent abdominal condition, and Tammy was hospitalized again for surgery. Successful graduates of the clinic are awarded a memorial badge, one that has a material worth of cents, but which clearly signifies a priceless personal invest-ment. Stevie Nicks would tell me that Betty Ford herself materialized at Tammy's bedside, the singer's condition being so serious, and pinned a badge to her medical gown. Instantly, I had a vision of an angel with an ex-president for a husband, or at least some latter-day Florence Nightingale, committed to ministering to a patient list comprised only of the celebrity drink- or drug-addled. Such a mission had made her as famous, for a while, as her husband once was.

Tammy Wynette would be allowed ten more years of a life that seemed, because of its scope and content, to have as much to do with soap opera – she starred in one briefly, a

Washington-based drama called *Capitol* – as it did with actual reality. On that *Arena* documentary, she'd been pictured addressing her concert audience in some mid-western venue or other. 'Here's a song that has a special meaning for me and, I hope, for a lot of you beautiful people out there,' she'd said, introducing one of her many country number ones, a story of emotional dependence entitled ' 'Til I Can Make It On My Own'.

Some months after screening of the documentary, Christine and I went to see her perform at the Royal Albert Hall in London. Appearing brittle, but still showbusiness-beautiful, in a short, spangled dress, with elaborately teased and back-combed hair, the star used the exact same words to introduce the exact same song. And did so again when I next heard her sing it in London, a full five years later. In between, she must have performed perhaps five, six times a week, for up to fifty weeks of the year, in venues all over the world. Each night, she must have used an identical script to introduce material authentically dripping with heartache. That meant her words were true and yet not true, sincerely meant and yet totally insincere. How willingly an audience suspends disbelief when the singer is someone who has won their love. And how central to that suspension, that love, is the audience's aware-ness of the trials and traumas of that singer's off-stage life.

More so than most artists, Annie Lennox's musical and public persona has been shaped by her identity as a private individual. Despite her singing and songwriting talents, and her ability to deliver a bravura performance in the spotlight, she has always struck me as an essentially shy and insecure person, uncomfortable at being the object of scrutiny. Of course, that made it no more or less sad to enter my local newsagent's one day to see a raft of tabloid headlines about her – that of the *Sun*, ANNIE'S BABY BORN DEAD, spelled out the facts as bluntly as any. But I felt that it must be an especial pressure on her, the awareness that every aspect of her life, even this, was up for public consumption.

I had known she was pregnant, but not when her baby was due. And the articles, when you read them, were every bit as sad as you would imagine. A son, Daniel, had been stillborn, without any apparent medical explanation. His suddenly worsened condition had been discovered when she arrived at hospital to await what she expected to be a normal labour and delivery. Instead, she had to wait to give birth to a child she had already been told was dead.

At home, I sat and debated the appropriateness, or otherwise, of writing to say how very sorry I was. Of course, my feelings were irrelevant in the matter. But we all know that messages of support, from whatever source, can be a comfort at times of bereavement. I opted to write, and was struggling to compose a suitable letter when I received a call from her manager. He told me that Annie wanted to give an interview to me, both to explain her feelings and to try to create something positive out of a terrible situation. The essential crapness of my potential as a tabloid reporter was brought home to me by my instinctive response: 'But surely she shouldn't be talking to any journalist. Isn't it a private thing? Why on earth would she want to speak publicly about it right now?'

'She just wants to. She thinks it's important that she does. Will you help us?'

Of course I would. Immediately, I phoned Lou to ask for advice. 'Get a written agreement that the interview you submit will not be altered without consultation and your permission,' she told me. 'And make sure, too, that it will not be sold on to other publications without your and Annie's approval.' Then she went off to speak to her editors. Naturally, they were delighted at their good fortune. They and all their competitors had sent reporters and photographers out to Paris, where they believed her to be. Here was someone able to deliver the story to them on a plate, and exclusively. I suppose I could have rung around and tried to auction it. As it was, I didn't even ask what the *Express* would pay me. I felt that if someone was trusting enough to open themselves up to me at a time of personal anguish, then I should do whatever was in my power to protect them. To deal with an unfamiliar paper would, I decided, represent an unacceptable risk. I called Annie's manager back again, and we talked the situation through.

Within twenty minutes, the singer was on the telephone to me from her bed at a west London hospital, her partner, Uri, by her side. I was sitting at our kitchen table, an empty notepad before me. There was little for me to do but listen and write. The accumulating lines of Teeline script told the story of a seemingly normal pregnancy, and the unexplained tragedy with which it had ended the day before. Only when she came to the end of what she had to say did Annie cry, and this closeness to the intensity of her emotion made me cry, too. She insisted that hers and Uri's situation was one faced every day of every year by many other couples, and that they took comfort from that fact. Even though they would never forget the son they had just lost, they would try again for the baby they longed for.

It was an uncomfortable feeling, standing in the *Express* newsroom the following day, accepting the congratulations of people I didn't know and had never met before. I could almost feel my journalistic stock rising, yet I knew that it was on the back of someone else's private misery. That was not the way in which I had hoped to see my career advance. And it was strange, too, in the days that followed, to receive scores of letters from parents who had also suffered the trauma of a still-birth, and who wanted to pass on their condolences and good wishes to another couple in pain. This brought home to me the extent to which we live vicariously through those in the public eye, investing the details of their unfolding stories with hopes and fears that are universal. It reminded me, too, that wealth and fame are no protection from the harsh facts of everyday life and death.

Rarely is the interface between a celebrity and the general public about anything other than self and product promotion. This, though, had been about making a real and human connection. This had been about the opportunity to focus attention on a medical issue that would never have won space on the nation's front pages had it not impacted on a famous, media-sexy life. I realized then that Annie had been not only brave, but right to take that opportunity, and I respected her all the more because of it.

In the weeks that followed, my journalistic currency remained improbably high. Papers and magazines I'd had no previous connection with got hold of my number and called me. Some simply wanted a route to Annie, or to encourage me to think of contacting them the next time I had a similarly newsworthy interview at my disposal. But there were offers of work, too, based on the unspoken belief that I would be able to produce such goods a second time and then a third. Even at the *Express* offices, I sensed the weight of this expectation: I'd delivered the goods once, so could be relied upon to do so again. There was the offer of a staff job, but I decided to turn it down. I know my own strengths and weak-nesses, and I'm simply not hard-nosed enough to go after the story, no matter what.

Listening, prompting even, as someone tells you voluntarily of their heartbreak is one thing, putting a foot inside their door and compelling them to do so is quite another. I had been no good at it in Norfolk, and I knew I'd be no better at it now. Happily, Paul at the *Sunday Express Magazine* had been among my callers. He wanted nothing more from me than the acceptance of a commission that involved spending a week in Los Angeles. 'It'll be hellish. You'll have to lie by the pool for days on end, occasionally stir yourself to do a little light chatting to famous people,' he said. 'Up for it? Course you are! Great! I'll call you back with the details, 'cos I've gotta go now. I'm late for lunch. Bahhh!'

8

Arriving back on familiar territory, I was disappointed to find no sign in the reception area of my old friend, the camp concierge. Mr Jackson had indeed transformed himself since he last stayed at the Sunset Marquis. Here he was, better dressed than before, with socially acceptable luggage and even a charge card to his name. These days, it would take more than a woman singing Christmas carols to frighten him out of a jacuzzi. Yet while I could spot the difference in myself, it would have been nice to have got the official seal of approval. No matter. There were at least some compensations.

This time, when the booking clerk said, 'Always a pleasure to welcome you back to the hotel, sir,' I could almost bring myself to believe him. After all, I really had stayed there before. And there was the additional nicety of being asked which of the available suites I would prefer. 'I can offer you poolside, sir, or end-of-corridor, second floor.' Poolside sounded jolly and, crucially, less far to walk, too. It was late and I'd been travelling for so long that I was able to undress, fall onto my bed and be asleep within two minutes of entering the darkened bedroom.

I woke eight hours later, my face mashed into a mess of pillows, and became aware of a faint sound of chatter in the air. It was like birdsong, but made by humans. Almost immediately, the telephone purred. 'Mr Jackson? So sorry if I'm disturbing you. It's Alex here, at the front desk. A rather delicate matter, sir. One of the waiters serving out on the terrace has brought it to my attention that your blinds aren't properly closed, and that you are visible from the table nearest your window. We felt sure you'd want to be advised of the fact.'

Slowly my brain came up to speed, assimilated and then acted upon the information it had just been given. I raised my head and looked over my right shoulder towards the window. Sunlight was streaming in through the angled vertical slats, and immediately beyond them, on the other side of a floor-to-ceiling expanse of glass, was the source of that chatter: two women, perhaps in their late forties, in animated conversation over coffee and croissants. Suddenly, comprehension dawned. If I could see them, it followed logically that they could see me. And I was lying on my stomach, naked, on top of the sheets. God, no.

Belatedly covering my blushing cheeks with a pillow, I slid firstly to the far side of the bed, then onto the floor. 'I can't tell you how sorry I am,' I said into the telephone. 'I had no idea. It was late when I checked in and I was so tired and . . . Well, anyway, could you please apologize on my behalf to the ladies concerned. I'm mortified, really.'

Alex sought to reassure me. 'It's not that there was a complaint, Mr Jackson,' he said. 'If anything, I think it was a source of some amusement. But I did feel that you'd want the situation pointing out to you. Now once again, I apologize for the disturbance. Be sure to have a nice day!'

I crawled across the floor, into the bathroom, and sat down on the cold tiles, still feeling hot with embarrassment. Then the telephone purred again. It was Dawn, the PR who was accompanying me to that morning's interview with choreographer-turned-pop-star Paula Abdul. 'We're going to do it over a late breakfast in the Polo Lounge of the Beverly Hills Hotel,' she reported. 'The Pink Palace, they call it here, apparently. Completely over-the-top old Hollywood. Anyway, I've booked the table for 10 a.m. But let's eat here first before going over there.'

The Polo Lounge had a reputation among people who cared about such things for being the ultimate power-breakfast venue. In particular, television and film executives of a certain age favoured it as a place to see and be seen. Dawn's legitimate fear was that, as a result of all this avid people-watching, it would be considered bad form – worse still, would mark us out as hopeless parvenus – to actually be seen eating anything. 'And I'm starving,' she said. 'Why don't we each get room service before taking a cab over there? That way we'll already be full, and we can just push small pieces of fruit around our plates like everyone else.'

Being hungry myself, but also unwilling to cause further ribaldry on the terrace outside my room by emerging there to eat, I applauded her logic. Within an hour, I had dealt successfully with a three-egg omelette and side order of bacon, two rounds of toast and a pot of coffee. Thus able to appear convincingly and sophisticatedly lacking in appetite, I felt ready for the Polo Lounge and all it could throw at me. Letting my belt out one forgiving notch, I went in search of Dawn.

'I couldn't eat another thing,' she said, as our cab moved enthusiastically in and out of the late rush-hour traffic on Sunset Boulevard. 'And, at this rate, I won't want anything more than a glass of water and a lie-down when we get to where we're going.'

I could sympathize and, in an attempt to distract the two of us from feeling nauseous, decided to recount to her the story of how my morning had begun. It became increasingly difficult to do so, given the horn-hooting and across-lane lurching of our driver. It's said that everyone you meet in Los Angeles is a resting actor, waiting for his or her break. It seemed more likely that we were at the mercy of a resting stuntman, one just waiting for that call from Schwarzenegger or Willis: 'Arnie! Bruce! What? You're lookin' for someone who can go the length of Sunset in just two minutes flat and on two wheels? Buddy, I'm your man!'

By the time we pulled up outside the elegant portals of the Beverly Hills Hotel, and two dazzlingly handsome young men in white chinos and purple polo shirts had stepped out from behind the topiary to open the cab doors for us, Dawn and I had turned a most unpleasant shade from the Dulux Weathershield paint card. Wheeler-dealers from the entertainment world? We looked like wannabe extras for a remake of *Night Of The Living Dead*.

'If looking not hungry is a sign of breeding, we'll be the smartest couple here,' she groaned, as we reeled into the lobby.

'Throwing up across a rug would be a step too far, though,' I hissed, smiling through gritted teeth at the succession of bowing, murmuring staff we encountered. 'Just breathe deeply. And if the worst comes to the worst, deposit your breakfast in your handbag. Lucky you for having one.'

The Polo Lounge did at least look splendid, its rose-pink and mint-green decor lit by filtered sunshine and the expensive sparkle both of crystal and the perfect dentistry of its patrons. Dawn and I smiled gratefully as we were shown to our table. Yes, a further two guests would be joining us. And no, we needed nothing more than mineral water right now, thank you.

'God, but we're fashionable,' I whispered, our hostess having turned on her heels. 'So fashionable that there's absolutely no food on our plates.'

'We've also been placed within projectile-vomiting distance of the kitchen doors,' noted Dawn, a true professional, even when afflicted with a malady. 'We can't do the interview here. It'd be disrespectful to Paula. Don't they know how many millions of albums she's sold this year? I'm going to have to get us moved closer to the middle of the room.'

A discreet, but obviously persuasive word did the trick. Within seconds, we and our water had been relocated to a satisfyingly prominent, roomy booth adjoining that of a party which included the actress Tracy Ullman and her producer husband. 'Perfect,' said Dawn, lifting a glass to her lips, not drinking and then putting it down again. 'Just perfect.'

She was right. Prominent was good but, as it turned out, roomy was even better. For when the doll-perfect Paula arrived minutes later – there was the Beverly Hills equivalent of a Mexican wave as she moved across the floor towards us, one table after another standing to air-kiss and 'Mwhah! Mwhah!' her – it was not just with her manager, Barry, in tow. It was both of her managers Barry. Mindful of the theory I'd developed after meeting my old chief reporter Barry in Norfolk, then the great Barry White, I checked to see if they were wearing safari suits. Theory disproved.

'Hi, I'm Barry,' said the first, who looked like Barry Manilow fresh off a sunbed.

'Hi, I'm Barry, too,' said the second, who didn't.

'Or Barry two,' suggested the first. I laughed, then noticed that the second Barry didn't seem to think this funny – it wasn't – and so stopped.

There was a quick reshuffle of table-placings and then we each attempted the embarrassing limbo dance which is the only way to take or leave your place at a banquette. Were we ready to order? The Barry on Dawn's left shoulder urged her to have pancakes with maple syrup, as he was doing. The Barry on her right applauded her wisdom in choosing the fresh fruit platter, his own preference. 'But only a very small one,' insisted Dawn, so pulling off a delicious piece of Californian one-upmanship.

I had fresh fruit, too, as did Paula, all three of us pushing it around our respective dishes, scarcely ever taking a mouthful. Across the table, real-estate prices were being animatedly discussed. I attempted to block out this conversation and conduct an interview instead. You're so beautiful, and I feel so ill, I remember thinking, staring glassy-eyed at Paula. If only I could just lie down, put my head in your lap and go to sleep.

Five years later, in London, I met her again. In the time that had passed, her record sales had slumped, a short-lived marriage to actor Emilio Estevez had broken down and she had publicly acknowledged a long-running battle against the eating disorder bulimia. So perhaps she too had been feeling wretched, toying with the overpriced berries and other bits and pieces on her plate that day. And for her it would have been a way of life, not just the product of a one-off pig-out and some reckless driving.

'The minute a little girl is given her first Barbie doll, the programming starts,' she told me then. 'It's equivalent to saying to that child, "This is what beautiful looks like, and so this is how you should aspire to look if you want to be considered that way." Well, my first Barbie was blonde, tanned and had legs that stretched to eternity . . . And look at me!'

Though born and raised in the San Fernando Valley, she had a lineage that included Brazilian and Syrian grandparents. Tiny and dark-skinned, she represented the antithesis of the conventional Californian beach babe. 'And when you're very young, you don't realize that you are genetically predisposed to look a certain way, and that's all there is to it. So you pick up your first teen magazine and you look at those fashion models, and that's what they become to you: models, in the most literal sense. You end up struggling towards some unattainable physical ideal.

'I don't remember a time when my friends and I weren't slimming or trying out some kind of diet. Always, we wanted to be thinner, taller, and I don't think we were untypical. There aren't many women around who don't say things like, "I'm so full" or "Just look at my stomach" or "These jeans fitted yesterday". There aren't many women who don't dream of being a dress size smaller. It's mad, isn't it?'

Yes, absolutely. But when I first sat gazing at her, trying not to be distracted by the energetic property-speak to which the Barrys were treating Dawn, I had none of this information at my disposal. I simply thought that she was beautiful, but that possibly she made a virtue of undereating in public, as so many rich and famous women do. Over the years, I've found myself worrying about the weight and, hence, personal stability of female artists I've met, ranging from Polly Harvey to Celine

Dion. The loss of Karen Carpenter and her voice was bad enough; we neither need nor want another celebrity victim of image-distortion. But just when does sleek and fabulous-looking also come to mean obsessive and self-denying? And even if you appear healthy and well-fed, are you really OK on the inside?

Some years later, I wondered about this on meeting Alanis Morissette. She was twenty-one. Within a year of its release, her album *Jagged Little Pill* had sold in excess of 12 million copies worldwide. With equanimity and total poise, and at an age when many of us haven't yet taken our first decisive steps into the world, she talked of previous incarnations. The first was as the ten-year-old star of a Canadian TV sitcom, *You Can't Do That On Television*, filmed in her home town of Ottawa. As a result of that show she had received long-distance hate mail. 'My character was introduced as the romantic interest for the two lead guys, and I guess some of the girls watching at home resented my presence,' she said flatly, twisting a strand of hair around her finger.

Four years later, she had been reborn as a bouncy pop singer. 'Back then, I thought the role of music was to make people smile, to distract them from their daily lives. And I enjoyed aiming for that, particularly because I was a really great dancer. Seeing the front rows grinning back at me was a lot more gratifying, and safer, than seeing them look disturbed or provoked or anything else that was a step towards intro-spection.' But though a willing partner in her record label's strategy to confirm her as a teenage icon, she found the attendant pressure to look and behave in a certain way played on her latent insecurities.

'I could talk on this issue for hours,' she said. 'But let's start by acknowledging that maybe only three per cent of the population meet what has become the prescribed standard for physical beauty. That leaves the other ninety-seven per cent of us in the ludicrous situation of feeling unattractive or, at best, quirky. Rationally, we know we're all so different, and so should be able to figure out that the prescribed standard is just one more obstacle to be transcended on the path to self-acceptance. But I gave in to tyranny for a long time. It's very easy to do that when you have low self-esteem and judge your worth in terms of external success and what you look like. And that's really unfulfilling, you know?'.

But back to that first occasion with Paula Abdul. She and I said our goodbyes in the native manner, with lots of air-kissing and exchanges of business cards. 'I've really enjoyed talking with you,' she'd said. 'Next time you're in town, call Barry and have him set up a lunch. It'd be fun. D'you promise?' I promised, but didn't follow through. Was I meant to? For a start, and on a purely practical level, which Barry should I have called? And would it have been in the least bit fun for her, the closet victim of an eating disorder? Fathoming the intricacies of human relationships are hard enough when both parties are on an equal footing. Doing so when one is rich and famous and the other not so is all but impossible.

Preparing to leave the Polo Lounge, and mindful of our earlier experience, Dawn took no chances with the return driver. 'Typical tourists, I know, but we're only in Los Angeles for a short while and we want to savour it as much as we can,' she told him. 'Could you bear to go as slowly as is reasonably possible for, let's see . . . here! An extra twenty dollars above the metered fare? We'd be really grateful.' As a result, we were borne along Sunset as if we were made of glass, arriving back at the hotel feeling revived enough to consider a drink and an idle hour by the pool.

'Oh, but Mr Jackson. Just a moment.' I looked round to find the male receptionist waving energetically in my direction. 'Hi! I'm Alex. We spoke on the phone this morning. There's a message here for you.'

There was no name on the unsealed envelope he handed me. 'Are you sure this is for me?' I asked.

'Oh, quite sure,' he twinkled back. 'It's from the ladies I referred to earlier.'

Puzzled, I went outside to where Dawn was now sitting. 'I hope it's not some sort of complaint,' I worried aloud. 'People here sue you if you so much as sneeze on them. Perhaps one of those women is saying the sight of me naked caused her mental and emotional trauma. I could be on the wrong end of a law suit.'

'Just open the envelope and order a beer, for goodness sake,' said Dawn, drawing her sunglasses down from her forehead and settling back into her chair.

I followed her first instruction. Inside, written in a flamboyant pencil scrawl on the piece of hotel stationery I unfolded, were just two words and an exclamation mark: 'Nice ass!'

'Obviously a forgery,' yawned Dawn, handing the note back to me. 'Do you send yourself extra birthday and Christmas cards, too. Ones with false signatures. "Dah–ling, can't believe we're not going to be together. But thinking of you always. I love you, Madonna. XXX."'

Our drinks arrived, and we sat for a minute or so in silence. Then, suddenly, Dawn sat upright. 'See that guy on the other side of the pool, third lounger from the right? I'm sure that's Bruce Springsteen.'

'He's face-down. How can you possibly know?'

'I just do. You're not thinking of having that note framed,

are you? I could recycle it by having it sent over to him. There's someone who really does have a nice ass.'

The itinerary of interviews Paul had planned for me meant my staying in Los Angeles for a little over a week. Dawn flew back to London. I negotiated a transfer to a first-floor suite, fearing that any further oversights with the window furnishings would win me a reputation as a serial exhibitionist. Thus installed, I got on with my work. I began by driving out beyond Malibu and, off Highway 101, waiting for a particularly ferocious set of electronic gates to open slowly and admit me. And then another set. And another. They guarded the home of Herb Alpert, the one-time Tijuana trumpeter turned jazz musician, painter, philanthropist and label boss. With Jerry Moss, he had co-founded the hugely successful A&M Records, home to acts that included The Carpenters, The Police and Janet Jackson. Run initially from a garage, it was bought out twenty-seven years later by Polygram for a staggering $500 million. Perhaps it stood to rights that a man who dealt in such sums would believe it took more than a Banham burglar alarm and a barking dog to guarantee security on his six-acre estate.

Once, late in my primary-school career, our family only recently having moved to the north-east, the next-door neighbours asked my parents if I might like to go on a short break to Scotland. I was to be company for their son, Brian, my exact same age. I didn't really want to go, but was told that I did. I remember very little about the resultant holiday, other than that, one perfect, sunny afternoon, we stopped at the side of some country road and went paddling in a stream. The water was icy, despite the day, and the stones underfoot felt as big as boulders. We two boys were hobbling and splashing in the shallow, fast-running water when, suddenly, the sound of music reached me from the car radio. It was Herb, singing Burt Bacharach and Hal David's 'This Guy's In Love With You'. I had never heard the record before, and it was beautiful. Even now, if I hear it played, I remember the concurrent feelings of cold and warmth, and the blue summer sky.

It was a similarly glorious day as I pulled up outside his house – split-level, self-designed, built predominantly of wood and glass – all those years later. An LA-based photographer had been commissioned to cover the assignment and was already at work photographing Herb, a tall, handsome man who was then in his early fifties. I was welcomed by his wife, the singer Lani Hall, and together we walked out into a garden so luxuriantly perfect that it might have been the work of a Disney animator on drugs. Ornamental pools teamed with fat orange koi, forever jostling and leaping into the air. The grass was greener than in a child's painting, and as thick and pliant as sponge. And beyond it, over a low stone wall that marked the cliff's edge, was the blue, blue ocean. 'Do you see that?' asked Lani, pointing to a thin triangle of rock pointing high above the water, midway to the horizon. 'At night, we can activate a spotlight that shines right on it. Isn't it just beautiful?'

As beautiful as money could buy. As I drank it in, Mrs Alpert spotted that her husband was accommodating the photographer to the extent of lying back on a section of the perimeter wall, arms folded over his chest. 'Herb, don't pose like that. It's macabre,' she ordered. 'Alan and I are going inside to talk. We'll be in the kitchen when you're finished.'

We padded back across the velveteen greensward, towards the house, me feeling secretly delighted. As a kid looking out at the world, a very few key things signified to me glamour and the possibility of a jet-set life being lived elsewhere by other people. European cars were one. The French Panhard was my favourite, even though I'd only ever seen it in pictures – every Christmas I would ask for the new edition of *The Observer Book of Automobiles*. The Martini adverts they screened at the cinema were another – all those beautiful people moving around on a terrace, smiling and chinking their glasses. And, most potent of all, was the voice of Lani Hall. It was she who took the lead vocal on the recordings of Sergio Mendes and Brazil '66, and who imbued versions of Antonios Carlos Jobim compositions like 'Mas Que Nada' and 'Desafinado' with that cool, light, international edge. And twenty years after first discovering her name in the small print on an album sleeve, here I was sitting in her kitchen.

Of necessity, I adopted a straight-backed, hands-folded-in-lap pose. I couldn't so much as rest an elbow on top of the circular table that separated us. Every inch of its surface was covered with small bottles and plastic tubs containing dietary supplements and the like. 'I admit that we're a little obsessive about our lifestyle,' smiled Lani, sipping steadily from a glass of filtered water. 'We grow every possible vegetable here, from artichokes to zucchini, plus our own apples, oranges and lemons, and we have chickens that we don't kill but whose eggs we eat. Herb's really into vitamins, as you can see, while my rule is that I won't eat anything not organic. I won't even eat in restaurants. If we're invited out some place, I'll prepare my own food in advance and take it with me, rather than risk putting chemicals or additives into my body. As for drugs or alcohol . . . You have to be joking.'

Other journalists I knew interviewed junkies. They mixed with musicians who were rarely to be found without a syringe hanging from their arm or a rolled banknote raised to their nostril. The only pill-poppers I got to meet were the sort who'd faint if they realized they were talking to a man who occasionally set foot in fast-food outlets and who had, once, sometime in the winter of 1979, actually munched his way through an entire late-night kebab. Just two weeks earlier, back in London, I had interviewed Roberta Flack, the singer whose duet with Donny Hathaway, 'The Closer I Get To You', I had played near-daily on that pub jukebox while at journalism college in Cardiff. A dumpling on thin legs, she had entered the hotel lobby carrying a handbag the size of her home state, North Carolina. It was, in effect, her mobile medicine chest. And over the course of the forty minutes we spent together, she extracted from it an entire Boots'-worth of pots and phials, and unconcernedly set about swallowing her daily intake of this and that vitamin. Now there was Lani.

I wondered if she knew that, in the diner close to the A&M Records lot, where I had eaten supper the previous evening, there was actually a burger that bore her husband's name. Was it his habit to sneak out for a quick grease-and-carbohydrate fix, before leaving the office and heading back home to organic, additive-free Fort Malibu? He had now entered the room, so it occurred to me to ask him. But not wanting to get him into trouble with the wife – illicit French-fry consumption might well have been grounds for divorce in Lani's book – I made do with an enquiry about the motivation for his current diet-consciousness.

'Back in 1983 I contracted hepatitis, dropped fifteen pounds in weight and felt like I might be about to check out of this life,' he explained, eventually adding that yes, he knew about the burger, and yes, he used to eat them there – but a long, long time ago. 'Then I was put on this very precise diet and noticed straight away that there was a direct connection between what I put into my body and how I felt. And as you get older, that link intensifies. In my twenties, I could line up at McDonald's alongside the next man, eat my way through the menu and bounce straight back. Now my system takes longer to right itself.'

Sounds fair enough, I thought, driving back along Highway 101, through Malibu itself. Seeing the sudden profusion of cafés and bars, I realized I was hungry and pulled over. Up on the boardwalk, I found Alice's Restaurant and, sitting next to an open window, savoured the ozone in the air and watched the surfers at play. 'Any relishes for you today?' asked my waitress, placing a giant, oval plate of superior junk food before me. I asked for mayonnaise and tried to imagine the Alperts' reaction to my lunch. A Laniburger, it was not. But then, a Laniburger was something you would have to make at home, slipping a few shreds of organically grown lettuce and nothing much else between some wholemeal, unbuttered buns, and then take out with you in a Tupperware box. The concept would never catch on.

Back at the Sunset Marquis, I took a swim. Although it was still warm, a covering of cloud had gathered, and the pool area was deserted at this dead, late-afternoon hour. Slowly, mindlessly, I made my way back and forth through the water, thinking of everything, thinking of nothing. Then, all at once, on approaching the shallower end, I found myself confronted by a laughing, splashing child, perhaps eighteen months or two years in age. Supported by his father, he slapped his palms down again and again on the surface of the turquoise-hued water, mouth wide open in delight. It was the sort of moment that makes you wistful for parenthood.

'He's having a great time,' I remarked, turning round in the water, without really looking up.

'Yeah,' confirmed the dad. 'He loves getting in here,

especially when it's quiet. And his mom loves it, too, 'cos it tires him right out.'

I swam away again, and continued lazily to make my way up and down, up and down. But each time I approached the shallow water, the little boy was there, smiling at me and the world, occasionally shrieking with pleasure.

'You've made a friend,' said his dad, holding him out towards me.

'I'm glad to hear it. He's a lovely kid. What's his name?'

'Evan. Evan James.'

'Pleased to meet you, Evan. I'm Alan. How're you doing?'

By now, I was grinning as widely as he was, and stood and held out my hand for a mock-adult shake. In response, the dad raised his son towards me. 'Say hello to your new buddy Alan,' he said. 'Alan, Evan. Evan, Alan.'

I pantomimed my side of the introduction and was rewarded with a megawatt beam from the little lad. Delighted, I smiled up at his dad. Fuck! Above the blue shorts and the toned torso was a bearded face that belonged to none other than Bruce Springsteen, a man whose exclusive interview every music journalist of the time dreamed of winning. Dawn had been right. He was using the same hotel. Now, what to do about it? How to get that interview? By diving underwater and whipping off his trunks, thus holding him hostage until he agreed to talk? By seizing the kid and threatening to drown him? Hardly. 'Good to meet you both,' I said, and swam off again, leaving father and son to enjoy their quality time uninterrupted.

Shortly afterwards, Springsteen's wife, Patti Scialfa, appeared with an older, similarly red-haired woman, possibly her mother. As the two fussed over Evan and dried him with a giant towel, the singer raised himself up out of the water, balanced on the pool's edge and then dived, neatly and deeply, back in. A plume of spray rose instantly into the air and then splattered down onto the hot ground. When he broke the surface again, a vexed Patti was waiting for him, pulling at her jeans and T-shirt.

'Bruce, that was such a dumb thing to do. We're completely soaked up here.'

He pulled an aw-shucks face and squinted up at her. 'Sorry, honey. I wasn't thinking.'

'Obviously.'

He grinned. She melted. Then Bruce, hauling himself out of the water, dripping, made as if to hug her. Patti pushed him away, laughing now, and threw a white robe at him. I looked away, feeling like a voyeur on a private moment. Smiling to myself, I went indoors and began to dial my home number back in London. Then it occurred to me to check the time. It would be one o'clock in the morning in England. I put down the phone, reminding myself that aw-shucks faces don't work as well long distance. And Christine and I had already talked earlier, and could do so later if I stayed up long enough to catch her before she left for work. Instead, I called Sheena Easton, who had become my one true friend in this strangest of cities. Yes, she was still free. We would meet for an early dinner at Genghis Cohen's, a Chinese restaurant she liked.

'How come no-one else here is drinking?' I asked, looking from my glass of beer to her glass of water, and then to all the many such others placed ostentatiously on tables around the room.

'Because if you have any kind of public profile at all, and you're seen out with a glass of alcohol in your hand, people assume that you're a lush,' she told me. 'Judgements like that are passed real fast, and are impossible to overturn. But then, this is a town where everyone eats early. So those who want to can leave their table by nine, drive home sober and then do whatever is their pleasure. And the rest of us are none the wiser. That's how things are here.'

I returned to the Sunset Marquis to find myself greeted in the crowded lobby with the cheerful exclamation, 'Chopper Jackson!' Instantly, I was enveloped in a bear hug. The man, whom I will call Greg, precisely because I know no-one of that name in the British music industry, was one of my very favourite London PRs – straightforward, funny and always good company. And here he was, newly arrived in the city, but with the small party of music-paper journalists travelling with him having already doubled in number. This happened everywhere he went. I'd been to New York with Greg and, on a previous occasion, to Los Angeles. In both instances, and within minutes of checking in, he was busy on the phone, address book in hand. The results were near instantaneous: bright, attractive people, old friends from school or college, would suddenly materialize in reception, often trailing bright, attractive friends of their own.

Such was the case tonight, and Greg's party was about to move on. A friend of a friend was apartment-sharing with the British boxer Gary Stretch, while both tried to break into acting. Gary was meeting various friends of his own in the bar of the nearby Mondrian Hotel on Sunset, and so everyone else was going there, too. 'You've got to come with us,' Greg instructed. 'Everybody! This is Chopper. He's joining the party.'

We arrived outside the Mondrian at exactly the same moment as two ludicrously *Easy Rider*-ish motorbikes. Dismounting awkwardly, and handing their crash helmets to the valet parking boys, were the singer Paul Young and Gary himself. 'The others are already inside,' Gary called to his flat-mate, the friend of Greg's friend, 'I see you've found a few pals of your own. Who's getting the drinks in?'

In the crowded twilight of the bar, we jostled for space, some twenty people, only a handful of whom actually knew each other. 'Stacy, I'd like you to meet Chopper,' said Greg, drawing me towards the glamorous, dark-haired woman he'd been talking to. 'Chopper, this is Stacy, Mrs Paul Young.'

'Delighted to meet you.'

'Likewise. That's a funny name you've got.'

'It's not my real one, just Greg's joke. I'm Alan.'

'So why does he call you Chopper?'

'It's a long—'

'Precisely!' Greg butted in. 'A very long story. But the gist of it is that he's got an absolutely ginormous—'

'Except I haven't. It's really very ordinary.'

I couldn't imagine why I was having this conversation at all, let alone this soon after being introduced to someone. Stacy looked appropriately iffy about what I assumed she viewed as silly lads' talk, so, with Greg's attention distracted, I asked how she was finding LA as a temporary home. She told me, in some detail, ending with a remark about how disconcerting it was to find so many uniformly attractive people gathered in one place.

'But I imagine you can soon get bored with conventional good looks, particularly if there's no spark behind them. I turned on the TV in my room last night and there was this beauty pageant on. Rachel Hunter, Rod Stewart's wife, was hosting it. I mean, yes, she's very good-looking, but talk about wooden.'

'She's a very good friend of mine, actually. Rachel's a lovely person.'

'Oh, I'm really sorry. And I'm sure she is. Wooden can be good. I mean, lots of beautiful things are made of wood. Trees, for a start. Trees are great. And . . .'

It was useless. Stacy had turned on her heel and was threading her way through the crowd in search of more congenial company. I never saw her or her husband again. I was standing on my own, finishing off my bottle of beer, when Greg rediscovered me. 'Paul and Gary are really good mates with Mickey Rourke. Gary's been teaching him how to box. And Mickey's got this club which is supposed to be just great. Everyone's piling off down there in a minute. Are you up for it? Apparently there's girls – y'know, dancing in cages. It'll be a laugh. Come on!'

I told him I was tired, because I was, and that I'd really rather just get an early night. I was interviewing Janet Jackson the following day. She was supposed to be painfully shy and, as a result, hard work. I wanted to be well-prepared.

'I know it's really boring of me, but I don't want to fuck up. I haven't been writing for this guy at the *Sunday Express Magazine* for long, and—'

'If it's just that you're tired, I can give you a line.'

I gave him a hug and said that no, I was fine as I was, and would really rather go back. But as the rest of my week unfolded and I became regularly absorbed into whatever evening plans Greg and his group of friends had made, I was reminded of the extent to which recreational drugs were a part of the world in which I now moved. Before starting out each night, for wherever, the party would gather in his suite and do their preparatory coke-snorting. Or, if supplies had been exhausted, the search would be on for more. For example, someone knew a model who had stuff she could sell on, but she was at dinner at this restaurant or that. And so I would find myself sitting outside in the restaurant carpark as Greg or whoever went in to join her table for coffee and covertly make the pick-up. I had no interest in doing coke myself, but I liked the guy who was the prime mover in all of this. As a result, I was the narcotics equivalent of a gooseberry in his relationship with the stuff.

Finally, on the last night before I left LA, I tired of pulling those none-for-me-thanks expressions and of being the only one in the room not hoovering up from a glass-topped table. There were perhaps fifteen of us in the room and everyone else had done their lines. 'Here, your go,' said a woman who hadn't been there on previous evenings, a producer from a British television company who had been instrumental in locating the evening's supply. It was the fact that she didn't even consider I might not be using that swung it for me. Everyone else is so OK with this, and you've never even tried it, I said to myself. Are you going to avoid every new experience that has an element of risk involved? It's not like you're being invited to mainline heroin or free-base crack.

People seemed genuinely pleased that, finally, I'd joined the party. I was clapped on the back by people who had taken delight in teasing me, four nights running, about my abstinence. Greg came over and ruffled my hair. And the woman from the television company, a complete stranger, linked arms with me as we walked through the lobby and out towards our waiting cabs. The schoolboy within me, the one who went to St Mary's RC Primary, had already intervened, however. He's a vigilant and tenacious little soul. It was he who had me make an excuse and dart into the bathroom upstairs. It was he who'd urged me to blow my lines straight back into a Kleenex.

211

Three days later, I arrived at a Soho preview theatre for the screening of a television film featuring an actor I was soon to interview. I had barely crossed the threshold into the darkened auditorium before I was grabbed by someone I couldn't – properly see. 'Christ, am I glad you've turned up!' came a fierce whisper in my ear. 'Got any coke on you? I'm desperate.' It was the woman from my final night in Los Angeles, acting on the only piece of knowledge she had about me.

I have never felt impelled to try a drug since that night.

Crossing Blackfriars bridge in the failing light of a late winter afternoon, I found myself walking straight into the chest of a familiar, leather-jacketed figure. 'Now then!' said my old scourge; the Freelance From Hell, looking suspiciously pleased to encounter me. 'Haven't seen you around in ages. Thought maybe you'd had to make a change of career? Anyway, s'pose you've noticed that I've been tarred with the brush of fame – I'm placing big features with the opposition these days. Top bands, and all. It was the best thing I ever did, telling you I was defecting. Wouldn't go back now, no matter how much they begged me. Well, got to go. Editorial meeting. I've hardly got time to scratch my arse these days. I hope things'll work out for you.'

He was gone. I walked on. Although he and I worked in a related medium, we inhabited very different worlds these days. Encouraged by Lou, Paul and other journalists and commissioning editors I'd been introduced to, and in order to guarantee myself a living as a fledgling freelance, I was plying my trade far and wide. Record companies had begun to actively court me. Today it was that of the American singer Stevie Nicks. She was, at the time, on leave from Fleetwood Mac, the band with which she'd had great success in the late

Seventies and early Eighties, and was in Britain to make a solo album, *The Other Side Of The Mirror*. I had been invited out to the Buckinghamshire home of its producer, Rupert Hine, where she was living and working.

I was well-prepared. I'd been sent a sheaf of biographical information in advance, plus photocopies of past interviews and profiles, and I had studied these at length. In amongst this weight of paper had been a selection of glossy photographs from a recent session, commissioned for promotional use. They showed her swathed in trademark bolts of black lace, her face thin and pale, her eyes huge and rimmed with kohl, her lips moistly painted. It was Stevie Nicks as the world has always known her.

But when she entered the room, paused awkwardly and then came forward to shake my hand, I had to make a physical effort to stop my face betraying dismay, both at how she looked and at my own naivety. Of course the camera lies. Those in the public eye depend on it to do so. Photographers and retouch artists make a living from colluding in the process. Stevie's hair, white-blond in those photographs, was hard and brassy and set in stiff waves about her face and shoulders. The ghostly perfection of her features, though still discernible, was blurred and caricatured by heavy make-up. And her body, no longer slim and youthful, looked even heavier than it might otherwise have done, due to the fussy, high-collared, floor-length dress she was wearing. It was deep red in collar and patterned with dark, overblown roses. It turned her into an armchair.

All of this would have been irrelevant had she seemed confident and happy in herself. But she didn't. She looked bloated and self-conscious, and at the first opportunity she sank down at the dining table which dominated the room.

There, she pulled in her elbows, placed her arms across her chest and hugged her shoulders tightly, thus making herself appear as tiny as I'd believed her to be. We were to have dinner together – for Stevie, whose habit it was to sleep all day and work all night, it represented breakfast – but food didn't tempt her. She could feign no interest in, or enjoyment of, the white fish and steamed vegetables which had been prepared for her, thus doing the Californian thing. She merely pushed them around the plate, scarcely ever raising the fork to her mouth.

The very second that this awkward ritual could have been said to be over, Stevie half stood in her chair and suggested we went upstairs to talk. 'It's quieter there. Fewer distractions,' she said, motioning towards a television visible through the open door of an adjoining room, and before which two male studio hands were slumped, plates on lap. 'Give us about an hour. No disturbances,' she told her PR, Brian. Then, seizing an open but untouched bottle of red wine, and asking for me, please, to bring some glasses, she moved towards the staircase leading to her bedroom.

Out of respect, I held back as she began to ascend its tightly winding spiral. Thus, as she did so, I was able to see, beneath the flounced hem of her dress, a pair of vertiginously platformed boots. It was a decade since such footwear had been fashionable, and it would be another decade at least before it came back into vogue. This intimate sighting of them made her appear oddly vulnerable. 'It can be hard work, being stuck in a timewarp,' observed Stevie, wryly, over her shoulder, in reference to the slow, deliberate way they forced her to move.

It was some sixth sense that caused me to look in the direction of the two men in the next-door room. Both were watching me and grinning. Having caught my eye, one offered a ripe, comedic, man-to-man wink. Clearly, they were reading the situation in seaside-picture-postcard terms: the little man, led upstairs to his fate by the larger woman. I wouldn't flatter myself. 'Are you all right down there? Come on up.' It was Stevie speaking. Knowing myself to be blushing, I began hurriedly to climb.

Hers was an old-fashioned, feminine room, dominated by a vast bed, covered in bridal white. Through the open curtains, the night sky was black. Inside, all was suffused with a rosy glow from table lamps which had been draped with fringed silk scarves. As I took my place in a low armchair that faced her bedside, Stevie poured wine for us both, then settled herself within the snowdrift of pillows and cushions at it's head. 'Our good health,' she said, raising her glass at me, 'and here's to a good interview.' I toasted her back, thinking how much she resembled one of those mock-Victorian dolls advertised towards the back of the Sunday supplements.

She needed so little encouragement to talk that I felt like some pretend psychiatrist, sitting quietly beside her and inter-jecting only occasionally, to prompt or murmur assent, or to seek clarification of some point or other. Articulate, and seemingly glad of the opportunity to air her feelings, she spoke of the stresses and anomalies of being a successful woman in what was still then an industry largely run by, and favouring, men. Of her romance with, and painful estrange-ment from, a colleague in Fleetwood Mac, Lindsey Buckingham. Of a subsequent, disastrous and short-lived marriage to the newly widowed husband of her late best female friend from childhood. And of a cocaine addiction fuelled not only by what had been a relentless work schedule, maintained over the course of many years, but also the overexacting standards against which she judged her own achievements.

For forty or fifty minutes she continued to expound in this easy, self-analytical way. I was surprised and flattered by such openness. To date, my experience of American celebrities was that they viewed interviews as little more than a promotional vehicle for their latest enterprise, and for the projection of a carefully prepared and maintained public image. Here was someone who was prepared to lay themselves open to intimate scrutiny, to admit their failings and the extent to which their life held disappointments. 'Getting older is no easy thing for a woman, famous or otherwise,' she said suddenly. 'I've got about two years left in which I probably still could have children. I'd love to have a baby. Would *love* to. I love children, love babies. But I don't know how it's going to happen. My diary is booked solid throughout those next two years and . . .'

She stopped for a moment, indicated for me to refill her glass and sighed deeply. 'Of course, if it were to happen with someone that I cared about, everything else would have to take a back seat. If I were to get pregnant, I would definitely stop being an overachiever. I would start taking better care of myself. I'd get more rest, not stay up all night, eat well and take my vitamins, all of that stuff and . . .' We never got beyond the 'and'. Almost imperceptibly, silently at first, she had started to cry.

It was not the first time this had happened to me in an interview situation, but still, I felt wretched for having just sat there nodding encouragement as she brought herself to such a point of unhappiness. Stevie accepted the tissue I fumbled for, but brushed aside as unnecessary my apologies and expressions of concern. 'Really, I'm OK,' she said, wiping her eyes and nose, and climbing down from the bed. 'I think it's time for another toast. To future happiness.'

We clinked glasses and drank, and then she began to move around the room, as if searching for something. She found it on top of her dressing table: a small, domed box, the kind you get from a jeweller's.

'Here!' she said. 'I'd like to give you this as a memento of our having met.' And she pressed it into my palm and closed my fingers around it. 'I went shopping in a little town near here the other day and, d'you know, I had a lot more luck in finding things than I usually do at Saks Fifth Avenue or Bergdorf Goodman. I got this dress I'm wearing, and a whole lot of other dresses, and these books here and that old family Bible over there. Lots of stuff. And then I also got this.'

From beneath her frilled collar she extracted an old gold necklace, set with turquoise and seed pearls. 'And that goes with it,' she said, indicating the small box I was holding. Inside it was a matching, oval-shaped locket, fitted with a tiny glass door, behind which a photograph could be placed. 'Not really a guy thing, I know,' she added, 'so I'm not going to pin it to your lapel. But, well, maybe you'll think of me, and the conversation that we had, whenever you see it. Please! I want you to have it.'

I told her how touched I was, and tried to think if there was anything in my little rucksack with which I could reciprocate. Only the hardback novel I'd bought that morning, and which I hadn't yet taken out of its bag. 'It's by Gabriel Garcia Marquez,' I said, holding it out to her. 'I'd love it if you would accept it in return.'

She said that she would be pleased to, but only if I wrote a dedication in it first. I did so and, on accepting it, she looked first at the message of thanks and good wishes that I had put inside, and then at the cover of the book itself. 'Wow!' she said, pulling a dubious face. 'What exactly is it that you're giving me here?' And with that she dropped my copy of *Love In The Time of Cholera* onto the bedclothes and gestured at our empty glasses.

'More wine?' she asked, finding her smile again. 'We might as well finish it off.'

9

In the September of 1990, after almost ten years of living together, Christine and I got married. The particular impetus was provided by her mother, Agnes, who had been widowed five years earlier and was now increasingly compromised with Parkinson's disease. She had raised seven children, Christine being the youngest. In a family that large and all grown up, there was usually some happy occasion for her to focus on: a forthcoming birth, christening, confirmation or whatever. The anticipation of such events helped greatly to maintain both her good spirits and a determination to battle against her illness. But, by chance, there came a period when there was no such occasion on the horizon and her will to live appeared diminished. This was the kick up the backside that we'd been needing.

Like any other couple, there were moments when we doubted the wisdom of our decision. 'Is there any favourite "Our Tune" you'd like me to play during the signing of the register?' wondered the enthusiastic young organist of the Yorkshire parish we chose. 'A Phil Collins track, perhaps? I find he's very popular. OK, OK. I was only asking.'

Because neither of us like a fuss to be made, we kept things as simple as we could. We gave our respective families just four weeks' notice of the event, asking them, please, to try and be there. We didn't invite, or even tell in advance, our friends or work colleagues. We hoped they would understand, telephoned as many of those closest to us as we could just before or after the ceremony, asking them to celebrate for us that night, and then caught up with them when we were back from honeymoon. And we both walked up and, twenty minutes later, down the aisle together. Suddenly we were Mr and Mrs Jackson, even though the priest put the rings on the wrong fingers.

On the day after the wedding, we drove south and caught a late-afternoon ferry across to Calais. In the dark mid-evening, while making our way through northern France, I pulled on to the hard shoulder and attempted to look through a bag of favourite cassettes and CDs I'd assembled for the two weeks of our stay in a remote house in the Lot. Several of my favourite albums have associations with the same colour: *Kind Of Blue* by Miles Davis, *Blue Train* by John Coltrane, *A Walk Across The Rooftops* and *Hats* by The Blue Nile. And, of course, *Blue* by Joni Mitchell. It was this that came first to hand, and it played as we drove along a deserted autoroute towards our overnight stop. I hadn't heard it in some time, so it sounded familiar and new and wonderful all at once. I remember wondering how many more times in my life I would feel such calm and deep contentment.

Christine's mother was to live for another seven years, despite her illness and, eventually, despite also having suffered a massive stroke. One morning, meanwhile, some few months after the wedding, the telephone rang and I went to answer it, face lathered with shaving cream. On the line was a doctor I'd never heard of, let alone spoken to before. 'I'm very sorry to have to tell you that your father died a short time ago,' he said as I stood there, razor in hand. 'I have your mother here. She'd like to speak to you.'

Mum left alone; a widow. My dad, dead unexpectedly at sixty-six, and after little more than a year of the retirement he seemed to have been working towards for ever.

'So, how's the job?' I would ask sometimes.

'Only another forty-eight salary cheques to go,' he would reply. Or forty-seven, forty-six, forty-five and so on.

I used to think I was a disappointment to him, and that he would rather have had a son who loved aeroplanes and cricket and wood-working. These were among the things he was most interested in, and I imagine it would have given him pleasure to share his knowledge of them with me. I'm glad that he lived long enough for me to get over that feeling, allowing us to settle into a kind of friendship. I'm glad, too, that there had always been some areas of mutual interest, most especially music.

My mother associates him particularly with the records of Ella Fitzgerald. I find that I think of him whenever I hear the cool, milk-white voice of Peggy Lee, another of his favourites.

I was a small boy, just three or four years old, when first I heard it. And what a voice. It floated lightly from my parents' radio, out across the sunny back garden in which I was playing. The song was 'On The Street Where You Live'. Even then, I paid attention to lyrics, but couldn't always construct a sensible meaning from them. 'I have often walked down this street before,' began Peggy Lee. 'But the pavement always stayed beneath my feet before/All at once am I several storeys high/Knowing I'm on the street where you live . . .' She'd lost me.

Within the small network of streets that constituted for me, at the time, the entire known world, the footpaths were static and the houses had only an upstairs and a downstairs – my dad cleared things up a little by explaining the difference between storeys, which I was previously unfamiliar with, and stories, the things that were read at bedtime. Still, the world she sang of seemed impossibly far-off and glamorous and, instantly, I loved the singer who delivered this troubling lyric to me.

In the dawning days of the 1960s, other fine voices would sometimes be heard on radio performing the same song, those of Mel Tormé and Vic Damone included. But no-one else's version came close to Miss Lee's. Elegant, and with an inherent sense of fun, her voice tantalized me whenever – and in those far-off summers it was many times – its unique timbre was carried on the air, causing me to stop whatever game I was playing and listen. Along with those of other, equally sophisticated singers, such as Frank Sinatra and Nat 'King' Cole, her songs helped colour my earliest perceptions of America. Using information drawn from popular music, news reports and things that I heard adults say, I built for myself the picture of a distant land, in which people lived in strange, skyward-reaching apartment blocks, drove long, pastel-coloured cars and enjoyed serenely clement weather – all of this to a constant background of smooth, light, cocktail-friendly music.

As I grew, I continued to hear Peggy Lee's voice intermittently on the radios that provided the musical soundtrack to my childhood. Occasionally, I would be made aware of her in other contexts, too. In 1971, for example, there was the televised news coverage of Louis Armstrong's funeral, at which she performed a solemn, unaccompanied version of The Lord's Prayer. From time to time, too, she appeared as a guest on one or other of the big-budget variety packages popular around that time. On one occasion, I remember seeing her on a Petula Clark TV special, singing some song of loss and regret from amid the pillows of a stage-set bed. And, of course, I would come across her image in the local record-store racks which I trawled so obsessively.

Always, that image would be one of studied glamour: the lips Mona Lisa-like, offering the merest suggestion of a smile; the hair butter-yellow and luxuriantly arranged; the costumes those of a movie goddess. Dusty Springfield once told me that Peggy Lee's iconic appearance had been the inspiration for her own exaggerated stage look. I could see why. Though superficially seductive, it offered someone shy and insecure the equivalent of a mask to hide behind. One of her record sleeves in particular caught my imagination. It was for an album called *Norma Deloris Egstrom From Jamestown, North Dakota*, the singer's real name and place of birth, and pictured her sepia-tinted, the face impassive and porcelain-smooth above a collar of sleek, dark fur. On the reverse was a road map of the part of North Dakota she came from, her home town just one tiny junction within an extended spider's web of roads and rivers.

This juxtaposition of where she had started out from and what she had fashioned herself into made a distinct impression upon me. Everyone begins somewhere, it prompted me to realize, but has at least the capacity to end up in a different place, and as a different person. As, indeed, I was hoping to do myself.

Still, though, I gave no real prolonged thought to the real

woman who lived behind that artful public face. Then, while in my first year of university, I read in *The Sunday Times* a review by the late Derek Jewell of an LP she was about to release. 'Several years ago I saw Peggy Lee at the Albert Hall and, despite the happiest memories of this sensitive singer, was disappointed,' he wrote. 'She seemed simply to be rehashing the moods and music of her past; her voice and middle-aged aura couldn't stand it. Now, however, she has astonishingly reappeared with a new album called *Mirrors*, which for wit, aptness and sheer musical value is a major popular creation. The reason is simple: she is being her age, in terms of both her voice and her songs.'

This was long ago and far away; 1975, in fact, when long-playing records such as this – as the review concluded by advising readers – had a recommended retail price of just £2.99. I bought my copy, loved it then and still love it today. It's a great and underrecognized piece of work, one of the finest-ever achievements within an easy-listening genre too frequently characterized by the formulaic and the bland. In fact, it makes very uneasy listening.

The singer's own inspired, sometimes black-comedic, performances, and her cast of supporting musicians – an orchestra of such size and quality that it would be beyond most record-company budgets today – each contribute to the project's chilly brilliance. More effective still is the strange, dreamlike quality of the words and music, and their surprising bleakness – one tempered only by the pragmatic acceptance of the aging process described in the opening song, 'Ready To Begin Again'. In it, Lee, the newly woken narrator, reflects on the various rituals and restructurings necessary before she can bear to face the world in the morning.

'When my teeth are at rest in the glass by my bed,' she sings, 'And my hair lies somewhere in a drawer/Then the world doesn't seem like a very nice place/Not a very nice place any more . . .'

Slowly, though, and with a kind of stoic dignity, she coaxes herself into the process of self-reassembly, slipping in her dentures, fitting on her wig, 'And a strange thing occurs when I do/For my teeth start to feel like my very own teeth/And my hair like my very own, too.'

Subsequently, by washing – 'I'm reaching for the soap/My heart is full of hope/Again, again . . .' – dressing and then decorating herself with bracelets and brooches, rings, pearls and pins, she completes her transformation and is finally able to declare, 'I'm ready to begin again/Looking fresh and bright, I trust/Ready to begin again/As everybody must.'

These words, coming from the painted mouth of a woman whose public persona, so rigorously maintained, depended on the conceit that her beauty was effortless and innate, were startling, shocking even. More than that, they sounded brave and defiant, as if she had finally decided to acknowledge the artificial mask it's deemed essential for female showbusiness legends to hide behind if they are to maintain their marketability and, accordingly, their self-esteem. What would her peers make of it? I wondered. All those other nipped, tucked, cosseted and cosmeticized women of a certain age. Would they empathize with the words Lee sang, or would they feel betrayed, as if in exposing her fearfulness and vanity she had also laid bare their own?

Like all nine other remarkable songs on the album, 'Ready To Begin Again' was written by Jerry Leiber and Mike Stoller, most celebrated for their hit compositions of the early 1960s – among them 'Hound Dog' and 'Jailhouse Rock' for Elvis

Presley, 'Stand By Me' and 'On Broadway' for Ben E. King and The Drifters. All ten songs were then arranged, and that vast orchestra conducted, to hypnotic, other-worldly effect, by Johnny Mandel, a man peerless at his craft. And, as Derek Jewell commented so persuasively, the result was 'the most triumphant assertion of over-fifties style imaginable, beautifully sung by a Benny Goodman band graduate, once compared for soulful emotion with Billie Holiday; the kind of album to maintain faith in the indispensability of quality pop.'

Two thoughts occurred to me. The first was that it must be wonderful to have Jewell's knowledge and authority, to be able to reappraise publicly artists who were deserving but overlooked, thus causing readers like myself to search out music they wouldn't otherwise have heard. And the second, which didn't strike me until some days later, by which time I owned a copy of *Mirrors* and was familiar with its songs, was that it would be more wonderful still to actually meet and talk with the singer herself. Though legendary, she was by then unplayed by all but the most nostalgic of radio stations. I wanted to help effect her rediscovery, or at least just meet her. It was to be some twenty years before I got my chance – two decades punctuated by a couple of almost-meetings in between.

The first was in 1990, when Bloomsbury published an autobiography, *Miss Peggy Lee*. A friend, Robert, then working as the chief pop critic of *The Sunday Times* – as such, a successor to the late Mr Jewell – phoned one Saturday morning to ask if I was free to have lunch. I was. First, though, he explained, he would have to pop in to a book launch-cum-press conference at the Groucho Club in Soho. I could come along if I liked, or just meet him afterwards. Whose book was it? I asked, and couldn't quite believe the answer. It was Peggy

Lee's. I'd had no idea she had written a book, but yes, of course I wanted to come along.

The bar was quiet when we arrived, but gradually filled with journalists from the broadsheets and middle-market papers. It was an unusual day on which to host such an event – most launches take place during the working week – and the sense was of people who would much rather have been somewhere else, but were attending through duty. Thus gathered, we waited and waited, with some of those present becoming visibly impatient as the minutes ticked by and the small talk lurched and, gradually, stalled. There was a palpable sense of irritation, if not complaint, by the time a PR stepped forward to address the group. Miss Lee had fallen recently and was having difficulty walking unaided, she told us. As a result, getting anywhere, especially in public, took longer than it might otherwise do. She was now on her way from her hotel, and sent her sincere apologies for the delay. She would be with us before very much longer.

Finally, a long black car emerged from amid Soho's habitually choked traffic and pulled up outside. Decanting the inconvenienced star from its back seat took time. In fact, it seemed an age before she finally appeared on the threshold of the room, leaning heavily on a walking cane, and with anxious minders at either side, ready to offer physical support should it be needed. 'I'm so very sorry to have kept all you ladies and gentlemen waiting,' she said in a slow, soft drawl. 'I had this accident, you see. Now I'm unable to get around quite as fast as I'd like to and . . .'

Her apology hung in the air, unfinished and unanswered, as she stood in the glare of our collective scrutiny. We saw an older, heavier-set woman, with a precise bob of platinum-white hair, dressed in a black trouser suit and dark glasses.

Unsurprisingly, she appeared a much-compromised relation of the airbrushed beauty pictured on the front of her book – they'd used that same photograph from the sleeve of *Norma Deloris Egstrom From Jamestown, North Dakota* – and in the publicity material displayed so prominently around the club. It shouldn't have mattered. She was Peggy Lee, and she was with us. Yet, for what seemed to me like a disrespectful eternity, she was rewarded with absolute silence. I could almost feel critical eyes taking stock of her.

Embarrassed, I willed there to be some response to her remark. I prayed for someone, anyone, to say something, anything. And, to my relief, my prayer was answered. A nervous voice spoke out across the room. 'It's just lovely that you could be here at all,' it said in a rushed, uncertain tone. 'Welcome to London.'

I exhaled with relief. Having felt protective of a woman who seemed too little appreciated, too harshly judged, I was immensely grateful that someone had taken the initiative and spoken on our collective behalf. Who had it been? Before I could identify which of my fellow journalists was responsible for the intercession, a slowly advancing Miss Lee lowered her glasses momentarily with her free hand and made eye contact with me. By reflex I smiled, but uncertainly. 'So kind of you to say that,' she purred. 'And so nice of everyone to be here to meet me today.'

Throughout the halting, excruciating press conference that then followed in an adjoining room, I sat wishing that I had been pre-advised of the book's publication so that I could have requested an interview. But, having no professional role to fulfil at the event, I felt I had no real mandate to speak. And anyway, could I be sure my voice would rediscover its proper register were I to feel impelled to do so? So, sitting in silence,

I found myself thinking increasingly about the aptness of the songs on the album *Mirrors*, by now fifteen years old, and in particular of 'Ready To Begin Again'. I later read that, subsequent to its recording, Miss Lee had judged the subject matter to be overly dark, and had decided never to perform any of the material publicly. Ironically, the album's striking cover image – a portrait showing her as a Disney-like witch, apparently staring into a looking glass – once cruelly self-revealing, seemed flattering now, a moment frozen in time.

Sitting at the front of the room, meanwhile, dark glasses still in place, the star struggled to respond to a series of syco-phantic, unanswerable comments on the book itself – 'You must be very proud . . .', 'Such a lovely memoir . . .', 'I really shouldn't ask you to pick a highlight from so distinguished a career, but . . .' – responding to them with as much grace as was possible. One of the younger journalists present asked if there were anyone among the now-emergent generation of female singers whom she felt might have been influenced by her own style and technique, and whom she thus felt special affection for. On beginning to reply, Miss Lee was interrupted by a coughing fit: 'Sh . . . Sh . . .' she managed, before having to motion for a glass of water.

'She means Cher,' interceded the showbiz correspondent of one of the dailies, turning from the front row to smile at the rest of us, as if in apology for the lapses of an elderly and infirm relative. 'No, she doesn't,' I wanted to call out but, to my shame, didn't. How could she possibly have meant Cher? Their singing styles could hardly be more diametrically opposed.

Later, when the invitees were drifting off and the whole sorry business was nearing a close, I heard Miss Lee say plaintively to one of her entourage, 'And I didn't mean Cher, I meant Sade.' There was no-one much left in the room to care, and the attention of those remaining was focused on getting her to a next appointment at Hatchard's, the Piccadilly book shop, where she was to make an in-store appearance. Having been told of this already, I had phoned and reserved my own signed copy of the autobiography, but hadn't taken up the offer of having it personally dedicated. I was prevented from doing so by that same mistrust of false intimacy that has stopped me wanting autographs from, or to be photographed with, any of the famous names I've met. I still have my edition of the book, though, and on the green fly leaf, written in silver ink on four separate lines, is, 'To you – Love, Peggy Lee, 1990.'

Two years later, I saw her in person again. I was in New York to interview Whitney Houston, who was, at the time, about to make her film début in Kevin Costner's production of *The Bodyguard*. I had booked into an uptown Hilton so vast and high-rise that ten minutes could easily pass between calling a lift in the foyer and arriving in your room. On entering the elevator car for the first time after checking in, I noticed a familiar face, shot as always in soft focus, looking out at me from behind glass. In cabaret at the hotel that week was, according to the framed announcement, Miss Peggy Lee.

I had only one free evening in the city, and learned that there were no available places for her show on that night. Disappointed, I went out to dinner instead and, on returning close to midnight, headed for the lift area and pressed the necessary button. The lobby was quiet at that hour, but in time I was joined by two other guests. Looking to my side, I saw a male attendant positioning a wheelchair beside me, within which sat a small, platinum-haired and silk-gowned figure . . . Miss Lee.

Her performance over, and the audience having dispersed, she was now being escorted back to her suite. I suppose I could have spoken to her, made some declaration of my admiration, but I was taken aback by finding that her condition had deteriorated and the fact that she looked tired. It just didn't seem to me the right time or place. Eventually, the lift arrived, but I decided to stand back rather than join her in it. At the last moment, two young girls in distressed denims and with big hair came running forward, squeezing through the doors just before they closed. They disappeared upwards, giggling, exuding energy and life, probably never even giving a second thought to the old, elaborately dressed woman in the wheelchair who travelled alongside them. Certainly, they were far too young to know who she was. Down below, and watching the floor numbers fly by on the gauge above my head, I rued the opportunity offered to me, and which I had failed to take.

A further two years later, a third chance came my way. Peggy Lee was to make a short series of appearances in London, and the arts editor of *The Times* had said he was prepared to carry an interview with her in advance of them, should I be able to secure one. A fax to the office she maintains in her home in Bel Air, Los Angeles, confirmed that she was willing to meet me. A date was suggested, and I was duly invited to join her for afternoon tea. How would she look? I wondered, when the day finally came around. No longer like the classic near-Hitchcockian blonde of her youthful publicity photographs, certainly; my sighting of her in New York had prepared me for that. Her appearance in a wheelchair at the Hilton had been no one-off, I'd learned. Though still making concert and cabaret appearances at seventy-four years of age, poor health dictated that she must now perform from a seated position. In spite of this, and a low public profile, a younger generation continued to discover her artistry. kd lang, for example, idolizes her, and had made the same pilgrimage I was about to make. And Madonna had sought her out, also. They both took flowers, and I resolved to do the same.

Leaving Sunset Boulevard at a point close to the UCLA campus, I drove up a steeply winding hillside, lined with expensive homes, mansions almost. It was an area within which the mere sight of an unknown pedestrian might trigger the armed response of residents' home-security services and, accordingly, I saw no-one walking. Very occasionally, another car would glide past on the immaculately surfaced road. Mostly, I was on my own in the kind of neighbourhood that the Beverly Hillbillies' truck lurched through, noisily incongruous, in the opening credits to the television series of my boyhood. I felt almost as much of an interloper as the Clampetts had, within a network of roads that seemed unnaturally quiet, as if hermetically sealed with wealth.

Finally, some thirty-five years after first hearing her voice, I was on the street where Peggy Lee herself lived. Her home stood at the very crest of the hill, looking down on what seemed like the whole of Los Angeles, heat-hazed and sprawling below. One of her two male personal assistants, Robert, welcomed me at the door, relieved me of the bouquet I was holding and asked me to wait in a large, formal, reception room while he went off to put the flowers in water. Alone, I looked around me. The vast floor space was covered with a peach-coloured carpet, so thick and luxuriant that I had left footprints behind me merely by progressing from the doorway to one of its several sofas. And because of the house's relative altitude, all I could see through the wall of windows looking out on to a terrace beyond was a cloudless wash of azure-blue sky. It was as if I were sitting in the state room of an ocean liner.

As always, in such situations, any impulse I might have had to move about, look around and assimilate details was tempered by the fear that I might be being watched, or, worse still, that I might be discovered standing where I shouldn't be. Here, too, there was the added disincentive of the carpet; any step I took would remain documented until the next appearance of a vacuum cleaner. I had also never quite recovered from the potential humiliation of my imagined theft of Don Henley's cowboy boots those few years before. Accordingly, I sat stock-still and listened to the sounds of preparation in the adjoining room.

There was a constant, brisk swish of starched linen as members of uniformed nursing staff moved back and forth, readying the singer for our meeting. There was the soft exchange of voices too, Robert's and another, presumably that of Miss Lee herself. Then, suddenly, Robert reappeared before me, holding out a vase containing my flowers. Motioning for me to follow him through a set of newly opened doors, he acted as my emissary. 'This is Alan from the London *Times*, Miss Lee. And look what he's brought you. Aren't they just lovely? So colourful, too.'

'They're very lovely. I thank you, Alan,' came the reply, but I couldn't yet see the person who was speaking. By now I was standing inside another vast room, this one suffused with a deep peach-pink glow. As my eyes adjusted to the half light, I was able to take in my surroundings. All the shutters had been drawn against the brightness of the afternoon, and a series of small, pink-shaded lamps had been lit. Three pink roses, in different stages of unfolding, were displayed in a trio of specimen vases – 'That's the Peggy Lee rose,' she would later tell me. 'Isn't it the most beautiful that you ever saw?' Cocktail jazz was playing softly on a CD system and, on an occasional table to my left, there stood a magnificently tall chocolate-mousse cake, a silver knife and cake slice placed beside it in readiness. I noticed that one tall, elegant wedge had already been cut and removed.

It sat, separate and proud, on the plate being balanced by Miss Lee, who was propped up on pillows in an enormous, white-counterpaned bed. I saw that, with her right hand, she was holding a fork close to her mouth, a morsel of cake upon it, and was maintaining this position as if for a photographer. Judging perhaps that I had been allowed enough time to commit the image to memory, she said, in a voice as slow as Mae West's, but warmer and more gentle, 'Forgive me for starting without you, but a lady gets a little hungry.' I wanted to hug her.

Miss Lee gestured at the chair Robert had just placed by her bedside, and I sat down on it. He then passed me a plate, bearing another large wedge of the cake, furnished me with a fork and starched napkin, then hurried off again to supervise the making of tea. Alone together now, and amid our mutual opening pleasantries, I had the chance to observe the singer at close hand, and to take in her appearance. I found myself humbled by the effort she had made, if not on my behalf, then out of personal pride.

She was wearing a bed jacket of thick peach-coloured silk. Her hair was covered by a green turban, also silk, its folds of material gathered beneath the dark jewel at its centre, high above the forehead. Her eyes were hidden behind wrap-around sunglasses, their frames frosted with diamanté, while pearls as fat as leeches hung from her ear lobes. Her lipstick was a fresh, glistening red. Speaking slowly, and no doubt sensing that she was being assessed, she said, 'I've been a little unwell and, ideally, I'd like to have waited until I was feeling fully better before welcoming you. But I know that you're going back to London tomorrow and that this was to be our only opportunity. Well, I was determined not to cancel. And now here you are. I hope that I'm not too much of a disappointment to you.'

Before I could assure her that she was anything but, I was distracted by a rustling sound coming from somewhere amid the vast expanse of snowy bed linen. Noting my puzzled expression, Miss Lee nodded in the direction of a hat box some twelve inches deep and made out of shiny white cardboard. 'Look inside,' she invited, and I walked all the way around the bed to do so. There, stretching and yawning within its nest of virgin tissue paper, was a cat of clearly aristocratic lineage. 'Baby!' Miss Lee addressed it. 'This is Alan. Did I tell you he was coming to tea? Why, no. I don't believe that I did.'

To me, she said, 'She's an American shorthaired silver chinchilla and, like all cats, she's very independent. She does exactly what she wants to do, when she wants to do it. I'd say that she has a very nice life. I even take her out with me, though she absolutely doesn't like short cars and is only happy riding in a stretch. A lot of people have applied to be reincarnated as her on the next plane.'

Baby, having inspected me briefly, and with a clear lack of interest, extended one thin, pale foreleg in elegant boredom, then closed her eyes again.

I returned to my chair, and told Miss Lee that I knew many famous people had, over the years, approached her in the way that I was doing now, all of them keen to express their admiration and respect. For example, in the late 1970s, Paul and Linda McCartney had been dinner guests and, instead of flowers, the now Sir Paul had brought with him a specially written song, 'Let's Love', which Miss Lee subsequently recorded and made the title track of an album. I remembered having bought a copy for my dad, in the W.H. Smith in Stockton-on-Tees. And what about Madonna? And what about kd?

'Oh, you can't imagine how gratifying it is to find that I have fans among the younger generation of performers,' she said softly. 'Madonna came to see me in concert, then afterwards visited backstage to give me flowers. She wasn't at all like the notorious person I'd read about. She was dressed very properly, very nicely and was totally on her best behaviour. I liked her very much. And afterwards, she recorded a dance version of my hit 'Fever'. I took that as a great compliment.

'As for kd, well, she came right here to the house. But what I didn't realize, until she reminded me of it, was that I'd met her once before. It was when I was playing a season up in Canada, and somehow she was always there, this sweet, shy little girl, whenever I came in or out of the theatre. Apparently, one day I'd stopped to talk to her, and she had never, ever forgotten it. To see her now, and to hear that wonderful, enormous singing voice coming forth . . . Well, she's just so very special.'

We were speaking only days after a Los Angeles charitable organization, the Society Of Singers – its then chairman of the board, Francis Albert Sinatra, its Director Emeritus, Ella Fitzgerald – had honoured Miss Lee with a lifetime achievement award at a dinner in the ballroom of the Beverly Hilton Hotel. When I asked how it went, she used an index finger with a long painted nail to tap the keys of her bedside telephone, summoning Robert forth with the relevant press cuttings. Within seconds he was there, handing me first a china teacup and saucer, then a selection of photocopied articles about the occasion.

I read out loud the introduction to one, published in *Variety*. It asked, 'Who was the blonde in the wheelchair being pushed down Beverly Boulevard with a prize cat in her lap last night?' Miss Lee clapped her hands delightedly and exclaimed, 'It was me! Somehow, our limousine broke down on the way and, fearing that we would be late, we decided to make a run for it. So there was I, with Baby on my lap. How you'd have laughed. But we made it. And what a wonderful evening it turned out to be.

'So many great artists performed for me: Jack Jones, Cleo Laine, the Manhattan Transfer, Mel Tormé, Rosemary Clooney, kd herself. And then Natalie Cole came out in this skin-tight red satin gown and sang "I'm A Woman" with every last little gesture of mine off pat. She knew exactly the way that I used to walk when I did that song. Truly, I had the loveliest time.'

I asked about this iconic aspect of her image – one so well-defined that, in America, there is a female impersonator, Jim Bailey, who makes a living from impersonating her – and the daily effort required to maintenance it. She told me, 'Your image is your trademark, and you have to look after it. I didn't realize that for a long time, but Cary Grant and I were great friends, and I noticed that he always paid attention to detail. He'd read every last thing written about him, vet every photograph taken – even at a time when other people would talk dismissively of "those damned bromides". And he had a perfect image, didn't he? Well, what is it that they say,

"Perfection is made up of trifles, but perfection itself is no trifle." In my life, I may not have lived up to that maxim, but at least I have tried.'

Miss Lee first moved to Hollywood in 1937, so had been resident there for over half a century. The days of the perfect image were long gone, of course. We were living in a cynical, scandal-hungry age, in which many celebrities have discovered that there's career advancement to be made from self-exposure, from holding up their foibles and failings for the scrutiny of us, the gawping public. The most affecting chapter of her otherwise bland autobiography was its opening one, a beautifully written, though restrained, account of her harsh upbringing in North Dakota. It had left me wanting to know more than she was prepared to tell.

These days, many celebrities would have made the absolute most of every factual detail, would even have embroidered the past to win sympathy and publicity for themselves. She had done the opposite. And so I wondered what she, someone clearly rigorous in her efforts to maintain what she felt to be a proper public image, made of this trend for self-exposure?

'To completely unburden oneself in public? No, I don't hold with that. Yes, there was more I could have said in my book about my early life, but why burden the reader? I wanted to reveal just enough for people to understand that I had to grow through something.

'I have seen standards change and, I think, not always for the better. Back when the screen magazines first started to show pictures of the pretty starlet in the kitchen, cooking, wearing her little apron and all, I remember thinking, They really shouldn't do that. And when they were shown going to the market, I thought they should at least have thought to put on a hat or dark glasses, or to try in some way to look neat and tidy and a little bit more like a star. Because it was my feeling that, in the end, it would catch up with them, that they'd lose a little bit of the audience's esteem for them. Of course, you can take it to the point of obsession but, well, all things in moderation seems to me a good rule.'

Peggy Lee's mother died when she was a young girl and, when her father subsequently remarried, it was to a woman who resented her presence and treated her so harshly that, at seventeen, she ran away and began life on her own. When I asked her about those early years, she said she thought of them as having been happy, but for the inner experiences, rather than the real-life ones. 'Daddy wasn't rich, and he lost everything in the Crash, as everyone did – or, if they didn't, they'd always claim to have done. But even in our modest circumstances, we kept up appearances. That was the influence of my mother, who had been to finishing school, and evidently she was a living example to me, because, to this day, I hold things like fresh linen and flowers to be important. Even on a day when I'm here alone I make sure I have them. I do it for the inner person.'

When I mentioned the album *Mirrors*, and my great admiration for it, she smiled slowly and said, 'Ah, yes. Songs that were a little ahead of their time, I think. People didn't seem to take too kindly to them, over here, at least. Maybe it's time to dust one or two of them off again. Perhaps I'll choose some to bring with me to London.'

My praise for its cover artwork was less appreciated, though. 'I didn't like that picture at all. I looked so dead in it. Maybe I was being just a little oversensitive, but at about that time one side of my face was paralysed, a Bell's palsy or something, and I had people writing about my "mask-like face".

Please don't write anything like that. There was a long time when I couldn't even smile. I had to retrain my face to do it. Now I can again, and I do.'

And she did so to prove her point. She then went on to say that she wasn't afraid of growing older, or of dying. But, I asked, wasn't the frustration hard to bear, when your body let you down and you were physically unable to do all that you wished?

'I think of it the other way around, Alan,' she said. 'I think I let my body down. I think it's all my fault. Being sort of a workaholic, I used to go all day without eating and, despite that, my body would struggle to meet all the demands I placed on it. Well, the body's a strange and wonderful thing. But when you're through with it and go on to the next plane, it's just left lying there, like an old suit. It's your soul that goes on to some place else.

'I do believe in life after death – life after life, I should say – so I'm not afraid of dying. I don't like the idea of it; I want to go on for ever right here. But it's very comforting to me to know that we'll all have another experience. I don't think necessarily we'll remain as Alan and Peggy – or maybe we will. But I do think that we'll go on. Yes, it's sad seeing people die, but I think we will all see each other again. I have to believe that we will. If we weren't to, it would seem to me that life was just a joke.'

For a while, after my visit, I would get telephone calls from Miss Lee. They would come just as I was waking in London, and as she sat up in bed in Los Angeles late at night, planning the programme for her London concerts. Half asleep, I would pick up the receiver by my bed, and the slow, familiar voice would say, 'Hello, it's Peggy here. I do hope I'm not disturbing you, but . . .' Then I would find myself in the unbelievable situation of advising a woman who had been singing publicly for over fifty years on what numbers she should include in her shows, and which she should leave out. My personal preferences did colour that advice in one instance, and yes, I persuaded her that she should sing some of the material from *Mirrors*.

The concerts never took place. Like so many veteran performers who have to trust whichever advisors are prepared to become involved with their dwindling careers, Miss Lee could be at the mercy of poor business practice. The finance for the trip fell through at the eleventh hour, and she was left at home in Bel Air, with bags packed and her set list completed, only to remain unsung. She never visited Britain again.

At around the time I finally met Miss Lee, my mother-in-law, Agnes, already confined to a wheelchair by Parkinson's disease, was recovering from her stroke. Both women were of a similar age, and when making visits with Christine, either to hospital or to the nursing home where Agnes spent the last two years of her life, I was often struck by the similarities in their separate situations. Of course, the material circumstances were very different, but the resilience, faith and humour of both women impressed me enormously.

One had enjoyed worldwide acclaim, lived in a vast house filled with collections of Baccarat crystal and Meissen porcelain and will leave behind her a legacy of timeless music. The other was known only within the small Lincolnshire town in which she had lived since the last war, had just a few trinkets and religious artifacts in her one small room, and left nothing much other than memories and the enduring love that she inspired in her seven children and extended family. Both took equal pride in getting dressed up for visitors, even if the end results were rather different. And the memory of their fortitude and wisdom reminds me always of how much there is to learn from, and respect in, people older than ourselves.

Peggy Lee was one of the guests attending Frank Sinatra's funeral in 1998. 'Not so much a *Who's Who* of showbusiness, as a Who's Next?' observed one writer of a guest list that included many of his ailing contemporaries. Cruel, of course. But she more than any of them would, I believe, have prepared herself for that moment when she, too, would be called upon to begin again.

10

How quickly and easily we are seduced by the good life. The first time I'd arrived at an American airport through work, I had been reluctant to believe that the man holding up a sign bearing my name was waiting for me. Soon, that sign became the first thing I looked for on entering an arrivals hall. And, back at LAX some seven years after my visit to meet Joni Mitchell, there it was. 'Sorry to keep you,' I said brightly to an improbably tall, lounge-suited driver, who was continuing to scan the advancing heads behind me. 'Immigration took for ever.' There was no reaction from him whatsoever to my words, and I was reminded suddenly of conversations attempted long ago with my Norfolk landlord, Jumbo. Perhaps this man, too, had difficulty seeing or hearing people significantly shorter than himself. Drawing myself up onto my tiptoes, I tried again.

'Hello? It's Alan Jackson. It's me you're waiting for. Look, here! This is my name on your piece of paper.' So that there could be no possible margin for error, I tapped it with my index finger. It seemed to be this action, rather than what I had said, which finally won me attention from on high.

'Just you watch where you're pointing,' said Mount Everest, defensively, at once raising the sign to a height beyond my reach. 'Damage this and Alan Jackson will have no idea that it's him I'm here to meet.'

I apologized again. 'But, you see, it is me. I'm Alan Jackson. Arrived from London on BA, going to the Mondrian on Sunset Boulevard. Here. Take a look at my passport.'

What other evidence of my identity could I offer? And, to make matters worse, it was my second such Kafkaesque encounter in a matter of days. Just the previous week, Christine and I had moved house. And as we stood there on the pavement, watching removal men carry our possessions into a new home, an older couple had materialized from just a few doors way, and had begun to make slow and deliberate progress towards us.

'Alan Jackson,' I'd said, again brightly, when finally they approached. 'And my wife, Christine. The new arrivals. Pleased to meet you both.'

'Alan Johnson,' corrected the gentleman, gravely shaking the hand I had proffered.

Puzzled, I had paused for a moment. Then, deciding it was important to correctly establish my name from the very start, I'd tried again. 'Er, it's Jackson. Alan Jackson. Not Johnson.'

'Alan Johnson,' agreed our new neighbour, still shaking away. The confusion persisted through two more such exchanges, and was cleared up only when his wife, becoming as exasperated as me, interrupted with, 'Yes, yes, we understand that you're Alan Jackson. But this is my husband, Alan Johnson, and I'm his wife, Betty!'

Back in the arrivals hall at LAX, the misunderstanding over who I was, and whether or not I was entitled to a free limousine ride, was less easily cleared up. Mr Everest, who later identified himself as an exile from the southern states, had, on receiving his job sheet for the day, leaped to the conclusion that the Alan Jackson he would be driving was not a small English journalist now writing for *The Times*, but his fellow Georgian, the multi-million-selling country-and-western artist of the same name. I could see how he would have had trouble reconciling one with the other. I am five foot six, have short dark hair and am clean-shaven. I cannot sing. That other, richer and more famous – though, mercifully, not yet in Britain – Alan Jackson is a skyscraper of a man, with bounteous golden locks and a moustache so luxuriant that animals and small children could find shelter within it. Over the years, when reading the American trade magazine *Billboard*, I have kept track of his accumulating success and, very selfishly, prayed that it never extends to these shores. Given our recent embrace of such fellow country stars as LeAnn Rimes, Shania Twain, Trisha Yearwood and Reba McEntire, there is an increasing possibility that it will. That will be the day I change my Christian name to something less embarrassing, like Michael or Janet.

It took a phone call for Everest to confirm his mistake. Yes, I was the man he was supposed to meet. But no, I didn't feel vindicated, let alone angry or even amused. If anything, I was embarrassed to be five-and-a-half-feet of disappointment, not six-foot-something of stetsoned, cowboy-booted superstar, and the fulsome apologies heaped on me during our walk out to the parking lot only made me feel more so. Not that my reluctant driver was a natural diplomat. Long before we reached La Brea, he'd rallied sufficiently to dial up his girlfriend and relate to her the details of our encounter. 'So, I'm looking down at this little English guy,' I could hear him recount, despite the smoked-glass screen raised in between us, 'and he's saying,' – adopts cod-upper-class British accent – ' "Oh, but actually I'm the Alan Jackson you're waiting for," and I'm thinking, Like hell you are, shorty!'

Shorty? Throughout adolescence, I was sensitive about my height, or lack of it, and, when the wheel of fashion turned in my favour, had attempted to augment my natural stature through the use of artificial aids. By this I mean the particularly nasty, three-tiered, black-maroon-black pair of platform shoes I'd bought during my first year at university to impress – how misguided I was – Christine. She and a group of friends I hadn't yet infiltrated were spending the Easter holidays in a cottage on the Isle of Skye. The only thing in my social diary was three weeks of moping around Darlington town centre. Lovelorn, for the first time in my life, I didn't even have the heart to put Petula Clark – or, for old time's sake, Marc Bolan – albums to the forefront of record-counter displays. In this fragile emotional state, it was hardly surprising that I should prove susceptible to the evil, corrupting influence of chainstore fashion.

Quite why I imagined she would swoon before a man wearing a pair of hip-hugging black viscose flares, ones that skimmed the ground around his ghastly platforms, is beyond me now. Believe it I did, though. My mum having hemmed the offending trousers to the requisite length, I wore them proudly to the pub on the first night back of the new term. All was fine while I was sitting down but, come closing time, I found myself in difficulties. Four pints of Newcastle Brown Ale, combined with the rarefied air breathed by someone who suddenly found himself to be five foot nine, rendered me incapable of getting home unaided. 'Here, let me help you,' said Christine, having seen me falling first off the kerb and then off my right heel. 'You don't want to break an ankle. Take my arm, now. One, two, three . . . and off we go.'

You set out for the evening feeling like Casanova and you end up being supported home by the object of your affections, one who sees you not as the lofty sex magnet of your fevered imagination, but as a little brother figure, pathetically in need of help. I never wore those shoes again. They went to a charity shop – aptly named, as it was the staff who showed that virtue in accepting them – shortly afterwards. Even so, the casual use of a term like Shorty could still reawaken old insecurities many years later. All at once, everyone in Los Angeles seemed taller than me.

'Always a pleasure to welcome you to the Mondrian,' said the desk clerk (tall), as I approached to check in.

'If there's anything I can do to make your stay more enjoyable, just ask for George,' said the yet taller employee who showed me to my room.

'Good evening, sir. I'm Leroy, your room-service waiter. I hope you enjoy your meal,' said the human Empire State Building who wheeled in my supper some thirty minutes later. He caught me trying to stow my luggage away. 'Need a hand putting that case up on the shelf? Here, let me do it for you.'

I was in town to interview Sade. We'd talked twice before, and I had strong memories of her cool, clear-eyed beauty, and of her surprisingly earthy, almost mannish laugh. But one crucial fact about her eluded me now: her height. I couldn't be 100 per cent certain, but it was my feeling that she was, at the very least, as tall as me, quite possibly taller. Picking glumly at the French fries accompanying my upmarket cheeseburger, I reminded myself that there was absolutely nothing I could do about it anyway. Or was there?

The next morning was free for me to spend in whichever way I chose. I decided to spend it at the mall. The Beverly Center is your average Arndale experience, given a glossy make-over and multiplied by ten. Were you so minded, you could spend the entire day there. Many people do. But I was a man with a mission, a hit-and-run consumer, interested only in one kind of retail outlet: the shoe shop. Ludicrous though it seems to admit it now, I was looking for something with a bit of a heel.

'Like, excellent choice. Those boots are just so-oo neat. My boyfriend got a pair last week and he just doesn't want to take them off. I think he looks, like, really sexy in them.'

The girl assistant had been grooving catatonically to 'Blasphemous Rumours' – the only Depeche Mode track I ever remember liking – for as long as I continued to move around the displays of men's footwear. But now, seconds after I'd stopped and picked up this, a kind of Chelsea boot with altitude, she was by my side, conversing in tones of relative animation.

'You don't think they're a bit too, well, young for me?'

'Like, my boyfriend's twenty-four.'

'That's what I mean. For me, even thirty-four is just a memory. I wouldn't want to look stupid.'

'No way. Trust me. You'll love what they do for you.'

What they did was cause me to walk about the store in a curious, stalking manner, backside thrust out and with my hands extended in a bid to maintain balance. Oh, and they also caused me to appear about two and a half inches taller. Obviously, they were to die for.

There is something about Los Angeles which causes me to take leave of what limited sense I have in relation to clothes shopping. A deep breath of the Californian air and I am suddenly a man without taste or standards, cheerfully buying shirts and trousers in garish colours, despite knowing that, at home, I will never, ever feel comfortable in anything that's not black, grey or dark blue. And I was about to prove myself equally fallible in the matter of shoes.

'Incidentally, what does your boyfriend do for a living?' I asked, accepting a bag containing the offending items. 'That's if you don't mind my—'

'Mario's the lead guitarist in a band,' she replied proudly. 'He's, like, really, really good. It's kind of a Nirvana-meets-Van Halen type of sound, with a bit of Prince thrown in. Totally cool.'

'I should listen out for them. What are they called?'

'Angels Outta Valhalla. Yeah, you listen out. They've not got a deal yet, but he's hopeful. Now, enjoy your boots. And have a nice day.'

Standing at the cab rank, I shook my head in disbelief. I, an English journalist in his late thirties, had just bought the same pair of boots as the doubtless poodle-haired twenty-four-year-old axe warrior in an unsigned and totally clueless-sounding Los Angeles band. Was Mario a bit on the short side, too? It would have been rude to ask. Anyway, I had enough shortcomings of my own to worry about. Clearly, I needed my head examining, and that was just the beginning. If I actually wore them, I might well need my ankles, calves and knees examining, too.

Wear them I did. A little covert perambulation back and forth in my room convinced me that not only were the boots tenable as a mode of personal transport, but that they even looked rather fetching – that Los Angeles self-delusional thing again. As a result, it was with a stiff gait and at a slight elevation that I accomplished the short walk along Sunset from the Mondrian to the famed Chateau Marmont, my journey punctuated by a harsh click-clacking sound which I was powerless to subdue. The sound seemed only to increase in volume as I entered the expensive hush of the hotel's lobby, pointy black leather toes twinkling at the end of either trouser leg. Click-clack, click-clack. Only by raising my heels off the floor and progressing on the soles alone could I silence the humiliating racket. If the male receptionist found my carriage strange or laughable, he was too discreet to let it show. Instead, he directed me to the penthouse suite's terrace, where I found Sade waiting for me.

Sitting at a wrought-iron table, and dappled with early-afternoon sunshine, she looked glorious. Her hair was pulled back from her face in trademark style, and she wore white jeans, with a red blouse knotted beneath her breasts. Seeing – hearing? – me approach, she rose and took a step forward. She was barefoot. How I wished I were, too.

'Good to see you again,' she said, smiling up at me. 'You know, you look different? I don't know quite how, but you seem . . .'

Taller? The possessor of a distinctly silly walk? I said nothing and merely smiled back at her in an interested but, hopefully, non-committal fashion. She then glided back towards the table at which she'd been waiting, me lurching along in her wake. Once safely there, I began the interview by first seeking to catch up on all that had happened to her in the four or so years since we'd last met.

'When was it that you moved from London to Spain?' I wondered, endeavouring to get straight in my mind the chronology of her personal life and, at the same time, distract myself from the fact that my feet were now throbbing wildly within my stupid, stupid boots.

'Let's see,' she replied evenly. 'It was just before I got married. That was three years ago, so—'

'To think, they said it wouldn't last,' I interrupted foolishly, barely able to concentrate on what she was saying because of the pain in my toes.

'It didn't,' said Sade. And before I could even register the fact that an exclusive had been placed in my lap, tears began to roll down her cheeks.

A scoop should be a trigger for great celebration, being one of the yardsticks by which journalists can measure themselves against their peers. But whenever one has come my way, I've never felt much like celebrating. Perhaps it's something specific to the medium of the celebrity profile, but inevitably, a scoop means someone telling you about a tragedy that has befallen them, or some deep unhappiness that has unfolded in their lives. So, while it's possible to take personal and professional pride at being the one selected to receive that information, then present it for public consumption in an accurate and, hopefully, sympathetic way, I haven't wanted to reach for the champagne the instant I've filed the story about someone's marriage having floundered, or their baby having died.

Furthermore, being chosen as the best person to process the details of someone else's misery is one thing. Building a career on your supposed ability to divine the next famous victim and then inveigle yourself into their confidence would be quite another. Which is why, on briefly having a currency among the tabloids and middle-market papers following my exclusive on Annie Lennox's stillborn son, I decided not to take up any of the offers of staff jobs or contracts that followed. Though glad to be of constructive help to anyone in so unhappy a situation, I knew I couldn't accept an increased salary on the false premise of being the man who could always make the stars talk. Sometimes, and quite rightly, they just don't want to.

So instead, from time to time, exclusives or scoops have been offered to me simply because a PR, artist, or both, have felt I was the best journalist to trust with a particular piece of information within a given situation. One such offer came from Regine who, first as a record-company press officer and then as an independent specialist, handles publicity for U2 and other major acts. At the time she rang, I was still pinching myself. My previous call had been from Barry Manilow. In town for the opening of his musical *Copacabana*, he'd been reading *The Times* over breakfast, and had seen my article on Peggy Lee. It is rare enough to be thanked for, or congratulated on, something you have written in a medium as disposable as newspapers, rarer still for someone famous to take the trouble of personally getting in touch. More especially when the article in question isn't even about them. I was completely charmed, so much so that I missed the opportunity to ask if, like some other Barrys I've encountered, he owned a safari suit.

'Aren't you the lucky one?' said Regine, possibly thinking I was hallucinating when I told her about the conversation I'd just had. 'Well, I'm afraid it's just boring old me this time. But I was wondering, would you like to come out to lunch sometime soon? There's a situation involving one of my friends . . . I was wondering if you might be prepared to help. I can tell you more when we meet.'

When we did so, she told me that the man in question had learned that he was HIV positive and, as someone with a public profile, he accepted that there was a danger of his diagnosis being exposed by a third party. He wanted to make the information public himself, in a non-sensational way, and in the context of a more wide-ranging interview. The time was not yet right, Regine said: despite several attempts, her friend had not yet managed to break the news to his parents. But when he'd done so, might I be interested in taking such an interview to *The Times*? Without knowing, or being able to guess who it was we were talking about, I told her I would.

Months passed, and I'd all but forgotten about the whole situation by the time Regine called again. The friend previously referred to was, she told me, Holly Johnson, the former lead singer of Frankie Goes To Hollywood, a band whose press relations she had overseen from the start of its controversial and highly successful career in the early 1980s. Suddenly, there was an urgency to his situation. He had been doorstepped by a tabloid journalist, asking if it were true that he had AIDS. Holly assumed that a fellow patient or member of staff at a hospital clinic he was attending must have tipped off the paper about his visits there. By now he'd told his parents, at home in Liverpool, of his new health status. Clearly, the next important step to take was that of making the information public before someone else did it for him.

Holly and his partner of long-standing, Wolfgang, share an elegant home in west London, and it was there that I went to meet him for the first time. It was an odd feeling, setting out that day in order to prompt the telling of a story that, naturally, all concerned wished wasn't true, let alone that it had to be told. If I was uncharacteristically nervous about doing the interview, Holly himself must have been more so. Our encounter proved surprisingly upbeat, however. Warm and funny, he talked me easily through a life which had progressed from working-class roots in Liverpool, through art school and a gay *demi-monde*, both in his home city and in London, to the explosion of success with the Frankies and beyond. This fluency was doubtless helped by the fact that, at the time, he was nearing completion of the first draft of his 1994 autobiography, *A Bone In My Flute*. Even so, by the time we reached the present day and his experiences of dealing with the HIV virus, he'd given me such a vivid picture of himself that it was as if I were learning about the illness of a friend, not of someone I was meeting for the first time.

Clearly, when being entrusted with a sensitive story, it's imperative that you can trust the editorial staff for whom you are writing it. In this situation, there was no-one I would rather have been dealing with than Gill Morgan, then deputy editor of *The Times Magazine* and now its editor. We had first met when she was working on the features desk of the *Sunday Express Magazine*, and over the years she'd become a close and valued friend. I had spoken to her of the potential interview when Regine first approached me and, even without knowing who the subject was, she had expressed her interest in commissioning it. Now she was as committed as I was to making sure Holly's story reached the public in exactly the way he wanted it to. Sickeningly for both of us, but more especially for Holly and Wolfgang, their friends and family, the completed article was accessed in some way that has never been identified, by staff on the *Sun*, and its contents revealed by them two days before the article's publication in *The Times Magazine*.

The first hint that normal security protecting two separate papers in the News International stable had been breached came on the Wednesday of that week. I was working at home when I had a call from the journalist Piers Morgan, at the time showbusiness editor of the *Sun*. He said that he understood I'd done an interview with Holly, which included the revelation that he had contracted AIDS, and he asked if I could confirm this. For an instant I felt paralysed and, in trying to form a reply, I had the sense I was playing one of those childhood games in which saying the words yes or no means you're out. I told him that I could say categorically this wasn't true, but that I wasn't prepared to comment further. He responded by congratulating me on getting the story. I put the phone down and called first Gill and then Holly to tell them what had happened.

There was no obvious explanation as to how the *Sun* could have got hold of my article: I hadn't shown it to anyone other than Gill and Holly, and had circulated no copies to third parties. At *The Times Magazine*, too, it had been worked on only by Gill and one sub-editor, and had been kept in a specially created computer file that no other members of staff knew of, or had access to. An internal inquiry began, but there was little comfort in this: all we could do was wait for the following morning's papers.

That day began as undoubtedly the worst of my journalistic career. I was outside my local newsagent when it opened at 7 a.m. The IRA's detonation of an explosive device in central London, two hours before a memorial service for the two schoolboy victims of the earlier Warrington bomb blast, prevented the revelation of Holly's HIV-positive status being lead story in the *Sun*. But there it was, in a side panel on the front, and across a double-page spread within, reported in exactly the sensationalist fashion he had wanted to avoid, and with extensive quotes lifted directly from my original text. To make matters worse, the following day's edition would include a near full-page article by the columnist Garry Bushell, illustrated with a picture of Holly and Wolfgang, and head-lined WHEN WILL THEY LEARN THAT SODOMY KILLS? 'Homosexual stars in pop and showbiz are dropping like flies,' it would begin. Meanwhile, rival papers had picked up the initial story from their copies of the *Sun*'s first edition, as had TV and radio. Even though I and *The Times Magazine* were credited as being the original sources of the story, I felt as if I'd been mugged in the street, or burgled. How Holly himself must be feeling, I could hardly bear speculate.

As I was trying to address myself to the question of how to begin to apologize to him, Christine, at the time deputy advertising manager of the Express Group of newspapers, was consulting the head of its legal department. As at the time of the earlier Annie Lennox story, I had solicited from my commissioning editor a letter confirming that copyright of the article remained with me, and that, in this case, it could not be republished or sold on to any other publication without Holly's and my permission. The advice we received was that, plainly, this copyright had been breached, leaving clear grounds for legal action. But top-flight and specialist legal representation would be necessary – a recommendation was kindly made – to stand up to so experienced and powerful an adversary.

Michael Skrein of the London firm Richards Butler was encouraging about the chances of my being successful in winning an apology and, possibly, some level of damages through litigation. Naturally, he was also straightforward about the implications of being unsuccessful: I would be liable not only for all my own costs, but also those incurred by the *Sun* in defending the action. 'Perhaps some of the artists I know might agree to appear at a benefit concert to help me out,' I said, not seriously. 'I hope you're thinking along the lines of Wembley Arena as a venue,' responded Michael, sounding only too serious.

I knew that, were things to go wrong, it might be necessary for us to sell our house. It's asking a great deal of your partner to contemplate any action involving the risk, albeit slight, of such an eventuality. Christine was unequivocal, however. Holly had been gravely wronged, and my integrity and professional reputation was at stake – on the very day of the story's publication in the *Sun*, one PR, missing the point entirely, rang to congratulate me and suggested that, as I was now writing for that paper, I might like to consider interviewing a particular client of hers. Of course I had to defend myself against their action, no matter what the implications might be.

When, later that morning, feeling more wretchedly sorry than I could ever hope to express, I managed to speak to Holly, he was calm and reasonable. 'I know that it wasn't your fault, or Gill's, but something has to be done,' he said. 'I'm glad to hear that you're going to take legal action because, if you weren't, I would feel that I had to sue you.' In the circumstances, I couldn't – wouldn't – have blamed him at all. To date, and mercifully, the action against Piers Morgan and the *Sun* remains my only experience of litigation and, accordingly, litigation lawyers.

It proved an elongated, sometimes scary and all-consuming process, but at least, in my case, it was a successful one. After months of watching correspondence fly back and forth between the *Sun*'s lawyers and my own, an acceptable out-of-court settlement was reached, allowing me and, by proxy, Holly to feel we had exacted some kind of retribution. The financial award was, to a large extent, irrelevant. For the injured parties, having one's copyright breached is not the moneyspinner that a successful libel action can be. In the circumstances, I aimed to behave appropriately by making a significant donation from it to The Terrence Higgins Trust, which works for the benefit of those who are HIV positive, or who have AIDS.

Through it all, Michael Skrein and his then assistant Rachel Miller provided me with the most excellent service, and I remain indebted to them in a moral, though not, thankfully, monetary sense. As for Holly and I, each subsequent Christmas we've exchanged cards, his always featuring a detail from one of his paintings: bold, figurative and *faux naïf*, and frequently depicting angels or sailors. When he had completed his autobiography and was in need of a literary agent, I was pleased to be able to recommend my own, Barbara Levy, who duly sold the book for him. Since then I have interviewed him on two further occasions, and have again been struck by what a remarkably sanguine and good-humoured man he is. He always strikes me as an embodiement of courage in the face of adversity. And he also serves as a reminder to me of why I don't work in the medium of breaking showbusiness news for the nation's tabloids.

The taking of flowers to those you interview could be viewed as creepy and manipulative. With just the odd, dishonourable exception – Courtney Love; it was because I was scared of you – I have done so only when genuinely motivated by affection, and when fairly sure that I wouldn't be left holding them publicly for too long, like some sad romantic whose date has stood him up.

I took flowers to Peggy Lee. I took them to Holly Johnson. Once, last-minute and spur-of-the-moment, I bought a small, rather sorry-looking bunch of something or other for Natalie

Merchant, the former lead singer of the American band 10,000 Maniacs, and she was so pleased that I was almost embarrassed. 'I'm leaving for Germany this evening, but I promise I'm going to try and carry them with me on the plane,' she said, holding the wilting bunch before her, as if she were a little girl playing at being a bride.

The flowers I gave to Lyle Lovett were rather more impressive, and not really from me. My interview with him had been scheduled, cancelled and rescheduled endlessly over a period of months, he being particularly press-shy at the time, due to the parlous state of his marriage to actress Julia Roberts. It was Christine who had chosen and bought them, hoping they might disarm him and make him less prickly. 'Tell him how much I loved his performance in *Short Cuts*,' she said, as we had recently seen Robert Altman's film adaptation of the late Raymond Carver's collection of stories. Lyle, a courteous and softly spoken man, seemed surprised, but also touched, to find himself approached by a male journalist carrying a small bouquet. By the end of our interview, and despite my having scrupulously avoided reference to his marital difficulties, he seemed to have forgotten, or lost belief, in my explanation of their origin. 'Thank you again for the flowers, and I'll be sure to pass them on to Julia when I see her tonight,' he said. 'I'm sure it was for her that you intended them really.'

More recently, there was Courtney Love and the discreet arrangement of something or other very expensive that I took her. Why was I frightened of her? Well, a certain reputation for difficulty and high-handedness goes before her. Also, the interview had been dependent on my agreeing to various provisions and prerequisites. Questions on her history of addiction were forbidden, for example. So, too, were any relating to her late husband, Nirvana star Kurt Cobain, who had committed suicide two years earlier. Questions about anything other than her current work projects would be greeted with silence. Perhaps fearing I might be amnesic, I was reminded of all this again, and in person, by first her American public-relations manager, then the British equivalent, when I arrived at her hotel. And just in case I was particularly slow on the uptake, the former, ushering me into Courtney's suite, drew my attention to the muscleman bodyguard managing both to look threatening and chew gum in the corridor outside. 'I'll be sitting in on the interview,' she told me. 'And, should you decide not to observe the stated conditions, I'll be calling on this gentleman to help you leave.'

His services weren't required. On the admittedly scant evidence of a strictly policed twenty-minute encounter, I was tempted to like Courtney, even if she did drop my peace-offering onto the couch with a bored-sounding, 'Gee, thanks.' But a cut-glass-accented member of her temporary PR presence had a different opinion. Months later, it was this woman who reminded me we had met before when, on arriving at The Dorchester to meet a different star, I began to introduce myself.

'You don't remember me, do you?' she demanded.

'Of course I do. How are you?' I lied unconvincingly. To my surprise, she replied instantly, 'A whole lot better since that bitch Courtney Love left town, I have to say. Never before has it been my displeasure to work with anyone more awful.'

But back to flowers. At a street-corner stall on New York's Upper West Side, meanwhile, and because I hadn't managed to locate a proper florist in the area, I once bought an armful of white tulips for the singer-songwriter Carly Simon. In my teenage years, and through into my twenties, she had been an object of erotic thrall to me, a famously playful series of album sleeves having made much of the Carly legs, lips, hair and *décolletage*. 'Just me playing with my image, dressing up the way a child would in her mother's high heels and an old fox fur,' she would tell me, when I commented upon them. 'Just me playing in front of a camera, pretending to be something I'm not. There is an erotic element, but it's not important.'

It had seemed quite important to me at the time. Which, combined with the beautifully burnished voice and the melodic, literate songs that represent her best work as a song-writer, is why I wanted to give her flowers. 'No journalist has ever, ever done this for me before,' she insisted, ushering me into the beautiful, high-ceilinged apartment that represents her winter home – like many wealthy east-coasters, she summers on Martha's Vineyard – and turning upon me the most dazzling of smiles. Instantly, my head was full of an old song of hers, 'Interview'.

In it she toys with the idea of seducing a writer who visits her at home. 'A sweet young man sat on my chair,' it begins. 'With a tape machine and a face of fear . . . Interview. Who's interviewing who? Are you interviewing me, or am I interviewing you?' Snapping out of my reverie, I realized the singer, still strikingly attractive at forty-nine, was looking at me expectantly. She had asked me a question and, not having heard it, I'd failed to respond. I apologized, and she asked again. Could she offer me some tea? Yes, of course, I told her. That would be very nice. Then, as she departed for the kitchen, my mind snapped back to that song. 'And how would it feel to hold me in your arms?'

Although Carly Simon is confirmed in her status as one of New York's top-tier liberals – she's a close friend of Bill and Hillary Clinton, and is a spokesperson or active campaigner for an impeccable range of social causes – her commercial star has waxed and waned dramatically over the years. Relevant to this process is the fact that she suffers from stage fright, and so only very rarely has she been able to promote her records with live concert appearances. Also, she has defined herself first and foremost as a mother to Sarah and Ben, both now in their early twenties, the children of an eleven-year marriage to fellow singer-songwriter James Taylor. But beyond any career constraints thus imposed, there is the cycle of fashion-ability to consider. The entertainment industry is largely obsessed with the young and the new. Few artists manage to stay at the top for longer than five years. Those that do, do so by evolving. 'It's adapt or die in this business,' Bette Midler once told me, 'and I learned to adapt.' Carly hasn't always done so as successfully.

I was interested to know how she had coped with her shifting fortunes, most particularly during that period in the mid-Eighties when her commercial star was at its lowest. A long-standing association with Elektra Records had ended, to be replaced by a short-lived contract with Epic. As someone who had made it their speciality to chronicle consistently and persuasively the neuroses of those for whom good looks and good fortune are still not enough to guarantee a happy-ever-after, it was perhaps unhelpful to call the resultant record *Spoiled Girl*. It proved to be the only one of her albums not to chart at all. Soon after its release, and for a second time, she found herself looking for a new label, and was urged into an umpromising new deal by her then-manager, Tommy Mottola. Now president and CEO of Sony Music Enter-tainment and the ex-husband and mentor of Mariah Carey, he was unequivocal in his advice. 'Take it,' she recalled him telling her of an offer from Arista that was dependent on no money upfront, and on the company's head, Clive Davis, having power of veto over whatever material she recorded. 'Right now, no-one else wants you.'

'It happens to a lot of people that they reach a low point where they find their options to be greatly reduced,' she told me. 'It's sad but true. There I was, close to being forty, with a lot of my old songs still active on the radio, yet, according to my manager, with no-one out there interested in me any more. I thought I was facing the end of my career, and that I could easily go the way of X, Y or Z, never to be heard of again. The bottom line was that I didn't want to be without a record contract, yet the only way forward for me was with a man who once said that I was a singer not a writer, and that I should only be doing other people's songs. I signed, but only because I'd been backed into a corner. Basically, I was acting out of fear.'

During the recording of their first project together, in 1987, she recalls being reduced to tears 'many, many times' by Davis. The worst moments related to his insistence that she not only record a song she didn't like, by Bryan Adams, but that Adams himself should be present in the studio as she did so to ensure she phrased it properly. 'Now obviously that was embarrassing for Bryan, but for me it was just the most tremendously demeaning experience, one of the low points of my creative life.'

Meeting Adams in London subsequently, I asked for his memories of the occasion. 'Listen,' he told me, 'and this is not off the record, OK? She went to the press afterwards, saying that working with me was worse than watching her ex-husband [Taylor] come off heroin addiction. I've got a clipping of it. No, you haven't touched a nerve at all. I was actually quite flattered by that. Plus, it was an interesting experience, technologically, trying to complete a track she didn't even finish singing before storming out of the studio. So it wasn't a nightmare, and I actually thought she was really, really nice. It's just that there seemed to be an awful lot going on for her at the time and, not knowing how best to handle her, it seemed to be down to me to bear the brunt of it all.'

Revenge, should she have looked for it, was eventually Carly's. The Adams-penned track was overlooked by radio programmers and is all but forgotten today. But one of the tracks she wrote herself, 'Coming Around Again', not only provided the album with its title, but was also adopted as the theme to Nora Ephron's film *Heartburn*, starring Jack Nicholson and Meryl Streep, and as such was a worldwide hit single. 'There is still a lot of struggle, but also much that's positive,' she said of her subsequent relationship with Davis. 'I think he now respects who I am and is no longer trying to shape me into someone else.'

At the time of our meeting, she was nearing completion of another Arista album, *Letters Never Sent*, and I asked if it were possible to hear anything from it. 'Come into my bedroom – the sound's much better there,' she responded, before leading me along a corridor lined with framed family photographs. Following behind her, I noted pictures of her late father, Richard, co-founder of the Simon & Schuster publishing house, with, among others, Albert Einstein, Ernest Hemingway and baseball legend Jackie Robinson, and of her recently deceased mother, Andrea, with the other Simon children Lucy, Joanna and Peter. It was in front of a picture of the singer and her second husband, advertising executive Jim Hart, on Martha's Vineyard with the Clintons, that I stopped and stared, however. The four, each arm in arm with their opposite number, looked like characters from a short story by

Cheever or Updike: prosperous, apparently confident and content, handsome in middle age. 'Don't you think we each seem to fit better with the other's partner?' she remarked, joining me in looking at the picture.

The bedroom was lamplit in mid-afternoon, and expensively appointed. Only the presence by the foot of the bed of a giant soft toy, a lemon-coloured duck, jarred. 'A present from a friend,' Carly pre-empted, patting its head in passing. It was as she moved around the room, looking for the relevant cassette, that I registered for the first time how very much taller she was than I. Only for a second, I regretted having left those ridiculous, high-heeled boots back in the wardrobe of my suite at the Mondrian in Los Angeles. For weeks afterwards, it had been my fear that an unusually efficient management would mail them on to me in London, assuming I had made a mistake when packing. But they hadn't and so here I was, several uncomfortable inches shorter than my hostess.

Having activated the tape machine, Carly proceeded to drape herself across the bed, her head supported with one hand and a faraway expression on her lovely face. Instantly, and for the second time, my head was full of that old song of hers: 'Interview. Who's interviewing who? Are you interviewing me, or am I interviewing you?'

What exactly was I supposed to do as she reclined in contemplation of the new ballad, 'Touched By The Sun', that had begun to play? Should I, too, climb onto the bed and lie down? Or perhaps just sit demurely alongside her, one foot on the floor, as if in deference to Hollywood's old Hayes Moral Code? I didn't have a clue, and the star herself seemed disinclined to offer me one.

So it was that I stood at the end of the bed, hands in trouser pockets and all but whistling. As I swayed self-consciously back and forth, in time to the swelling music, I asked myself the old unanswerable question: How friendly do famous people mean you to be when they act as if you are their friend?

'Whenever you hear I'm in town, you've gotta call up,' Liza Minnelli once insisted, saucer eyes brimming with sincerity. 'I sit here in my room and no-one calls. So, promise me. Promise me you'll call.' I promised but, of course, have never done so. I can't believe she would remember someone with whom she'd spent only forty minutes of her lifetime. And yet, somehow, I don't doubt that she meant it when she said it.

By the time I'd interviewed her for the third time, Janet Jackson, too, had decided I was like family. Coming from so large a one, it's possible that she was genuinely mistaken. 'Momma, I want you to meet Alan,' she said, thrusting me towards her mother backstage at Wembley Arena on one occasion. 'He's like a brother to me.'

A faraway look entered Katherine Jackson's eyes, as if she were wondering if I really was someone to whom she'd given birth. Then came Janet's invitation. 'Next time you're in LA, you've got to let me know, OK? Come and hang out at the ranch. I mean it. Spend some time with us. Do you promise?' I promised but, again, have never done so. It's hardly surprising, really. Janet forgot to give me her telephone number.

None of which was any help in knowing how best to behave at the foot of the bed slept in nightly by the woman who wrote 'You're So Vain'. She'd already told me that her husband maintained a separate apartment: 'I think it's a very good way for a marriage to work, even though Jim spends nearly all of his time here, my place being the nicer.'

I admit that I described the moment to various male friends on returning to London. I disagreed with the retrospective verdict of some. I told them no. Again, I wouldn't flatter myself. And anyway, Carly had already talked very warmly about her partner, and had asked about mine. So perhaps I was right simply to have stood, undulating and foolish, in the middle of her bedroom carpet, looking anywhere but at the siren of my teenage dreams. If only I hadn't looked to my extreme right, though. There, revealed through an open door, was the *en-suite* bathroom. That's Carly Simon's toilet, I found myself thinking, incredulous, as I stared distractedly at the relevant arrangement of elegant white porcelain. Visually, it was more information than I felt entitled to receive.

When the three tracks she had available to play me were over, we moved back to the drawing room, and she asked if Christine and I had children. 'No? Oh, I'm sorry. Well, I suppose you wouldn't want copies of my books,' she said, referring to the children's titles she had written for the publishing house Doubleday, where she was edited by her close friend, Jacqueline Onassis. I said that I would really, really like to have them, if that were OK, and, looking pleased, she went off in search of copies. Each had a frontis-piece in which you could record the owner's name, or that of the person making a gift of it, and in the first three, *Amy The Dancing Bear*, *The Fisherman's Song* and *The Boy of the Bells*, she wrote, 'To Alan and Christine, with love, Carly Simon.' But in the fourth and biggest book, *The Nightime Chauffeur*, she put, 'To Alan, with thanks for the nicest interview I have ever, ever done. Love, Carly. XXX.'

I was thrilled, and have kept the books carefully. Back then, having put them into my briefcase, I offered my thanks for her time and kindness. She made some gracious rejoinder. Then a housekeeper entered with the news that her husband was on the telephone. 'You can see yourself out, can't you?' she then said vaguely. And, having kissed me quickly on both cheeks, she left me standing in a hallway thick with coats and umbrellas. I could and did, but I felt just a little disappointed.

If only she could have kept up the pretence for a few seconds longer, if only she could have waited and waved me off, then I would have left believing she was just as enchanted with me as I was with her.

I began this chapter by detailing embarrassments I've suffered in America, due to the growing popularity of my name-sake, the country singer. Garth Brooks is a yet brighter star in that same firmament, a man whose albums have regularly outperformed even those of U2, R.E.M., Michael Jackson and Madonna. And he set the record straight for me with regard to the rightful ownership of the two combined words: Alan and Jackson.

Given the accelerating global popularity of Nashville-generated music, it was only a matter of time before I was sent there to report on the phenomenon. The occasion came courtesy of Mr Brooks, who was due in Britain for live concert dates.

'So, not *the* Alan Jackson, then,' remarked the receptionist, disappointed, as I checked into the city's Union Station Hotel. 'Well, well! So there's more than one Alan Jackson,' exclaimed a waiter, when I signed the check for breakfast in its dining room. By the time I had handed over a credit card at Tower Records later in the day, only to elicit the same response, I was just a little fed-up with the name that appears on my birth certificate.

That night, before seeing him perform in an out-of-town stadium, filled with the excitable, bedenimed and back-combed citizens of middle America, there was a meet 'n' greet opportunity backstage for competition winners and assorted media and retail representatives, myself included. Feeling out of place, I ushered one after another tried-and-true fan to a place ahead of me in the queue. Then Garth's British PR, Richard, spotted me hanging back and duly propelled me into the presence of a man who has sold some 50 million albums in less than a decade. Already, I had watched and listened as he called each approaching male 'sir' and each woman 'ma'am' and doffed his stetson. Now he turned his considerable professional charm full-beam on me.

'Alan Jackson from the London *Times*,' said Richard, pressing me forward.

'Er, not *the* Alan Jackson, of course,' I qualified, mindful of recent experience.

'Not true, sir,' said Garth, pumping my hand warmly. 'As far as I'm concerned, you're the one and only man to bear that name. To me you are *the* Alan Jackson.'

He smiled a Nashville smile. Instinctively, I recoiled in the very same way I once did when, mid-conversation, Michael Bolton threw back his head and, without warning, began to sing 'Nessun Dorma' to me. To be the sole audience for someone else's star performance is to bear the weight of great responsibility. Perhaps being mistaken for somebody else wasn't such a terrible thing after all.

11

In Manhattan's meatpacking district, animal flesh is traded by day, human flesh by night. 'So what is this building, do you think?' I asked, indicating the gum-pink, featureless edifice next to which we were standing.

'It's a whorehouse,' replied Deborah Harry matter-of-factly.

'And over there is one of the city's most famous sex clubs,' volunteered Michael, her make-up artist and personal stylist. As he spoke, he made a final adjustment to the vast bustle, completing a floor-length but entirely see-through black Yamamoto outfit, chosen by the singer for her *Times Magazine* photo shoot. '*Voila!* Now, how long are you in town for? Perhaps you'd like to go there. You might find it quite an eye-opener.'

There are those of us who cringe before a camera lens and others who, like Debbie, come magically alive. The final touches of powder having been applied, she threw her head and shoulders back and vamped imperiously in response to the photographer's urging. Up and down along the grimy, sawdust-strewn sidewalk she whirled and stamped, the layers of black gauze clothing beating around her body like an insect's wings. Though the area sees little traffic at this late hour on a Saturday morning, what passers-by there were stopped and stared on finding her at the centre of our little media circus. Some stood silently. Others – two joggers, a grizzled down-and-out, one cab and one truck driver – whooped or called out in appreciation of Debbie's impromptu performance, and were rewarded with waves and a succession of sweetly appreciative smiles. Just one lone male was stupid enough to show a lack of respect.

'Hey, hooker,' he shouted, leaning from his open window. 'Wanna come for a ride? How much are you chargin' for a blow job?'

Suddenly assuming an almost regal demeanour, despite the fact that her lingerie was on display, the star began to stalk towards her accuser, a spell-casting finger held out towards his face. 'Pervert!' she hissed, magnificently malevolent. 'Are you big enough to get out of your car and say that to me, you filthy-mouthed pervert?' At which point an NYPD squad car rounded the corner and pulled up, its arrival a further entertainment for the straggle of onlookers. A squeal of tyres announced the hasty exit of the man with the mouth.

'OK, OK, so what exactly's going on here?' asked Officer Simonetti of the Sixth Precinct, West 10th Street, approaching our group with hands outstretched in a don't-anyone-move sort of gesture. Then, at a distance of perhaps ten paces, recognition washed across his face like sunlight.

'Man, I loved you when you were in Blondie. You were terrific.'

I hoped he would stop right there and let her bask in the moment. Instead, he pressed on. 'Minute I saw you, I

271

thought how it looked like you. Of course, a little older than I remembered, but . . .'

Silence was all I could hear for a second or two. Those seconds felt equal to a minute. Then, with all eyes upon him, Officer Simonetti rallied successfully.

'But, hey, aren't we all?' he resumed, beaming and gesturing at his hair and waistlines. 'I'm the last person who can talk.'

'So you finally made it to twenty-one, too, eh?' Saying this, Debbie grinned, and in doing so made it possible for all of us to relax. An autograph with a little personal dedication? It would be her pleasure. 'Give my love to New York's finest back at the precinct,' she called, as he walked happily away. Then, turning to me and still smiling, she observed, 'That was a cute little meeting. Very cute.'

By lunchtime, photographs over, the two of us repaired to the Moonstruck Diner, a café near her rooftop apartment in the Chelsea district. Now dressed in shorts and a loose shirt, and sporting an ankle bracelet above her sandals, she won a warm greeting from its proprietor.

'Hey, Debbie!' he exclaimed, ushering us towards a booth at the back of the room. 'Nice to see ya! You're looking sunny today.'

'That's because I'm feeling sunny today,' she responded warmly. 'In fact, I'm feeling very sunny.'

I had feared it might be otherwise. At the time of our meeting, she had only recently parted company with her record company of long standing, Chrysalis, and was as yet unsigned to any other label. Three solo albums had failed to replicate the chart domination achieved during her time as vocalist and public image of Blondie. There had been some small, though well-reviewed, film roles, most of them low-budget and independent. She had sung on a record with Talking Heads, and was about to tour Europe with the Jazz Passengers collective. But the recent, triumphant career upswing of the Blondie reformation was still two years away and, she readily admitted, there had been some days when the telephone hadn't rung at all. Such days had involved a test of nerve. 'What's going on? My God, nobody wants me any more. I've been deserted.'

Rummaging in the rucksack by my feet, I managed to find a fax that had been waiting when I checked in to my hotel the previous evening. Sent by Colette, assistant editor on *The Times Magazine* and a besotted fan of Debbie's since adolescence, it read, 'Please tell her I think she is the most talented, inspirational and beautiful woman to have walked the earth.'

'Someone actually wrote that about me?' Her eyes, previously so cool, even lightly mocking, welled up as soon as I handed her the proof. 'My God, that's so sweet. Really it is. Well, hey! All right!' In a split second, she'd progressed from near-tears to jubilance. She would have the melon and a glass of water, she told the waiter, while still smiling broadly. Heck, no. She wanted a whole bottle of water.

Yet while Debbie could clearly be moved and uplifted by an admirer's sentiments, she was on guard against anything that might represent journalistic flattery or ingratiation. When I introduced into the conversation the names of Madonna and Annie Lennox, and suggested that their much-praised facility for image manipulation might owe a debt to her own earlier cleverness while with Blondie, she put down her fork and fixed me with an appraising stare. 'Cleverness?' she repeated, her voice acquiring a chillier edge. 'I wish I were more clever. Because if I were, I would be selling records at the rate that they are. And that's the truth, isn't it?'

The expression on her face as she delivered these words wasn't hostile or accusatory. Rather, it was sweetly, un-blinkingly reasonable. I fumbled for the right thing to say, and managed only, 'Well, er . . .'

'It is. It's the truth. If I've really done all that ground-breaking work, and all of your kind postulates are correct, then how come my cleverness isn't working for me now, eh?'

Debbie was at pains to say she wasn't bitter, and I almost believed her. Certainly, she was a supreme diplomat. When asked if it didn't hurt, being set free by the company that had reaped the benefits of the entire Blondie catalogue, she would say nothing more than, 'Partings are rarely the most auspicious or happy of occasions, and I don't really want to get into the nitty-gritty of it all. Someone's always left feeling a little let down.' I had only to look across the table to see who that someone was.

Knowing that I wouldn't be able to flatter her into a resumption of her earlier, cheerful mood, I tried instead to offer an honest observation. To my mind, the three solo albums she'd completed for Chrysalis seemed racked by compromise: it was as if she, or they, were unsure whether to proceed by perpetuating the image of the peroxide pop goddess of old, or to enter that more adult territory so well patrolled by the former Sixties *ingénue* Marianne Faithfull.

'You're right. I agree,' she responded firmly. 'But then, it's very difficult when you have an identity that locks you into a format. On the whole, I think the songs on my solo albums were good, but that the interpretations were limited. There should have been more hits off them, but then, I imagine every recording artist thinks that about their work.

'Perhaps, had I stayed with the identity of Blondie, the industry would have considered me more of a sure thing. But because I veered off, it was hard for anyone to grasp – or be bothered grasping – where I was headed. But hey, onwards and upwards! I'm free now. Free to be creative. Free to be my little artistic self. And that's a great liberty, a great privilege.' And to ensure that I understood this was the official line, one from which no amount of blandishments would tempt her to stray, she then fixed me with the most dazzling but blank and subject-closing of smiles. I admitted defeat.

Oddly, though, and after a few conciliatory minutes of conversational back-and-forth, it was she who returned to my earlier subject. 'You know, it just seems very odd to me,' she said. 'I can go anywhere in the world to perform and be sure I'll draw a good audience. I'm a good singer and, I think, a really good performer. I can also write songs and make records. Yet people in the corporate world look on me as not being a safe bet . . . It's just a bizarre position to find yourself in. It's not something I'm really worried about. I play the hand I'm dealt, always; it's what has pulled me through in life. But don't you think there's something wrong with a picture like that? I do. I think there's something very definitely wrong with that picture.'

With which she readdressed herself to a plate now only half full of melon, unaware, as was I, that in little more than two years she would be topping charts once again all around the world.

At some point early in 1991, stuck in traffic and looking to make the best use of my time, I put my hand into a bag of pre-release cassettes I'd been sent by various record companies, pulled one out, sight unseen, and loaded it into the cassette player. The opening track was unpromising, an uptempo but thoroughly undistinguished pop song, and I considered pushing the eject button and making another choice. But there was something about the singer which encouraged me to stay with it and, though the quality of the songs on the first side scarcely improved, I eventually found myself flipping the tape over and listening right through to the end. On getting home, I sought out the press release that had accompanied it, in order to find some biographical details about a woman whose voice, though previously unknown to me, was so strong and so distinctive.

I learned that she was a twenty-one-year-old French-Canadian, and that the recordings in question represented a first departure from her native tongue. She had been a star in the francophone market since late childhood, however, having recorded nine albums which had amassed combined sales of several millions. She had even won the Eurovision Song Contest – a fact her label would soon try to forget – singing for Switzerland. Now she was trying to break through into the lucrative English-language market. Given that, previously, no French-speaking pop star had managed to do this with any sustained level of success, I thought her situation was interesting and duly phoned the press office at Sony Music. And that is how I came to do the first-ever British interview with Celine Dion.

Some time shortly afterwards, she performed a three-song showcase at a Covent Garden bar to officially launch that album, *Unison*. Such events can be dispiriting for the audience: the much-hyped artist may well be worse than awful. I would imagine it's still worse for the performer, however, walking out into a room full – if he or she is lucky – of assorted media types, all on their way to somewhere else, yet lured in by the thought of free alcohol and the possibility of meeting friends, and who feel no particular obligation to stop talking when you open your mouth to sing. I felt apologetic towards her as she climbed onto a small dais at the back of the room, an unfashionable singer of unfashionable songs, and began to perform to prerecorded backing tracks. Her between-songs smile never wavered, despite the unceasing hum of chatter which emanated from around the bar, even while she sang. And by the time she'd reached her final number 'Calling You' the eerie theme to the film *Bagdad Café*, I knew without question that she had the potential to be one of the world's greatest stars. Christopher Neil, producer of *Unison*, had told me she was a frighteningly good singer, comparable even to Streisand. Now I knew what he meant.

Less than a decade later, Celine sells more records than any other woman in the world, and when she sings in London it is from the stage of Wembley Stadium, not while standing on a box in front of a club's fire doors. Over the intervening years, we have met again perhaps six or seven times, and it has been through watching her development as an artist, a sales phenomenon and an individual that I have learned my best lesson about what it takes to be successful in the music industry today. What it takes, in addition to talent and good fortune, is total motivation and a relentless capacity for hard work. Celine all but embodies these qualities. As she stood before the chatting, quaffing British media in Covent Garden that first night, with her not-quite-right hair and her not-quite-right clothes, they weren't immediately evident. Yet they were undoubtedly there in someone who was the youngest of fourteen children, with a father who had supported his family by working variously as a lumberjack, a butcher, a youth counsellor and the leader of a part-time folk singing troupe. That was how she had become a French-language star in the first place. Now, deliberately, she had learned English, and was committed enough to humble herself by starting all over again. 'I want to thank my Sony Music family world-wide for giving me this wonderful chance,' I remember her saying, above the buzz of audience indifference. Rebellion is fine, but it's a smart, calculating and usually successful artist who realizes the importance of playing the corporate game.

By the time we met again, Celine had a couple of Top-10 British hits to her name, but still no-one was taking her par-ticularly seriously. She was sitting barefoot, amid mounds of silk cushions, in the expensive tastelessness of a Mayfair hotel suite and, though increasingly proficient at conversing in her second language, she had to be pushed and pushed again before she would depart from what was, I suspected, the party line some US adviser had devised and coached her in. Only after I had mentioned the names of Whitney Houston and Mariah Carey, at the time both considerably more successful in the same musical field as her, did Celine say anything that sounded remotely spontaneous. Wasn't it frustrating to have to deploy her voice on material which was unworthy of it? I persisted.

'There are only so many good songs available at any one time, and when you're an unknown quantity the writers don't want to gamble on you,' she said with perfect reasonableness. 'They'd rather send them to someone sure-fire, like the names you've mentioned.'

We met again two years later. It was 1995, and she was supposed to be on honeymoon, having some weeks earlier married long-time manager Rene Angelil, twenty-seven years her senior, in a lavish ceremony at Montreal's Notre Dame Basilica. But he was now 3,000 miles away at a PGA golf resort in Florida, and she was in London working, a necessary concession, given that hers was the rare achievement of having both a single and an album top the British charts consecutively. And it wasn't all quite as business-minded and unromantic as it might sound: the post-marriage break had been scheduled to last not two short weeks but a full three months. 'This time off has been so great for me,' she enthused. 'Take cooking, for instance. I never knew anything about it before, yet I find I can do it. I cook good! My husband loves my cooking! And each night I've been so tired, my feet burning from having been on them all day, making pies, cleaning floors, ironing clothes, living a normal life for the first time in years. I tell you, I've been so happy. I've loved the way our life has been since the wedding.' Almost all of me believed her. Just a tiny part felt that this time it was hearing not extracts from a text written for her by some professional image-maker, but the let's-pretend dreams of the little girl she had once been.

At this point in her transition from aspirant English-language star to world-class diva, Celine still looked awkward. Just before I met her, the photographer from a tabloid colour supplement had persuaded her to pose amid the artfully rumpled sheets of her hotel bed, the straps of a black lace bra hanging from her shoulders. Now she was wearing a silk blouse, patterned with big, splashy roses, above skin-tight trousers, fishnet stockings and high, strappy shoes. 'You look beautiful,' purred a member of her entourage, as a make-up artist finished fussing around her. 'I don't, but thank you anyway,' she replied, glancing briefly in a mirror.

On her left hand was an engagement ring which featured a diamond the size of a postage stamp – a symbol of the world of wealth she now inhabited. The wedding band beside it confirmed her new status as a married woman. Not only could she now buy whatever might be her heart's desire, but incontrovertible success and a settled private life were hers, too. Even so, she looked oddly like a child who has been let loose in the dressing-up box. 'I never really needed to grow up, because I was old already, even when I was little,' she said when asked if she felt she had sacrificed her youth for her career. Meanwhile, the facts of her early life, in particular its struggle, were recalled now, as if she were reading from a script. 'I'm just a hick from the sticks,' I recall her saying. 'I'd come home from school, pull a carrot from the soil, wipe it on my jeans and eat it. And boy, that carrot tasted good.' Even the memory of a wardrobe full of hand-me-downs had acquired a rosy hue. 'Do you know what? Those clothes felt great,' she said, 'because they were full of love and experience and important stuff like that.'

I next saw Celine two years later, in 1997, at Midem, the annual music industry gathering that takes place in Cannes. Celine was now outselling all her female rivals, and her record company was using the occasion to launch a new album. Personnel from all their global territories, plus selected guests from media and retail, had been flown in to see her perform in concert and then attend a late-night dinner held in her honour. Other artists, having already spent two hours on stage, would expend only the minimum time and effort on attempting to charm some 200 functionaries and, worse still, strangers. She, reed-thin, newly elegant in Chanel, worked the room harder than any presidential candidate, and with more sincerity. She went from table to table, dispensing handshakes and kisses, speaking here in English, there in French, thanking people for having taken the trouble to come, asking if they had all they needed to be comfortable, eventually bidding them good night. Her schedule the following day began with a similarly scaled lunch for yet more functionaries and strangers. There was a different Chanel outfit, of course, but the smile was exactly the same, the greetings as warmly delivered.

Most artists hate this part of the star-making process; they are either awkward and half-hearted at it, or glibly professional. 'I'm not very good at turning into plastic,' observed fellow Canadian kd lang to me, backstage in a Boston theatre some few weeks later. 'It's definitely my downfall. I need a clone kd who can do all the handshakes-and-hugs stuff for me, and do it well. Because absolutely it's what sells records these days, and absolutely it's what people expect from you. It will sound immodest to say that I'm not very relaxed being superficial, but it's true. And I'm hugely jealous of other artists who don't have my qualms. It gives them such a big head start.'

The easy inference to make is that Celine's career is based firmly on professional insincerity. I don't believe this to be true. Recently, I interviewed Simply Red's Mick Hucknall once more and, in the course of our conversation, he mentioned that she'd been on the same Concorde flight as him from London to New York some weeks earlier. The girlfriend Hucknall was travelling with was a big fan, but baulked at the suggestion that he might introduce her to Celine. On arrival at JFK however, and while waiting for their driver to collect them, the pair became aware that a stretch limousine was reversing towards them and that the rear passenger window was being lowered.

'I didn't like to approach you on the plane, but I just wanted to say hi and that I really love your music,' said Celine, leaning out of it.

'Do you know how many million records she sold last year?' Hucknall asked me, shaking his head in wonderment. 'And there she is, saying that to me. I couldn't believe she would be so nice. It made the girlfriend look at me with new respect, too, I can tell you. She was impressed, but so was I, too.'

When I last saw Celine, Christmas was fast approaching. She was sitting in her dressing room at a London television studio, waiting to prerecord two appearances for a top-rated show which had turned her down as a guest only two years earlier. 'It's just how things are,' she shrugged, when I asked if that fact made her cynical about the effusive welcome the host had given her earlier. 'It's the same with writers. On the way up, you struggle to get strong material. But once people see you sell 25 million copies of an album, it's like, "Hey, I think maybe I'll send her one of my songs after all." So no, I'm not cynical about it. I'm just grateful to be in a position where people are offering the best of themselves to me.'

I asked her if she would be home in time for the holidays. She would, but only just. Normally, she enjoyed buying her Christmas gifts personally; stores were kind enough to open specially out of hours, so that she could shop undisturbed. This time a sister was having to do it all for her. 'We're phoning and faxing each other all the time, to make sure everything's just right,' she said. 'Thirteen older brothers and sisters. All those nieces and nephews. Then there's Rene's family. It's an awful lot of presents.'

Soon she was in another Disneyesque reverie. 'I'd love to be sitting at home, before a blazing log fire, a cup of hot chocolate by my side, wrapping everything up myself,' she said, hugging herself at the idea. 'But it's not to be, I have to work.'

At which point an aide put her head around the door and told Celine that rehearsals were about to begin again. 'I want you to have a wonderful Christmas,' she told me, kissing me first on one cheek, then the other. The smile she offered me was in her eyes as well as on her lips. She couldn't have made that smile warmer or more plausible if she'd tried. For just as long as it mattered, she managed to convince me that my happiness was her utmost concern.

The plane had landed, but the exit door had, as yet, failed to open. Half sitting, half standing in my seat, I smiled to see again the mahogany-tanned neck and shoulders of Peter Andre, a singer known chiefly for his six-pack stomach, and whose short-lived career as a teen idol was just now beginning to wane. It had not been warm when we left London, but still he and his travelling companion, an older male who I assumed must be his manager, had entered the business-class cabin wearing nothing more than low-cut white singlets and some conspicuous gold jewellery on their upper bodies. Their arrival on board had caused an audible ripple of excitement to sweep through the galley behind me, where assorted stewards and stewardesses were preparing trays of complimentary drinks. From the young guy in the seat beside me, younger brother of one of the crew members and thus travelling on a freebie, it prompted a single-word exclamation, 'Wankers!'

Absorbed in the book I was rereading, William Trevor's *Felicia's Journey*, I had soon forgotten about Andre's presence two rows ahead of me. The two small bottles of warm white wine I'd drunk with my meal put him further out of my mind, and caused me to fall asleep during that dead, dark time after the in-flight movies had come to an end. And then I had woken, suddenly aware of an urgent, rhythmic panting sound coming from somewhere all too near me. I blinked and tried to ascertain its source. Right there! So close I could have reached out and touched it, a male body strained up and down, up and down, oblivious to all but its own exertions. This Mile High Club stuff is getting right out of hand, I thought to myself. It used to be confined to the toilets. Now they've started doing it in the aisles.

But as my eyes adapted to the semi-dark, I realized that the activity taking place beside and below me was of a different nature. Only one person was involved, and that person was wearing a baggy white singlet. It was Peter Andre, helping maintain that celebrated six-pack by doing one-armed press-ups.

I was distracted from the relishing of this recent memory by the realization that I knew one of the fellow passengers whose faces I'd been mindlessly scanning for the past few seconds. The curtains delineating first class had been pulled back and there, on the right-hand side of them, was Danny Boyle, director of the films *Shallow Grave* and *Trainspotting*. I knew him tangentially as his twin sister, Maria, had been a close friend of Christine and myself since university. He, Maria – now a teacher – and I had all been born on the same day in the very same year.

Danny recognized me just as the door was at last opened and the aisle became clogged with anxious-to-disembark travellers. 'So, what are you in Los Angeles to do?' he asked, reaching through the throng to shake my hand.

I hesitated, realizing that I could be about to trigger a wave of anti-luvvie nausea that would envelop all of those around us. Even so, there was no alternative but to answer. 'Good to see you, too. I'm here to, er, interview Madonna. What about you?'

He also hesitated before replying, 'Oh, I'm just here for one night. A meeting with an agent. Then, well, I'm off to Utah in the morning to do some location scouting for my next film.' It was to be *A Life Less Ordinary*, starring Ewan McGregor and Cameron Diaz.

At that moment, the line began to move and Danny and I were separated. Reapplying my mind to the task ahead, I joined the slow shuffle through immigration and went in search of a cab – no man with a sign this time. You hope to do any interview well, but it was imperative that I get the most out of Madonna. I was the only British press journalist she was meeting while promoting the *Evita* soundtrack, and *The Times Magazine* was planning to run the results not as one self-contained article, but two. That meant something that was twice the usual length, with twice the usual number of insights and quotes, and which sustained the reader's interest for twice the usual time. Luckily, Madonna is at least twice the star of most of her contemporaries. That left me as the one potential weak link in a chain which had begun when her British record-company PR, the indomitable BC, had called to vaunt the possibility of my talking exclusively to the single most famous of her very many famous charges. I owed it to everyone concerned, not least to myself, to carry the day.

'Later on I've got a meeting with someone very important, and I'd like to take a gift,' I told the concierge in my hotel, who was all but dwarfed by the splendid arrangement of blooms which dominated his counter. 'You obviously have the services of a very good florist. I know it's short notice, but do you think they could come up with something appropriate?'

He was certain they could. 'But it might help if we could tell them a little something about the recipient. For example, would they have a favourite colour, do you know? Might they prefer something formal or informal? Any preference in—'

'It's for Madonna. I don't really know.'

'Ah, Madonna.' Possibly, he thought I'd just swum ashore from Fantasy Island, and was really *en route* to having tea with my granny. 'Something big and flamboyant and colourful, perhaps?'

I cast my mind back to Peggy Lee's description of the lovely bouquet of cabbage roses the younger star had brought when visiting her. Then I recalled the lurid arrangement I had been forced to hand over, having asked for something similarly low key to take to Miss Lee myself. Big, flamboyant and colourful? That meant something that looked like a municipal flower bed, as depicted by an acid casualty.

'The exact opposite, if possible,' I told him. 'Something discreet, tasteful, old-fashioned and not too big. And something that'll be ready for when I leave at three p.m.' I pressed into his hand a thick fold of $10 bills. 'Will this be enough?'

Clearly, it had been too much. When the resultant order was delivered to my room it was indeed exquisite and exactly what I'd hoped for. But so much money had been left over that the store had felt it necessary to arrange the flowers in a blue glass bowl, around which strands of ivy had been carefully wound. All well and good. It was beautiful. It also contained at least half a gallon of water.

'You ain't coming in this cab carrying that.'

'But I've got to. It isn't far.'

'I said you ain't. I don't care if you only want to go across the road. My upholstery is gonna get soaked.'

I promised to be very careful, but to no avail. I offered to pay double the metered fare, plus tip. Eventually, I struck a deal. But only because I further agreed to sit on the grubby woollen blanket which was produced from the taxi's boot, and with a rumpled towel from the driver's gym bag stretched across my knees.

Thus swaddled, and with the bowl of flowers further contained within a cardboard box produced by hotel reception, I travelled down Beverly Boulevard for my appointment with one of the most famous women in the world. The ten-minute journey was conducted in hostile silence. My driver was keen to prove his caution justified, meanwhile. We seemed to encounter more potholes than can be explored in the whole of the Peak District, and some of them felt as deep. There were also violently sudden, swinging, told-you-so lane changes to be made, unnecessary ones mostly. The point was duly made. By the time we arrived at the headquarters of Maverick Records, the label Madonna had created to show-case new talent, Alanis Morissette included, much of the water intended to sustain the flowers was instead darkening the crotch and thighs of my jeans. I looked like an incontinent.

'Flowers. Wow! They're fabulous! Who are they for? D'you need me to sign?' The receptionist reached out across her counter to accept the soggy box advertising a brand of peanut butter which I was holding.

'They're for Madonna. And I'm not delivering them. I'm here to interview her.'

Within seconds, a personal assistant was at my side, ready to guide me through a large, open-plan office, in which conspicuously busy young men and women were interacting animatedly or conducting telephone conversations of a clearly vital nature. I felt as if I'd stepped onto the set of a television commercial for chewing gum, or a haircare product that added body, bounce and shine, while halving the number of bottles you carried into the shower.

'Here. Can I take those from you? Is there a card? Who are they for?'

By the time I'd rounded a corner into the calm of an ante-room, not one but two young men had been helpful enough to try and relieve me of my burden, and I was beginning to

287

feel defensive. Did I really look like a flower-delivery person? Clearly, I did.

Exasperated, I smiled ruefully at the lemon-haired young woman now standing before me and complained, 'Everyone seems to want to take these off me. If only there hadn't been so much water in the bowl. This is just what I don't need right now. See, it looks as if I've wet myself!'

'Your flowers are beautiful,' she said, with an expression of light amusement. 'So beautiful that someone might actually want to take them home, rather than just leave them in their office. And who are they for?'

'Madonna,' I said again, wondering why her face seemed so strangely familiar. 'I'm here to interview her.'

'Well, hello then, and thank you,' she said, extending her right hand. 'You're here to see me. So perhaps you'd like to step into my office? You can leave the box right there.'

I had said I would like to hear some selections from the as-yet unreleased *Evita* soundtrack and so, making a geisha-like bow or two to signal the absurdity of the situation, Madonna set about satisfying my wish. She went in search of a CD, found one and duly placed it in the player, all the while somehow maintaining perfect balance on high-heeled mules, her heavily pregnant body skimmed by the opaque waves of a Versace reinterpretation of that old man-made fibre classic, the baby doll nightdress.

She looked marvellous – trim, taut and toned to a degree that belied her status as an expectant mother. But there it was, nonetheless, the proof: a proud, round bump, low on her stomach, at which I tried not to stare. Then, all at once, she turned her back to me and bent forward to activate the music. Wow! I thought, deciding it was safe to stare whilst she couldn't see me doing it. And there *it* is, be-thonged and barely a yard away from me: Madonna's bum.'

When the song had finished and I'd remarked on her performance of it, we settled down to talk in a room that was predominantly Italian contemporary in style, with just an ironic touch of boudoir. Observing the conventions of the promotional interview, I began by asking her in detail about her experience of playing Eva Peron in director Alan Parker's film. Then I congratulated her on her pregnancy. 'I'm trying to hide it,' she giggled, fanning out the filmy folds of her dress. 'As for these shoes . . . Well, they're simply more practical. I can't bend to tie a lace any more.' While she spoke of them, I looked down at the beautiful pink mules, objects of art in themselves. They were planted wide apart now, for comfort, not effect. As for the hands, they had settled on her lower belly, in support of the weight of her child. From time to time, as we spoke, and unconsciously almost, she would move a thumb gently back and forth across her stomach, as if to soothe the baby's brow.

Commentators have consistently used as grist to the theoretical mill the absence of any maternal role model in her life – Madonna was six years old when her mother died of cancer. It is why she's such a relentless high achiever, they had said. It explains why she must be the object of total emotional and erotic fascination, not just for audiences but for any man she becomes involved with. She shrugged at the very mention of such theories and said she felt they were overworked. 'I have lots of friends who are lucky enough to have mothers, yet who are completely consumed by their work and who don't want a family. A lot of women are, like me, waiting until they are in their late thirties to have children. It's possible that the absence of a mother in my own life has made me want to have a child even more than I might otherwise have done, just so that I might have a chance to understand the reality of a relationship I haven't personally known, but . . . Well, there were a lot of other things that I wanted to do first.'

She readily acknowledged the irony of the fact that she, someone famed for exerting such control over her body, had become pregnant by her personal trainer, Carlos Leon. She also admitted that it required a considerable mental adjustment to accept the fact of that body being taken over by something – someone – else. 'Some days are great. You feel really good and are really confident about how you look. Then, on other days, you look in the mirror and go, "Ugh, I'm a whale!" It's all so different. You find yourself getting totally tired after walking up just a couple of flights of stairs. The only rationales are that the feeling is temporary, and that what you get for a very small amount of suffering is quite worth it.'

When I reminded her that she spoke – as, obviously, I did, too – as someone who hadn't been through the process of childbirth, she raised her hands to her ears, as if to block out the sound of a maddening and persistent clamour. 'I know, I know, I know.' She laughed. 'Everyone tells me that. What can I say, other than that I'm prepared for all the suffering that lies ahead? At this point, I've had so many people tell me what lies in store that I'm like, "OK, no more horror stories, thank you!" I think it all stems from the fact that women don't go off to war. They have babies instead, and that provides them with a very particular equivalent to male war stories. Some have no problems, others have lots, but they all want to tell you what happened to them personally. In the end, you have to tell them just to shut up.'

I asked if she knew the Philip Larkin poem 'This Be The

Verse' – it was unlikely that she would, his appeal being so very English – and, when she confirmed that she didn't, I quoted to her its opening lines, 'They fuck you up, your mum and dad./They may not mean to, but they do./They fill you with the faults they had/And add some extra, just for you.' Madonna laughed again, then nodded her head vigorously in acknowledgement of the essential truth behind the words: that a child enters the world as a blank canvas upon which all the negative, as well as positive, aspects of its parents may be painted. Yes, she acknowledged, that aspect of motherhood concerned her.

'I agree, it's a huge responsibility,' she said. 'But I think the best way to be a good parent and role model is to be happy – with yourself, with what you do in your life. I think that, a lot of times, people make the big mistake of not ever really doing what they want to. They grow up, have their kids, then either live vicariously through them, pushing them to do the things they themselves never could, or else they're bitter about something and keep them down, so as not to highlight their own lack of accomplishment. I think it all starts with your own happiness and self-esteem, your self-possession, and radiates out from there. We've all seen it. The child who is raised by parents who are happy is different from the one who's raised by those who are not.'

It was a given, I remarked, that any child of hers would be born into an atmosphere of great privilege. But wouldn't it also be a rather tough introduction to the world, growing up as the son or daughter of the global icon called Madonna? Previously relaxed and friendly, she turned chill in an instant.

'Why?'

'Because of the level of media scrutiny they'll be exposed to.'

'Well, let the media scrutinize. But they're not going to have access to her' – at this late stage in the pregnancy, it was known the baby was a girl – 'in the way that they have to me. I'm not going to drag her out in front of the world to be photographed. I'm not going to exploit her in any way, shape or form. I want her to have as normal a life as possible. Yes, on the one hand she will have a privileged upbringing because I, her mother, consider myself to be a very evolved, intelligent human being. But she's still going to clean her room, make her bed and do all those kind of things. And I'm not just going to send her away to boarding school, either. I guess I'm just not as worried about that aspect of things as everyone else seems to be. I'll find a way.'

'But personal security has been a problem for you in the past. You've been stalked, had unwanted approaches—'

'I don't live in fear, and I don't think my daughter will, either.'

'And are you enjoying pregnancy enough to think you might want more than one child?'

'Yes, I do want to have several children. Definitely. I love them, and have spent a good deal of my life, to date, taking care of them.' She paused for a second, and raised an eyebrow theatrically. 'Grown-up children, that is. I've had plenty of practice where they're concerned.'

It had been a widely promoted theory that Leon, the baby's father, was little more than a sperm donor. 'It's all just part of the view the media likes to have of me. That I'm not a human being, that I don't have any feelings, that I don't really care for people, that I'm just ambitious, cold and calculating,' she responded, when I asked if such speculation was hurtful. 'It's all just part of the image that unhappy people like to construct for me. I'm not surprised by it.'

She maintained that their relationship was a genuine, loving one, and that she was greatly offended that anyone should think otherwise – that it was reported as having dissolved within months of daughter Lourdes's birth does not necessarily invalidate this, of course, although it did provide additional fuel for the cynics. But would she consider marriage a second time, having divorced first husband, Sean Penn, after four years? 'I don't think marriage is a religious thing,' she told me. 'I think it's an economic thing. In fact, it's more about money than anything else. It evolved out of women not being able to take care of themselves financially, and so having to become a man's possession, promising to love, honour and obey him. I don't know what I think of marriage any more, other than that it's an institution which grew out of a very sexist way of thinking and living.'

Yet there could have been no financial imperative for her to marry Penn, who, though at the time a young actor whose star was rising, must have had a significantly lower income than she?

'True, but then I was also younger and hadn't thought things through properly.' She smiled and sighed. 'So, marriage? I don't know if I believe in it any more. I don't know what function it could have in my life. Because if I love someone and want to be with them, I'm going to be there with them. If I don't, I'm not. And there isn't a piece of paper or a ceremony in the world that is going to change that. I think marriages are more about what society expects from you than what God expects. Are you married? Yes? You are? Oh, sorry!'

As our conversation moved towards its close, I remembered the final verse of that Larkin poem and, interested in what her reaction would be, repeated it to her: 'Man hands on misery to man./It deepens like a coastal shelf./Get out as early as you can,/And don't have any kids yourself.'

She looked at me carefully, then asked if I had any children of my own. I told her no.

'Well, go off and have some then,' she instructed, giggling, making as if to rush me out of the door and into congress with a waiting partner. 'You don't know what you're missing, so get to it. Go on! I'm serious! Hurry! I command you, go forth and multiply!'

Outside, the sky was darkening and most passing cars had switched on their lights. I'd considered asking the receptionist at Maverick to call a cab to take me back to the hotel, but there was nothing waiting for me there and I decided to do that most un-LA and frowned-upon of things and walk. Sheena was playing dates in Japan. What few other people I knew were also out of town. So while I would have liked to go out to eat with a friend, to tell them what it had been like to spend two hours in the company of the most famous woman in the entertainment world, I couldn't do so. No matter. Time for contemplation was a good second option, I reasoned, as I came up to an intersection that, for some reason, looked familiar. The low-rise building opposite me was shabby and boarded up, with a 'To Let' sign posted above its utilitarian entrance hall. Why did I think I'd seen it before?

Because it had once been the James Corcoran Gallery, venue for the Joni Mitchell reception I'd attended on my very first visit to Los Angeles. I crossed at the 'Walk' sign and approached its canopied doors. Through panels of reinforced glass I could see only a drifted pile of uncollected mail and some discarded telephone directories. I turned and looked back down a path that, those few years ago, had been cordoned off and covered with red carpeting. The flash bulbs of paparazzi photographs had lit up the sky that night. Now, the only prevailing light was that of the neon sign announcing an adult book store directly opposite.

A song of Joni's, 'Chinese Café', came into my head as I stood there, remembering. Just four words of its lyric are, I suppose, the nearest I have to a personal philosophy, whether life and circumstances are good at any given time, or bad. 'Nothin' lasts for long, nothin' – lasts – for – long . . .'

I made the few steps back down onto the sidewalk of Santa Monica Boulevard and turned towards my temporary home. Back in the hotel room, I picked up the phone and asked for a bottle of champagne and just one glass to be brought up with my room-service meal. I felt I'd earned a celebration drink, even if it was to be a lonely one. Later that evening, I fell into bed tired and half drunk, a different track now playing in my head. It was one Leiber & Stoller had written for Peggy Lee, 'Is That All There Is'. 'Let's break out the booze and have a ball,' she was singing. 'If that's all – there – is . . .'

12

As a small child, I was so shy that I hated even to have to acknowledge my name among strangers. In the gloom of the dentist's waiting room, I would be fearful not at the thought of the drill and the gas, but of an assistant entering and asking of those assembled, 'Alan Jackson?' On the day I was called up onto the junior-school stage by Sister Paul, it was only my sister's tugging hand – and the sight of the giant Easter egg which was supposed to reward our Black Baby Fund endeavours – that gave propulsion to legs which otherwise would have been incapable of movement.

Of course, in being so reluctant to acknowledge your own identity, you are in danger of casting yourself forever as an observer, rather than a participant. From there it is but a short step to living vicariously, to looking for others who can move through the world on your behalf. These many years later, I have achieved a healthier balance. Still, it is my inclination to observe all that goes on around me. But mercifully, I have learned to do more than that alone. One day, somewhere, I just looked up and found that, yes, I'd got a life.

The wide-eyed little kid I once was has had his influence on it, certainly. Not wanting to be famous himself, but just to get closer to those who were, he is the primary reason I gravitated towards the job I do now. And still, from time to time, he can leap out from nowhere and tug at my sleeve. He did so on the day that, more than thirty years after first falling in love with her, I was offered the chance to interview Petula Clark. He had to go along in the company of my older self, however, the one who feels increasingly alienated in a society which seems to value celebrity above all else.

Ironically enough, the meeting came just as Petula prepared to take over the role of Norma Desmond in the London stage production of *Sunset Boulevard*. Life, I'm glad to say, was not imitating art. Despite having spent a lifetime in the public eye, here was no self-deluding monster obsessed with past glories. A true Norma wouldn't have had a new grandson she was eager to show me Polaroids of over tea and biscuits. A true Norma wouldn't have apologized for wearing a skirt that she'd forgotten to iron.

At the same time that I was becoming disillusioned with it, the rest of the world seemed to be falling more deeply in love with the concept of fame. And that concept was metamorphosing into something different, too. What had first seduced me was the belief that famous people had a level of talent and glamour denied to the rest of us – that they were, at best, potentially heroic and, at least, something more than merely ordinary. But now it was the resolutely and incontrovertibly ordinary who were crowding the spotlight. Suddenly, confessional discussion programmes, docusoaps and make-over shows of people, their houses, their gardens were all over the TV schedules. The papers, meanwhile, were full of kiss-and-tells. Everyone wanted to be, and anyone could be, a star.

And stardom, as they all knew, not only guaranteed you attention and reassured you that you were special, it was also a licence to print money. The successful British launch of the glossy celebrity mags *Hello!* and, later, *OK!* must have proved a financial godsend for the (never) rich (enough) and famous. Now they could invite the public into their lovely homes, grant access to their every family occasion, and for a price. Sell your wedding pictures, sell those of your child's first public appearance, sell your soul . . . And for what reward? All that money. All that publicity. The self-validation of having your picture appear endlessly across a succession of pages. The un-written promise that no awkward question or critical comment would make its way into the accompanying text. What could be better than that? Only the fact that you didn't even need to be famous in your own right to reap this rich harvest.

Because there weren't enough genuine stars to feed this voracious new media, increasingly it had to fall back on those who were working the system in order to claim their own fifteen minutes' worth. Run out of Spice Girls? Then why not buy up a Spice Girl's sister? Run out of angles on the aging rock god? Well, write out a cheque to the wannabe model, actress or TV presenter whose career move it was to sleep with him. Increasingly, I found myself agreeing with the title of Blur's 1993 album, *Modern Life Is Rubbish*. And they and I weren't the only ones to think so. 'Do people really think I've spent all these years honing my craft specifically in order to sign up for something like *Dumb & Dumber*,' Bette Midler demanded of me, indicating her belief that Hollywood was pandering to the lowest common denominator, too.

It seemed as if a gulf now separated the adult I had become and the starstruck kid I used to be. Yet that gulf was nothing compared to that which I sensed between my young self and some of his successors, the harder cases among the current generation of young pop fans. Having spent four years reviewing concerts for the arts pages of *The Times*, I had seen such teen idols as Bros, Jason Donovan and Take That play before audiences of weeping, screaming, needy little girls. Thus I had witnessed the mass articulation of mini-love and, as the respective fortunes of those acts subsequently waned, had witnessed, too, the speed with which that love could fade, be withdrawn or redirected. What I hadn't noticed before was the phenomenon of mini-lust.

Shortly after Take That announced their disbandment, and in order to write about the act that had taken over as chief claimants on both the hearts and pocket money of Britain's younger schoolgirls, I spent three days observing Ireland's Boyzone while on tour. Its five members, all from solidly working-class north Dublin, are talented to varying degrees, and it is generally accepted that its two main singers, Ronan Keating and Stephen Gately, have the best chance of translating their current success into long-term showbusiness careers. It was these two, their fellow band member Keith Duffy and a pair of mountainous personal security staff that I accompanied on a walkabout through central Nottingham during what represented their two free hours of the day.

From one smart, expensive men's clothes shop to the next, the three young stars grazed, obtrusive in designer sunglasses, with mobile phones clenched in fists, and the good-natured Ronan delivering a constant stream of awful jokes for the benefit of nobody in particular.

'I hear they've straightened him out,' he observed, while waiting for his purchases to be bagged in one store.

'Who?' I asked, because it seemed nobody else was going to.

'Oliver Twist, of course,' he replied, bending to sign an autograph for one in what proved to be the endless succession of breathless, too-excited-to-speak young girls we encountered that afternoon.

Finally, shouldering bags that contained items by Dolce & Gabbana, Red Or Dead and Armani, he, Stephen and Keith acknowledged their need to purchase other more mundane items. So, from Superdrug – toothpaste, Nurofen – to Boots – contact-lens solution, royal-jelly capsules – we wandered, followed all the while by one especially persistent fan, pale as water and wearing a cheap, pastel-coloured short skirt and jacket. Perhaps thirteen years of age, fifteen at most, something about her put me in mind of the character played by Jodie Foster in the film *Taxi Driver*.

It was as we waited in an untidy line at the checkout that she stopped staring from a distance and approached one of the security men to whisper something, wriggling and giggling as she did so, brazen despite being barely five feet tall. An easygoing, seen-it-all kind of guy, his face nevertheless registered clear distaste for what he heard, and in motioning her away he also took a step or two backwards himself. What was that all about, I wondered? What on earth could she possibly have said? At first, he was reluctant to tell me.

'OK, OK,' he relented eventually. 'She said she'd like to fuck them. All three of them, all at once. She wanted to know would they be up for it?' As he spoke, he shook his head in disbelief.

Stephen, pocketing the change for his purchases, was oblivious to this exchange. Ronan, too. 'D'you know what I can't understand?' he was asking. 'Chinese writing. I said, Chinese writing . . . D'you get it? Because it's in Chinese, d'you see?'

Overlooked and unwanted, the girl hung back now, picking up and then replacing items from a nearby display of haircare products. Still, though now blankly, she continued to stare.

If I, who had never even experienced it at first hand, was feeling sated with and let down by pop fame, how did the artists themselves cope? 'Please, you mustn't tell anyone that we did this together,' kd lang urged as we huddled together in her hotel suite high above Boston harbour.

'It's too late to ask that. Now that I've seen for myself the sordid reality of your rock 'n' roll excesses, I'm going to have to call the *National Enquirer*.'

'God, no!' she wailed in response. 'I can see the headline: GAY SINGER LURED ME INTO JIGSAW SHAME. You'll reveal how I plied you with mineral water, then made you join me in attempting a one-thousand-five-hundred-piece puzzle, featuring an oil painting of a bowl of fruit. My career will be over. Oh, I'm so ashamed.'

Lang's sense of humour had come in useful to her. After making her commercial breakthrough with the 1992 album *Ingenue*, she had moved from Vancouver to Los Angeles, epicentre of the entertainment industry. Suddenly a person whom everyone wanted to know, she found herself in danger of being debauched by the city's value's system and, five years later, had retreated back to Canada. There she wrote the songs that formed the basis of *All You Can Eat*, a record she was currently promoting on a US concert tour. 'And basically, they're all about my discovery that, when you reach a certain level of wealth and fame, life becomes a smorgasbord, and it's up to you whether or not you make yourself sick,' she explained.

'I had somehow gotten added to the "A" list and, as a result, everyone wanted me at their parties. When that happens, you start to believe you're really special. You begin to think that you may, after all, be beautiful. That you might have something interesting and original to say. In short, you get treated like some superbeing and, for a while, you're able to believe that indeed you are. Sooner or later, reality hits, of course, but while you're still under the spell, it's hard to walk away. For myself, I'm only glad I did so before I experienced the move back down. When your status slides, you get relegated real quick. That must feel terrible, like the coming-down from any drug you can think of – just not worth the original up.'

But superficiality and a caste system can be found in any corner of the world, I suggested. 'Yes,' acknowledged lang, 'and it's all made worse by the fact that most of us are living in this state of suspension, thinking that if only we had this or wore that we would be happy and fulfilled. But in LA, especially, your ideas about success, sexuality and confidence can become so totally product-based and designer-led and, for a while, I admit I was taken in. There I'd be, front row at the Calvin Klein catwalk show . . . Oh, it's a real temptress, believe me.

'I don't want to put that lifestyle down completely, because at times it can be fun. But it's so easy to slip into this all-pervasive mindset, where everything's surface and real values are totally masked. And how I feel now that I'm away from it, trying just to live an honest life, is like I've managed to survive an addiction, as if I tried heroin and walked away from it. I'm left with this massive sense of relief, yet still I feel a little violated – by myself, rather than by anyone else.'

The singer's elevation to superstar status occurred shortly after she came out to the public. Suddenly cast as the most successful and high-profile lesbian in the American media landscape, she saw attitudes and behaviour towards her change instantly. 'And do you know what I noticed the most? That straight women began flirting with me more. I'd be in a restaurant, or wherever, and I'd catch them glancing over, or sort of swishing around me. It was flattering in a way, I suppose. But really, straight women bore me to tears.

'It's nice to flirt; we all know that. It's kind of sickening too, though, to find yourself on the receiving end of attentions that are ultimately insincere. Very attractive women who had ulterior motives showed interest in me, and it was hard to sort it all out in my head. At first, you think, Hey, this beautiful creature is totally into me! Yahoo! Sooner or later, though, the truth surfaces and you're saddened. Inevitably, you become suspicious of people, simply as a form of self-protection.

'Living in LA and experiencing all of this, I found it more and more difficult to retain an accurate sense of my own worth. Difficult as it was to admit that the life I had built for myself had no foundation, I realized I would have to break out. I'd made friends who weren't really my friends, and was left alone. I still feel that I'm very much alone. Not lonely, but like I don't fit in anywhere. Not amid the Hollywood scene, certainly. Nor, because I'm famous now, amid the totally natural, just-hangin'-out-with-my-buddies scene, either. I'm left floating around in between somewhere, feeling unnerved.'

When next I met up with lang, some few months later, she was grinning widely. Yes, she had fallen in love again, after all she'd said to me about doubting that she ever could. And yes, it felt and was going great. 'You find love when and where you least expect it, I suppose. She's been wonderful, mopping up all my bitterness. I've even moved back from Canada to Los Angeles just to be with her. So there I am, right back in the heart of the beast. But, hey! I've found out that when you're head over heels, you just don't care where you are.'

The suggestion that a happy ending was still possible – I was massively cheered. But then, just a couple of weeks later, I interviewed Luther Vandross, the American soul singer, and found my spirits sinking again. On previous occasions I had talked to big Luther and trim Luther – his body weight is said to veer between extremes of approximately 190 and 320 pounds – but this time the man who welcomed me to his splendid temporary quarters at London's Dorchester was medium-sized and melancholic of mood.

'No, I have not had any great love affairs in my life,' announced the voice which can sing in such an achingly beautiful way about romance. 'And yes, I feel the lack most severely. In part, it's due to the alienation that other people feel when someone else has a successful career. But also I blame this constant battle to lose weight, and the feelings of inferiority that stem from it. It's such a public struggle, too. You can have a drink or a drug problem and, if you're careful, no-one need know about it. But I walk into a room when I'm overweight and I can almost hear everyone thinking, Uh-oh, Luther's losing his battle.

'For years I have tortured myself over it – I mean really tortured myself. I've given myself migraines, worrying about it. I've cancelled engagements that I really wanted to fulfil, simply because I couldn't face turning up at some event and feeling myself to be a less worthy person than everyone else there. But finally, I don't feel like acting that way any more. I've resigned my chairmanship of the Let's Attack Luther

Society, and have decided that I'm not such a bad person after all. I'd certainly rather be me than some skinny terrorist, or a serial killer with perfect abs.'

I knew that, in this situation, to be reminded that his voice had given pleasure to millions would be of no genuine comfort whatsoever. And oh, what an unhappy irony that the man who had provided the soundtrack to so many trysts and carefully planned seductions should appear to have enjoyed so few himself. Nor could I expect it to help if I said that, were I to be granted the gift of being able to sing, I would plead, if not to sound like my friend Paul Buchanan of the Glasgow band The Blue Nile, then like some glorious, if small and white, approximation of the wonderful Luther himself. I kept quiet, and merely nodded my regretful appreciation of his situation. That was enough to prompt him to continue his sad dissection.

'Do you know, I have had just two serious relationships in my life and both came late: one was four years ago when I was forty-one, and the other was about twelve months ago,' he said. 'Neither lasted long, because neither person was prepared to meet me halfway. And, as a result, I've formulated what I call my Alphabet Theory. Let's say that I'm at A and the other person, someone I'm really attracted to and want to be with, is at Z. Now ideally, what should happen is that we get together around M or N. But in neither relationship did it happen like that. I wasn't met anywhere near the middle, meaning that I would end up going as far as X or Y just to convince the other person that I was worthy of being with them. And if you have to go all the way to the opposite end of the alphabet, rather than finding yourself met in the middle, there is no way that things are going to work out for you.'

By the time he entered his forties, Luther says he felt so

deprived of personal affection that he was grateful, honoured even, if an object of his affection would allow him even to be good to them. As a result, he found himself vulnerable to exploitation. 'My whole purpose in life became the quest to do whatever I could to make life easier for that other person. And I'm not just talking about buying them cars and clothes and paying for trips to Monte Carlo . . . I mean that I, Mr Work-Right-Thru'-Till-Midnight, broke the habit of a lifetime and started leaving the studio at six p.m., just so that I'd be free when they got out of work. But, as I say, I wasn't met halfway.'

To illustrate his point, he described the circumstance in which he recorded a particular track for the album he was then promoting, *Your Secret Love*. Assembled to play on it, and at dizzying cost, was a sixty-piece orchestra, led by the esteemed conductor Jeremy Lubbock. 'It was such a big day for me,' Luther recalled. 'And all I needed was for that other person to show up at the session, just to prove they gave half a cahoot about what was important to me and the way in which I make my living.

'But no. I spent the whole session trying desperately to concentrate on what should have been a great occasion for me, yet secretly staring at the door. It never opened. Then, when the recording was over and after the members of the orchestra had left, one by one, I sat alone in this vast, high-ceilinged room, so alienated, so humiliated. I didn't feel angry. Just stupid. At times like that you die a small death. And I have vowed never to let anyone kill me in that way again.'

It was hard to know what to say in response. Had it been an ordinary person speaking, I wouldn't have thought twice about crossing the room and giving them a consolatory embrace. Instead, I sat in what I hoped was sympathetic silence and Luther began to talk again. 'It's funny, but I think of Eleanor Rigby as having been a real person,' he said. 'The graveyards are full of people who died lonely and didn't deserve to. It's a simple fact of life. Often I fear that I'm going to be one of those people. And that is why I've decided to make the most of this career of mine instead. I'm going to enjoy it for all that it's worth.'

The expression in his vast, almond-shaped eyes contained no suggestion of enjoyment at all and, in my desperation to offer some, any, comforting words, I fell back on those said to me so recently by kd lang. 'But so often, people find love when and where they're least expecting it,' I told him. The remark sounded hollow and platitudinous, even as it was leaving my lips.

'If that's true, then it will come to me right now, because I no longer have any expectation of it whatsoever,' Luther replied. 'Love will land right outside on that balcony and walk through those doors.'

I turned and, like him, gazed towards the French windows behind me. Of course, they remained shut. There was nobody and nothing there.

Driving home that day, with the lyrics to Eleanor Rigby nagging in my brain, I thought, as I'd done so many times before, about the person who first opened my eyes to the truth that fame, wealth and acclaim bring with them no guarantee of happiness. Stevie Nicks had lately returned to the spot-light in a reformed Fleetwood Mac, and every emblem of success in the music industry was hers again: a number-one album, a high-grossing concert tour, the inevitable awards for lifetime achievement. She was looking wonderful, too. Superficially, at least, her life was in perfect order. But had she found contentment? I wondered. It was some few months later before I found out.

It was Sheryl Crow who was able to update me. As we waited for lunch to be served at the table booked for us by her London publicist, she remarked that, while completing her latest album, *The Globe Sessions*, she'd been called by Stevie and asked if she would produce a couple of songs for her, for inclusion on the soundtrack to the film *Practical Magic*. 'We'd done a fundraiser together once and she knew I was a big fan. She said that of everyone she's met and all the records that she's bought over the last fifteen years, it was in me that she could see the most of herself – that we seemed to have the same influences, the same philosophical outlook on life. She said that she knew I had no time right then, but that she was looking for someone fresh to produce these two tracks for her, someone with an understanding of who she is. Of course, right then and there I said that I would make the time.'

I told Sheryl of my encounter with Stevie ten years earlier, and asked how she had found her. 'Stevie's an intelligent, wise and remarkably open woman,' came the answer. 'She's been very hurt in the past, and she remains outspoken about it. But I would say that she's much more comfortable with who she is and the way things have gone for her now than she was when you met her. She's turned fifty now, and told me that she had found a sense of peace, and a new resolve, after coming to accept that her life wasn't going to be about having the be-all-and-end-all relationship, or about getting married and having children. She said her life was great, even without all of that, which was encouraging for me. I'm thirty-six now and think that maybe I would like children myself. But I'm still single and I'm starting to look at what I have besides music, and there's not very much. So will I have those children? I don't know. I think that things go the way they're supposed to.'

After we'd eaten, I walked Sheryl back to her hotel on the fringes of Covent Garden. It was low key to the point of near-invisibility, and I'd walked past it scores of times without ever really having registered its presence. 'I guess you get people using it who don't really like a fuss,' she commented. 'This morning, I was having a meeting over coffee and Jarvis Cocker walked through, and I was like, Wow! Look who it is! and really wanted to run up to him and introduce myself. Except that I couldn't, because I was talking to this other person and it would have been rude.'

As she finished speaking, and while waiting to cross at the busy intersection of Shaftesbury Avenue and Charing Cross Road, we became aware of two pale, urchin-faced youngsters bobbing and weaving beside us, their eyes wide with excitement. Who were they, these mid-teens, with their bleached hair, thin, shiny tracksuits and cheap trainers? Runaways, perhaps, or, given our proximity to the slot-machines-and-neon end of Old Compton Street, even rent boys. Whoever they were, they were too tongue-tied to speak.

Sheryl smiled encouragingly at them and it seemed to help. One pushed the other, who, in turn, pushed him back. Then, finally, they managed to say it: 'You're Sheryl Crow, aren't you?' She told them yes, which rendered them speechless again. We moved forward, Sheryl giving a little over-the-shoulder wave as we did so. The encounter had made their day. I knew this because, when I looked back, the pair were hugging each other and doing a little circular war dance on the pavement, McDonald's drinks cartons held extended in their right hands for safety.

When I pointed out this scene to the singer, she raised an eyebrow wryly, but didn't look at all surprised. From this, I inferred that it represented nothing out of the ordinary for her.

But why would it? She had felt a similar thrill on catching sight of Jarvis Cocker just hours earlier. The thing is, weird stuff happens around famous people all the time. And, clearly, not even those who are celebrated themselves are immune from staring at others, glassy-eyed.

The trick, I have decided, is for the famous to keep sight of what made them so famous in the first place. You have to remember it was the fact of being a singer or an actor or whatever which initially gave you visibility, and you must continue to define yourself as such. It's when stars convince themselves, or allow themselves to be convinced, that they are bigger or more important than their basic function that it all starts to get messy. To believe in the myth created for you by your publicists is to take a big first step down the path to madness.

Norma Desmond may be a grotesque, a parody of self-delusion, but there are lots of younger, less extreme and outwardly normal Normas and Normans busying about the streets of showbusiness. Yes, talent should be rewarded. It should be respected. But then, we are all due respect at a basic level, unless we demonstrate otherwise. So what about those who really believe that they're especially important, that their celebrity is a confirmation of the fact that they are fundamentally better than the rest of us? Perhaps some people are just genetically predisposed to think of themselves that way. After all, we have each encountered examples of the not-at-all-famous who believe they are better, more special, too.

The mistake, I have decided, is to let the attainment of fame – the fact of your enhanced status – take your life in a direction you are uncomfortable with. Of all the artists I have met, it is undoubtedly the 1960s hitmaker Scott Walker who took the most radical action to stop this happening to him.

His was easily one of the best white male voices of his generation, yet from the start there was a divergence evident between what was commercially successful for him, and his own musical inclinations. The melodramatic sentiments and wall-of-sound production of epic Walker Brothers hits like 'Make It Easy On Yourself' and 'The Sun Ain't Gonna Shine Anymore' still draw record-buyers towards compilations of their work more than thirty years later. His taste, though, was for the work of Jacques Brel and, latterly, for self-written material that was, musically and lyrically, almost wilfully impenetrable for mass audiences.

With collections of such songs having failed commercially – 1994's startling solo album *Climate Of The Hunter*, though lauded in the music press of the time, is said to be one of the lowest-selling Virgin releases ever – it became increasingly difficult for him to find funding for the kind of work he wanted to do. 'A lot of people wanted to sign me up just as a singer, a commercial item,' he said with distaste, when I met him in 1996. 'They'd call wanting to have lunch with me, but in a way that made it clear I had become the Orson Welles of the music industry. They were hoping to get from me a mainstream record, something they could sell easily. "If you'd just do this," they'd say, "or if you'd just do that, then we could proceed with a record." But doing this or that would have been to return to the old horrendous groove. Before you knew it, it would all be happening again.'

Scott, by now fifty-two, was referring to the unhappy fallout from his brief tenure as the man who had it all. Good looks, an enigmatic quality and the brooding romanticism of those Walker Brothers hits had conferred upon him the status of teen pin-up. Meanwhile, the particular quality of his voice, the intelligence and sensitivity with which he deployed it and the purity of his musical ambitions made him a critical and intellectual darling, too. Artists today dream of encapsulating such bipartisan appeal. Biographical accounts of his life speak of alcoholism and suicide attempts in the wake of that early success. 'I had too many bad experiences in the 1960s,' he told me, of a fear of live performance which has kept him off the public stage for over twenty years. 'They just left this kind of scar. I was drinking and all that stuff. To me, it was a living nightmare.'

When we met, he was in reluctant promotion of a new and, even by his own latter-day standards, supremely inaccessible record, *Tilt*, his first since *Climate Of The Hunter*, eleven years earlier. What had he done in between? 'I've just existed, like everybody else. I do the day-to-day. It's not that interesting.' He allowed that he had a home in west London, that he appreciated being able to travel the city on public transport without attention or recognition, and that he had reactivated a teenage interest in art, taking one or two local-authority-run courses. A couple of relationships had followed an earlier, short-lived marriage. One of them had been long-term, but was now over. The other was on-going. 'But I live alone and it's important that I do. I need my own space, as I think everybody does ultimately. It's the only way through a lot of this.'

Because of his disinclination to exploit the past for profit – no reunion tours, no colourful autobiography recounting his years amid the glitterati of the swinging Sixties – finance had frequently been a problem. 'It's been ducking and diving,' he shrugged. 'Luckily, I've had one or two good friends . . .' It was with a kind of anthropological interest that he noted how the near-horizontal public profile he had maintained over the years – combined with his talent and inability to compromise

– had nevertheless won him semi-legendary status in music-business circles. 'Very strange that you should be thought of as a recluse, just because you don't want to be a celebrity,' he said.

I put it to him that, were it not so, and should he find himself able to play along with just a suggestion of enthusiasm, then he could be crowned King of Las Vegas virtually over-night. Walker gave his first smile of the afternoon in response. 'Precisely,' he told me. 'You said it.' What an unwavering rejection of the accepted showbiz game. I was impressed.

It was with Walker in mind that I voiced to Sheryl Crow the opinion that, for far too many young artists coming into the business, a desire for attention was the great motiv-ating force, more so than any wish to excel at what they did. 'Well, for me it's always been about looking for respect,' she countered. 'Which is why having Bob Dylan call and say he wanted to give me one of his songs means so much more than knowing I've sold eight million copies of this record or five million copies of that one. To have the respect of someone you've worshipped all your life? God! It's a defining moment. What else is there?'

For me, it was significant that she had mentioned Dylan. Some months earlier I had met him myself, having been granted his first interview with a UK journalist in almost ten years. The path that led to the securing of this, on behalf of *The Times Magazine*, had not been straightforward. As is often the case when American-based PRs enter the picture, it was requested that I submit some examples of previously published profiles I'd written. I didn't flatter myself that it was Dylan who was interested in Alan Jackson, journalist – this was to be for the publicist's benefit alone, so that he could be sure he wasn't sanctioning his artist's exposure to some well-known British hatchet man.

'What sort of thing do you think they'd like to see?' I asked Karl, head of press at the London office of Dylan's record label, Sony, and the man who was brokering negotiations. 'Madonna? Whitney Houston? Sting? Jon Bon Jovi? Alanis Morissette? I've done all of them recently. Which do you think?'

The word back to us was emphatic. 'More than anything, he hates being approached as a celebrity. All that Dylan, the living legend stuff – he just loathes it. He's a working musician. He wants to see stuff about other working musicians. Has Alan talked to any of his contemporaries, perhaps?'

I racked my brains. There had been J.J. Cale. Leonard Cohen, too. And Joan Baez. Would they be the right sort of people? They would, it transpired, and so copies of the relevant articles were faxed to America. And, came the answer subsequently, yes, I was a suitable candidate to talk to him. But even then, progress was maddeningly slow. When and where the interview might take place was impossible to say, apparently. 'Still nothing definite, but Bob's going to make a decision on it before tonight's show.' I would hear this almost every morning, during a three-week period prior to his arrival in Britain for a short series of concert dates. Then, each afternoon, there would come an apologetic, 'No word yet, I'm afraid, but we're hoping that Bob's going to give it some thought in the morning.'

This pattern continued, even after he'd arrived in the country, with the result that I had become convinced the interview would never take place; it had all been wishful thinking, on the part of myself and the two PRs. Then, on a Friday evening, with only two days left before Dylan left the country, I took a call from a shocked but excited

Karl. 'We're on,' he told me. 'Tomorrow afternoon at four.' Finally, Dylan had said yes.

Immediately, I was thrown into a panic. When Karl had first approached me with the possibility of the interview, he had ended with a cautious, 'Of course, you are really familiar with his back catalogue, aren't you? That's really important. He's been known to test out how well writers know his work, so I'm told.' I had assured him I was, though I was stretching the truth. Like most of the world, I knew all of the celebrated albums, but had passed on those that critical opinion had deemed disappointing or self-indulgent. That was quite a few.

Perhaps suspecting as much, Karl had biked over a box of some twenty-five Dylan CDs, and it was these that I arranged face-down, with the track lists showing, on our kitchen table early the next morning. There were seven hours left before I needed to leave for Old Park Lane's ultra-fashionable Metropolitan Hotel, to my mind a surprising place in which to install an artist so oblivious to trends. That meant that I should be able to memorize exactly which songs appeared on which albums, so being able to keep face if asked a trick question by the great man. By three o'clock I'd all but done so, and had a thumping headache. I also had a new awareness of what Dylan's admirers have always held to be fact – that his is the greatest canon of work assembled by any one non-collaborative songwriter in the second half of the twentieth century. Forgetting that my head hurt, I began to get excited at the prospect of just who I was about to meet.

Perhaps because he is here among us so infrequently, our collective impressions of Bob Dylan are like snapshots, images formed at specific times and places, captured as if with a flashbulb and then frozen in time. In my own mind, three in particular hold sway.

There is the sweet-faced youth seen on the cover of 1963's *The Freewheelin' Bob Dylan*, the one who was just about to capture the attention of almost the entire world. He had his hands stuffed into jean pockets, his shoulders hunkered down into his jacket and his body braced against the cold, as he hurried through the New York City snow, with a laughing, long-haired, in-love girl upon his arm.

Then there is the colossus of popular culture, the wiry-haired, hook-nosed, multi-million-dollar success story and media ubiquity, revered throughout the second half of the Sixties and into the early Seventies, mixing with the great and good, and wryly assessing the world from behind his dark glasses. He is secure in his genius, this early- to mid-period Bob Dylan. Undisputed in it.

And then there is the latter-day picture, that of a grizzled and significantly older man, his legend undiminished, but his commercial standing heavily diluted and, we fear, his talent, too. This is the Dylan who released a series of indifferent albums to harsh reviews and equally indifferent sales; who, and too many times, has made bumbling, stumbling concert appearances; who has converted from Judaism to born-again Christianity to no-one is quite sure what – and he declines to say. This is a man we feel we no longer know or understand and who, again, we fear, looks increasingly to have lost the plot.

All three of these snapshots were in my mind when a door opened in a daylight-flooded hotel room of determinedly monochrome and minimalist ambition and in walked the fifty-eight-year-old reality. A slight, self-effacing man, he appeared dapper, even dandyish, in a horizontally striped black and white silk shirt, black jeans and shiny loafers. His face – he had only recently recovered from a life-threatening viral illness – was heavily lined, the skin putty-coloured and framed with hyacinthine curls, themselves only lightly flecked with grey. He was all three of my Polaroid images in one: a Holy Trinity, and then some.

He was also – and I hadn't anticipated this being the case – charming. Bright-eyed, too. And softly spoken. Infinitely more welcoming than I had dared hope. Of course, he wasn't about to ask me to recite the track listing of some record he'd released twenty-five years ago – it was a good job, too, for the unexpected sense of awe I felt had scrambled all the information I'd so diligently stuffed into my short-term memory. All in all, the longer hair and sharp clothes aside, he could be any kindly, personable Jewish man of late middle age. Someone coming up to retirement, perhaps. Somebody's grandad. Anything but a rock god.

Wincing at the autumn sunshine, meanwhile, Dylan smiled and shook hands. As aides struggled with the electronic system which controlled the vast room's retracted window blinds, he and I performed a small but intricate dance of good manners in front of an L-shaped sofa, both of us encouraging the other to select a seat and make himself comfortable first. Acknowledging our mutual awkwardness, and seeking to put me at my ease, he laughed, shoulders shaking softly, just like the dog Mutley in *Wacky Races*. 'Heh-heh-heh!' he went, settling himself at a close right-angle to me. 'Nice of you to come by.' As if I had, just on the off chance.

In that very week, Dylan had released *Time Out Of Mind*, his first complete album of new material in nine years, and one good enough to remind us how great he once was. Although he couldn't yet be sure of it, the record would collect almost universally excellent reviews, enter the Top 10 both in Britain and America and win him his first awards in years, Grammies included. But was the likely prospect of receiving critical and commercial endorsement again satisfying after so many lean years? He shook his head doubtfully. 'I'm not used to it any more and, having gravitated instead towards bringing my work alive again night after night on stage, I find that to be what's important to me now.

'I can't say that it's never been my turn, that I've not known the feeling of having a record top the charts, because it wouldn't be true. But to have it again? I'm not really counting on it – I don't want to set myself up for a disappointment. I'm used, now, to just a certain amount of people buying my albums and then them falling out of sight. And I'm aware that the record market belongs to much younger people these days. As it should. As it should . . .'

The concert performances he referred to have been christened by some particularly slavish devotees The Never-Ending Tour. This mystifies and irritates him. 'I don't know where that came from. I didn't call it that. Crosby, Stills & Nash play the same sort of number of dates as I do' – Dylan and his band appear between 100 and 150 nights each year – 'and they're not said to be on a never-ending tour. Lots of other people, too. And it's easier that way. When you play live, you just do the show, and it's over and done with. Then you're gone, on to some other place. The strain is more physical than mental, and that's why I choose to do it. Writing can be harder. I'm just an intinerant tradesman plying my trade.'

Equally, he found it meaningless to speculate as to whether a more authentic music, his own included, was coming back into vogue. 'I just plough my own furrow, regardless. The people I listened to – still listen to – were never fashionable, as far as I'm aware. Woody Guthrie? Was he ever fashionable? I don't think so. Or Leadbelly? Or the great Robert Johnson? How many records did he sell in his lifetime? Very few. Whereas Al Jolson, now he was fashionable. And what happened? In every era, fashionable people go out of fashion as soon as the prevailing wind changes.

'For myself, if I wasn't working live and had no other avenue of expression, then maybe there would be some kind of sense to it [the courting of a wider popularity]. But I have no great need to appeal to kids in high school. I wouldn't want to seem as if I had gone fishing for a younger set. A certain crowd comes and sees me play, and I assume that they're the ones who naturally relate to what I sing about. And that seems to be enough for me.'

Protective in the extreme about his private life, Dylan answered even the most respectful enquiry about it in terms so vague as to be impenetrable. It can be said with certainty that he has four grown-up children from a ten-year marriage that ended in divorce in 1977 and that the youngest of these, Jakob, is lead singer in a highly successful band, the Wallflowers. Their current LP of the time, *Bringing Down The Horse*, had then sold in excess of three million copies, reportedly more than any album Dylan himself has ever released. 'I get asked about that in a way that suggests I mightn't be pleased,' the proud father said, genuinely bemused by this. 'How does anyone think I feel? My feeling is that it's fantastic. I hope he sells a hundred million.'

Dylan's general unwillingness to discuss all aspects of his off-stage life, to be approached as anything other than Bob Dylan, Travelling Song Salesman, has bolstered the sense of him being a man who exists only within the spotlight. Of being someone who comes alive again each night on some stage somewhere around the world, a forever rootless and willing slave to that never-ending schedule of tour dates. Of course, the fact is that he does have a domestic life, and a very comfortable one – a mansion in Malibu, say the biographers, and a farm outside Minneapolis. He even likes to tread the greens and fairways, like so many other older men who, occasionally, find themselves with a little time on their hands and in need of some gentle exercise. 'How come everyone is so interested to know my handicap?' he demanded, not understanding the fact that I and everyone else was fascinated by the fact that Bob Dylan, voice of a generation, now plays golf.

Ultimately, all the various polite evasions underlined his own original point: that his is a trade like any other. Because that is so, because he isn't another self-promoting celebrity, selling pictures of himself relaxing with his children, or teeing off in some celebrity golf fixture, the sub-text has to be that we have no right to any further information, and should expect no heart- or soul-baring insights. I accepted that entirely. And when, after our stipulated hour together, both the American and the British PRs made their presence felt in the doorway of an ante-room, my only regret was that a thoroughly enjoyable encounter was about to end. I'd felt myself to be in the presence of greatness: Dylan really did have that aura about him. That being so, I didn't need to know his shoe size, or who he might be sleeping with. But just a second – although we were about to be parted, he was drawing me back for a final observation.

'I'm just so glad that you like my record,' he said, clasping my hand. 'In fact, I'm very overwhelmed. I'm used just to my records being slagged off and my shows misrepresented.

That's what I'm used to. You do get used to it. You have to. If you expect to go on, you have to get used to being slagged off and misrepresented in all kinds of ways. I'm no longer used to the acceptance of a record. I think it would take me a while to get used to it. So, thank you. Heh-heh-heh!'

And then he was gone, and I was left behind, hardly able to believe that Bob Dylan had just said such a thing to me. That he should have needed to at all, and that he, despite his protestations, one of the most famous men of the second half of the twentieth century, had actually meant it.

a postscript

This is not a good time to be a hero, and for that we are all to blame. It is a confessional, expositional, scandal-hungry and information-sated age that we have shaped for ourselves. As a result, we know so much about those who stand above us that we can no longer expect or believe them to be demigods. The famous may fly high, but still they fail and fall from grace. They err as we err. They too cry, bleed or die. And we, their ravenous audience, want all the details of each defeat and downfall, and pour over the slo-mo replays with undisguised delight. Who would want to put themselves before so fickle and unforgiving a public? Why imagine that love, loyalty or validation could ever grow up out of such stony soil? That I, by the very nature of my profession, have been complicit in the dismantling of the dream is an irony I am only too well aware of.

I chose to be a journalist specifically because I wanted to meet the beautiful, the talented, the heroic. Because I wanted to get close to those who possessed what seemed to me that magic and seductive quality, fame. Be careful what you wish for, runs the adage, for that wish may come true. Mine did, and as a result I found myself disappointed. Something corrosive had seeped into too many of the lives I'd fantasized about. Too often, and from close up, I'd witnessed a distortion of the perfect images I had admired from afar, one that revealed the loneliness and insecurity beneath the unblemished skin. Elsewhere, vanity and ego had run amok. And that distorting mirror, that corrosive element, the fertile ground in which the seed of superiority and self-satisfaction could flourish, was fame itself.

But let us remove fame from the equation for a moment. At heart, and though some clearly felt themselves to be much more, these were just ordinary men and women who had sat down to talk with me. I would be the first to admit that many had extraordinary talents. Still, though, they were human beings, not Superman or Wonder Woman. And strangely, after finally recognizing and coming to terms with this, I found myself able to like and understand them more. For they drag about with them such a weight of expectation, these golden people. Mine and your expectations, as well as their own. No matter how rich, they cannot pay for someone else to lift that burden. It remains the one piece of luggage that the famous must always carry for themselves.

Sooner or later in life, reality taps all of us on the shoulder. Sometimes, it even hits us in the face. There is no escape, even for those I once thought of as invulnerable, heroes and heroines, safe on high, way up above it all. And unless they are like Norma Desmond, deluded and grotesque, they must accept their essential ordinariness, the fact of their own mortality. 'Such a lot of people in my past situation really bought into their own mythology. Still do,' said Annie Lennox to me recently. 'I don't understand that. Of course, music is one of the most powerful communicating forces in the world, but to believe that you yourself are so very special, just because you make it? To start believing in your own myth . . .' She paused, and then gave a hollow laugh. 'I know what happens if you think that way. You become calcified.'

Yet while I have had to accept the falseness of the gods I worshipped for so long, ones that seemed to me so much more shiny and glamorous than that which I was taught to pray to as a child, I can have no real regrets about the job I chose to do. It remains a source of wonderment to me that I can be moved or uplifted or enlightened by the creative work of others, and then ask and be allowed to meet them. Only a relative few are given such access, and therein lies the challenge and the responsibility within the kind of journalism I do: to then transmit to readers an accurate and objective sense of the individual who you have met on their behalf. To succeed in doing so is the medium's best reward.

For all my reluctantly won cynicism about fame itself, I remain grateful to have met so many extraordinary/ordinary people along the way, and to have learned so much from them. So many artists that I'd looked up to. So many that I continue to look up to, because they didn't let me down. For that, and one additional thing, I sincerely thank them all – those who appear in this book and those who don't. And that is the gift they shared and the pleasure it has brought not only to me, but to so many others. That, after all, is what is important. That, hopefully, is what endures. That's entertainment.